UNDER INDICTMENT:
RACE, JURIES & JUSTICE IN LOUISIANA

UNDER INDICTMENT: RACE, JURIES & JUSTICE IN LOUISIANA

ANGELA A. ALLEN- BELL

DEDICATION

Oretha Castle Haley (1939-1987)
Photo credit Okyeame Haley

This dedication was conceived long before I ever imagined writing a book. I have transported it in my thoughts for over thirty years. Giving it a home is an act of reverence. Oretha Castle Haley, in a matter of months, completely reconfigured me. I remain grateful for her selfless final act. The world knows Haley as the bold, unapologetic, uncompromising Black woman who descended upon segregated New Orleans with hurricane force winds. To those who embraced inequality, she was no ordinary hurricane. She was a category five. She was the pulse of the New Orleans Civil Rights Movement, ushering in a departure from the pacifist patience that had prevailed before she took the reins as a founding member of the New Orleans Chapter of the Congress of Racial Equality (CORE).

As a student at Southern University at New Orleans, she participated in numerous protests in the city involving segregated accommodations and discriminatory employment practices. She was charged with criminal mischief in one instance. That was a minor inconvenience to a woman like Haley. She and her co-defendants took the matter to the SCOTUS and promptly continued their efforts to end segregation, completely undeterred. She worked to register voters throughout the state and beyond. She supported other activists in their pursuits and through their arrests, which was, in the 1960s, expected as an ancillary aspect of social change work.

In 1963, the SCOTUS vindicated her and her co-defendants in Lombard v. Louisiana. A year later, she organized the case that desegregated Charity Hospital in New Orleans. She also organized the New Orleans Sickle Cell Anemia Foundation and worked on several political campaigns to ensure the presence of Black elected officials. Dorothy Mae Taylor, another earth-shattering weather system in her own right, was one. Haley's body of work is extensive.

The aspirations that made Haley an enemy of the state were quite reasonable. She explained, "[a]ll I ever wanted was the basic dignity that every human being ought to have. That basic dignity to function as a free person."[1] I met Haley in the late 1980s, knowing none of what's been described above. To me, she was simply the intimidating figure over the camp for aspiring Black medical professionals. I met her shy and full of self-doubt. By the end of the summer of 1987, her confidence and courage was pumping through my veins. The old me died. I returned to a new school year a new person with a new purpose, a new confidence and a new determination. Haley's course would be tragically different.

About three months later, she departed this world. I am convinced cancer was the only opponent she ever lost to. I owe much of my evolution and professional success to that brief encounter. In 2005, I penned this poem in memory of that encounter:

Segregation. Separate but equal.
White only. Jim Crow.

You weren't hearing it.
You protested, sat in and demonstrated.
There is a school and a street
Named in your honor now.

Not so well known is your imposing
Presence in my 16-year-old face that summer
Telling me not to fear...not to doubt...
To rise and take my place.

Not so well known is the affirming
smile and the convicting nod you
gave me from the audience,
creating a woman immune to self-doubt.

Not so well known is the timing
of our meeting.
Not long after you armed me,
God disarmed you.

A plot orchestrated by the greatest,

understood by few, accepted by all
as the finale, but known only to me
as also the crescendo.

(Angela A. Allen-Bell, © 08/16/05)

I now dedicate what I believe will be my most important work as a lawyer to the giant of a woman who: interrupted the execution of my esteem at the most critical hour; helped me uncover my voice and showed me, through her example, how to use it; taught me the importance of claiming my place in a social struggle; showed me how not to be defined by the prevailing stereotypes about Black women, but, instead, imposed on me a duty to recreate them; and, silently passed a baton when it became clear to her that she couldn't carry it any longer. Through this book and dedication, I attempt to carry it a bit further.

CONTENTS

INTRODUCTION

UNDER INDICTMENT: RACE, JURIES & JUSTICE IN LOUISIANA

Opinion is the lowest form of human knowledge. It requires no accountability and no understanding. The highest form of knowledge... is empathy. For it requires us to suspend our egos and live in another's world. It requires profound purpose larger than the self-kind of understanding.

BILL BULLARD

Twenty-six years ago, I was granted a license to practice law in the state of Louisiana. The pride I felt entering the profession as a first-generation attorney defies description. I approached law with a veneration, believing it to be a faithful partner worthy of my adoration and devotion. Over the ensuing years, we have been inseparable. It was my research that catapulted the movement to end the use of non-unanimous juries in Louisiana. And I was one of the founding members of the advocacy team that led this effort to reform Louisiana's jury system through the adoption of legislation requiring unanimous juries in criminal trials in Louisiana state courts.

The House of Representatives of the Legislature of Louisiana has commended me for my "achievements as a legal scholar" and has recognized and recorded "the tremendous pride and honor" that I bring to the state of Louisiana.[1] I have the distinction of having worked on several other historic advocacy campaigns, such as the Angola 3 case, the case of Soledad Brother John Clutchette, the case of Vincent Simmons and the case of Robert Holbrook. These various experiences acquainted me with aspects of law that law school failed to acknowledge. My vows to law have now been tested.

At the beginning of my career, I could only appreciate the virtues of law because my view of its imperfections had been obstructed. Today, I see law for what it is and not what I had hoped our years together to be. Law has been an unfaithful, abusive, inconsistent and deceptive partner. At intervals, law has been a friend. At times, law has been a remedy. Sometimes, it is a solution. Often, law is power. In instances, it is trauma. Law is an occasional opponent. Law is, at times, an ally. In some situations, law is hypocritical. Law is frequently violent. Law can be a weapon (and a dangerous one at that).

This book is an act of resistance. It punctuates the sentences thought by the maroons before they were killed during chattel slavery because they refused to simply go along.[2] I join them in refusing to simply go along. I join them in demanding another way–a better way. As an activist scholar, I do not write to fill my resume with publications and presentations or with a craving to attain promotion. I write to cause revolutions. I confess the same intention here.

Four years ago, I set out to write a book that would memorialize the change from non-unanimous juries back to jury unanimity in Louisiana. That book would have had a happy ending. The ending was going to celebrate the death of Jim Crow juries. Before the ink could dry on that project, there were signs of Jim Crow lurking still. This time, it was not non-unanimous juries. It was the jury of twelve that we sought, but it was not the jury box that we imagined. Now, the twelve jurors, more often than not, were all white. People of color still–even after the death of non-unanimous juries–were not experiencing the unique power that the jury box could grant them.

And accused people still weren't experiencing the full protections of the Sixth Amendment.

The work of ending non-unanimous juries was a monumental feat, but, in the truth, it did not end Jim Crow juries or jury suppression in Louisiana. In its 2021 report *Race and the Jury Illegal Racial Discrimination in Jury Selection*, released years after non-unanimous juries ended, the Equal Justice Initiative protested the continuing legacy of Black juror suppression. The truth is that the unanimous jury campaign addressed one infinitesimal aspect of a larger pathology when it comes to Black jury justice. It was a reform, but it did not transform.

What was accomplished when non-unanimous juries ended must be understood in context less the victory becomes inflated and the resulting lessons forever lost. This book is an attempt to seize upon those lessons. To do justice to the topic of Jim Crow Juries or jury suppression, the discussion must long predate non-unanimous juries. In fact, it can't begin with juries at all. By necessity, the beginning has to be at the beginning–at the point law and race were joined to create diminished procedural safeguards for those of color, as well as different rights and different restrictions. To be credible, conversations about race and juries must always be anchored to this history.

Chapter one performs a groundbreaking social and historical audit in an effort to advance an understanding of how non-unanimous juries and Black juror suppression lie at the center of a boundless stratosphere where race and supremacy, through the evolution of time, came to intersect with: labor; law, policy and custom; religion; education; justice; medicine; data; and, policing. Changing the future is tied to being able to link people's understanding of what they are witnessing to a seemingly unrelated past. This audit attempts to impart that understanding.

"While the Emancipation Proclamation may have formally ended the system of slavery as it then existed, it did nothing to reverse the economic gains made by whites or to stop its mutation into other forms of systemic racism."[3] When the slavery era ended, little about the chattel slavery system stopped. The social, political and labor dynamics remained intact and shaped life during Reconstruction and beyond. The jury box is connected to this historical reality. Chapter one concludes with four audit findings that help explain the complexion of the jury box and its longevity as a forbidden space for people of color.

The initial finding involves the failure of the country to establish a meaning of freedom for the emancipated people when they were *freed*. This has caused a lack of clarity about the spaces, such as the jury box, Blacks should occupy and how much power is appropriate for Blacks. The jury box is a site of power and a chamber of control. When one sits on a jury, they are no longer amongst the ranks of the ordinary. Momentarily, they claim heightened powers that are tantamount to judicial powers. They, for these moments, are also the functional equivalent of political office holders. As a juror, a person participates in deciding matters that no one outside the jury can have a say in. Those decisions are highly consequential and they have far reach. They set guidelines for society.

Second, the audit finds that individual acts of racism mutated and led to systemic racism. Carter G. Woodson was correct in his observation that "we have been lied to about the inferiority of all things associated with Blackness and the superiority of everything associated with whiteness."[4] In actuality, race is nothing more than a "social construct, a bankrupt attempt to biologize a political system."[5] Yet, we find ourselves locked in an embrace with it. "White supremacy is not a marginal ideology."[6] "It is the early build of the country."[7] "It is the foundation on which social edifice rises, the bedrock of institutions."[8] We haven't been able to extricate ourselves from it. "American society and mainstream culture are premised on the belief in a false hierarchy of human value."[9] Our failure to part with this tendency comes at a cost. Way back during Reconstruction, a warning bell was rung by a member of Congress:

> The negro...will remain here an inhabitant of this country...Political history discloses no folly comparable with the attempt to rid a nation by force and violence of a numerous race of people indigenous to it, as it records no usurpation or royal crime at all equal to it....All attempts in this country to keep alive the old idea of orders of men, distinctions of

class, noble and ignoble, superior and inferior, antagonism of races, are so many efforts at insurrection and anarchy.[10]

The jury is a specific site of systemic racism both for the accused person of color and for the juror or prospective juror of color and the jury is situated in a carceral state polluted with added layers of bias, supremacy and racism, as well as an urge to respond punitively to the most basic of human transgressions. This explains why non-unanimous juries originated, why they survived as long as they did and why there is such resistance to totally ridding the state of the remnants of them.

Thirdly, the audit concludes that the aforementioned became sutured into the veins of a carceral state. Finally, the audit determines, because of these findings, Black juror suppression cannot be viewed in isolation, but, instead, must be analyzed for how it overlaps and intersects with other systems to maintain and rationalize white power and privilege and, systems that, by design, responds punitively to human transgressions, big or small.

"Prior to the Civil War and the subsequent enactment of the thirteenth amendment, African-Americans' exclusion from jury duty remained a national, uniform badge and incident of slavery."[11] Through an inquest, chapter two attempts to explore why this is. Suppressing Black presence in the jury box became the surety for maintaining and rationalizing the white privilege and power design of post-slavery Louisiana. Support for this conclusion emerges as an examination of the intersection between race and political rights–voting, jury service and office holding–in Louisiana is conducted. This inquest concludes that political rights achieve something greater than freedom; they confer power.

To render Blacks powerless, Louisiana exploited a fatal error made when the United States Constitution was written:

> [T]he framers made a consequential mistake when they drafted the Constitution and the Bill of Rights, the Constitution's first ten amendments. They failed to enshrine in these pivotal documents...the right to vote, not just for men or even only white men but for any American. Among many enumerated rights that the government cannot

abridge, the right to vote remained conspicuously absent and remains so today. All subsequent amendments protecting the voting rights of racial minorities, women, and young people....are framed negatively, stipulating not what the states must do to ensure people's voting rights in America[]...but what they cannot do.[12]

Chapter two also exposes an overlooked union between voter suppression and jury suppression in an effort to provide an additional reason why juries can't be approached in isolation. Instead, they must be viewed as entangled with a larger grant of power that the state (and country) has been unwilling to share with Blacks. This inquest is done so change agents can begin to appreciate the shortcomings of reforms and the rewards of transformative change, as well as to understand how to mount a challenge when the desired change involves longstanding ideologies and systemic practices.

Chapter three endeavors to perform an assessment of Louisiana's present legal system. Through an evaluation of cases, stories, policies and laws, the chapter shows, in graphic detail, what has been produced by the systemic inequities and the suppression of political rights explained in the earlier chapters. It illuminates a legal system that operates much like an assembly line. It moves fast, is solely interested profits and production and is automated and impersonal.

The post-script ends the book. It contains images from the final celebration of the non-unanimous jury victory, which took place inside the governor's mansion and included the key players from Phases I, II and III of the campaign.

In her book *Caste: The Origins of Our Discontents*, Isabel Wilkerson, likened caste in the U.S. to an old house with major structural issues. She said, in such an instance, appraisers are hired to find the problem. After, someone else comes along to fix it. Wilkerson goes on to explain, "while it's true that Americans who are alive today had no part in building the uneven pillars, joists and beams, they have taken possession of the house and thus must make the repairs."

This book serves as the appraisal. My book *Diversity in the Jury Box and Beyond: A Formula for Transforming Louisiana Injustice System* should be viewed as the building plans for the new house. My book *The Summons: Advocacy Insights for Systemic and Transformative Change* serves as the tools to be used for the construction of the new home.

As a young girl, my great grandmother showed me the way Biblical love looked. When I was in her care, I felt treasured and special. An intruder caused her death during a robbery. Her crime remains one of many unsolved crimes in New Orleans. What happened that day caused life-long trauma for me. Since that childhood experience, I have been a crime victim a few more times. These firsthand experiences with crime has produced a heightened sensitivity for crime victims.

I ache at the thought of inflicting further harm on any person who has been made a victim of crime, so exploring the various narratives in this book left me in a precarious position. Do I risk harming a victim by sharing some of these stories and in questioning judicial outcomes or do I risk creating a victim by choosing silence? I chose the latter, believing in the medicinal effect of truth. It is my prayer that my analysis proves sound. If I fall short, know insensitivity was never at play.

I entertained the risk of appearing to misrepresent a system by mentioning, in the larger scheme of things, what is actually a relatively small number of incidences. I concede that this is not a scientific study and I acknowledge that the limits of this work prevent a more comprehensive compilation of cases and incidents, but I remain adamant that a fair representation results from what is presented. And I add that, more than an attempt to produce results that can pass muster as a scientifically accurate study, this work seeks to use cases, stories and incidences to bear witness to a seemingly never-ending human struggle for freedom and against the consequences of racial hierarchies. Readers should approach this work with this understanding.

Admittedly and unapologetically, this book amplifies the plight of Blacks. In so doing, there is no intention to inflame racial tensions, indict all white people, diminish the genocide committed against Native Americans, the internment of Japanese Americans during World War II or the collective struggle of people of color. I merely attempt to fill a void that exists relative to the experience of Blacks when they interface with Louisiana's criminal legal system. The oppression of Blacks that I speak of refers to an embodiment of many people of color, represented in the stories of the few.[13]

When it comes to racial inequities or civil and political rights, Confederate states were largely on one accord. Often, methodology for maintaining supremacy was shared amongst some Confederate states, making for a comparable experience amongst Blacks in these jurisdictions. Perhaps less formally, but this spirit of collaboration amongst former Confederate states remains. At pit stops along this journey, the conversation comfortably vacillates from Louisiana to the South and back, such as when voter suppression tactics or the disenfranchisement movement or the sovereignty commissions are discussed. This acknowledges Louisiana's actions as part of a larger Southern trend in an effort to showcase how deeply entrenched the racial inheritances that undergird Louisiana's jury system are. The use of these out-of-state examples or Southern references should not detract from the focal point of the book, which is Louisiana.

While Louisiana is the setting for this story, this story should not be dismissed as a local one. For decades, Louisiana has had the highest incarceration rate of any of the U.S. states, which itself has the highest incarceration rate in the world. Racial hierarchies continue to shape life in Louisiana. Louisiana's criminal legal system continues to need transformation, despite the eradication of non-unanimous juries. From that vantage point, there is something very universal about what might have initially appeared to be a local story. The challenges discussed here exist in workplaces, institutions, schools, agencies, municipalities and systems across the country. This journey begins on local soil, but this is so much more than a local story. The lessons contained herein are boundless and transferable. I hope this book inspires audits, inquests and assessments of all systems that harm.

PREFACE

My work in ending non-unanimous juries in Louisiana inspired this book. I was the only Black female on the initial advocacy team. Because, as a Black woman, marginalization was a lived experience, the plight of the excluded Black juror resonated with me. As a Black person, having race be the outcome-determining factor in most things was also relatable so there was a oneness with all those accused people whose fate rested in the hands of a supposed process and all those excluded Black jurors who had something meaningful to offer, but who were being silenced by exclusion or marginalization. My efforts as a genetically predisposed intermediary begins by centering these dual perspectives—that of the juror of color denied their rightful place and that of the accused person of color denied their rightful process.

When the United States Congress refused to include jury service as a right of the newly emancipated people in the proposed 1872 civil rights bill, Senator Charles Summer correctly warned that, without this protection, "justice [would] find a new impediment in the jury box."[1] This book uses one aspect of Louisiana's justice system—the jury provisions of the Sixth Amendment to the United States Constitution—as an access point into a larger conversation about the legal system and the way it disadvantages people of color by yielding to racial hierarchies and giving shelter to systemic racism, supremacy and bias.

To experience what this book has to offer, one must first understand what a non-unanimous jury is, why they came to be, why Louisiana continued using them for over one hundred and twenty years and the long path of resistance undertaken by Blacks who refused to be denied access to the jury box or who would not acquiesce to attempts to deny them the protections that a jury assures. These are the ambitions of this preface.

A non-unanimous jury verdict occurs when twelve jurors are selected, but a conviction can be obtained upon the vote of less than all twelve members. For example, if jurors one through ten vote "guilty" and jurors eleven through twelve vote "not guilty," a conviction will occur under a non-unanimous jury rule because the vote does not have to be unanimous. Under a unanimous jury rule, all jurors have to vote "guilty" in order for a conviction to occur. In 1803, when Louisiana became a territory, unanimous verdicts were required. From its creation until the end of Reconstruction and the withdrawal of federal troops, Louisiana required unanimous jury verdicts.

Non-unanimous jury verdicts were first introduced in 1880, after slavery ended, when, through newly enacted code provisions, defendants could be convicted by vote of only nine of twelve jurors.[2] Non-unanimous jury verdicts made its way to the Constitution of 1898 by way of article 116 where state officials proclaimed the need for a "system better adapted to the peculiar conditions existing in our state."[3] By 1898, Louisiana had over one hundred and seventy-years of experience as a society that—by law, policy, practice and custom—relegated Black citizens to a status of inferiority and whites to a status of superiority. With civil rights and civil liberties protections largely sidelined, efforts to prevent the exercise of political rights assumed a place of greater priority.

And this was not secreted. Jury service, a political right, was formally reshaped at Louisiana's 1898 Constitutional Convention. Ernest

Benjamin Kruttschnitt was President of the convention. Mr. Kruttschnitt had a far reach in Louisiana politics. He was President of the New Orleans School Board, a respected member of the bar, a member of the White League and Chairman of the Democratic State Central Committee. A series of publications foreshadowed what occurred at the 1898 constitutional convention.

Concerning Blacks voting, another political right, Mr. Kruttschnitt told the *Times-Democrat*: "I favour the plan which will eliminate the largest number of negroes and the smallest number of white men from the electorate in this state." He spoke in harmony with Lieutenant Governor R.H. Snyder who revealed:

> I am in favour of a proposition which will say every white man in the state shall vote because he is white. And no negro shall vote because he is Black. Of course, we cannot put in those words, but we can attain that result. They aim at disfranchising 75 per cent of negroes. Why not disfranchise them all? If we leave the right of suffrage to ten or twenty thousand negroes in this state and the whites divide...these negroes will hold the balance of power, and what could be worse? Could you imagine a greater curse to this state?

Delegate Mr. J. D. Wilkinson told the *Times-Democrat* that he was "opposed to any clause that will let in the negroes. Even if there were only 10,000 negro voters in the state they would prove a disturbing element." These men legislated a change from the unanimous jury in criminal cases that had been used since the Louisiana Purchase to a non-unanimous jury system. The 1898 Constitutional Convention, a convention of all white men, required segregated schools and established literacy tests and poll taxes, which resulted in a reduction of available Black voters. Mr. Kruttschnitt closed the 1898 Constitutional Convention by confessing their success in "Rear[ing] [a system that would] protect the purity of the ballot box, and...perpetuate the supremacy of the Anglo-Saxon race in Louisiana."[4]

Governor Murphy J. Foster, elected in 1892, was only twelve at the time of the Civil War so he did not serve amongst the ranks of the

Confederates, but he definitely shared their ideals. Governor Foster relayed to the legislature in his 1898 message:

> The white supremacy for which we have so long struggled at the cost of so much precious blood and treasure is now crystallized into the Constitution as a fundamental part and parcel of that organic instrument.... With this great principle thus firmly imbedded in the Constitution, and honestly enforced, there need be no longer any fear as to the honesty and purity of our future elections.[5]

Louisiana citizens were not afforded the opportunity to vote to adopt the 1898 Constitution. At the time of the 1898 Convention, 44% of the registered voters in Louisiana were Black. The disenfranchisement movement of the South was well underway.[6] Its "aim was the rejection of the new state constitutions which had gone into effect (under Congress' Reconstruction program) during the 1870s."[7] As the state's 1898 constitutional convention was ongoing, Louisiana lawyer Louis Andrè Martinet, a member of the *Comité des Citoyens* (Citizens Committee in English), an Afro-Creole civil rights organization based in New Orleans that was formed to oppose segregation, was sending letters to various elected Louisiana officials, local judges and the attorney general of the United States complaining of a pattern and practice of dismissing qualified Black jurors from jury service in Louisiana merely because of their race.[8]

In those letters, he complained of frivolous charges being used to incarcerate Blacks and later entrap them into the state's lucrative convict leasing system. He also had misgivings about the effort to convert from a unanimous to a non-unanimous jury system. Martinet expressed this divination: "The purpose is to permanently disenfranchise the colored citizen. The problem uppermost in the minds of the members of this Convention is how to disenfranchise as many colored men and disqualify as few white men without too apparent violation of the Constitution of the United States." Martinet later visited Senator Chandler of New Hampshire who shared the Citizens Committee's concerns with the Senate Judiciary Committee and demanded a full investigation into jury service in Louisiana.[9]

Martinet's efforts weren't entirely in vain. Just a week before the 1898 convention, the U. S. Senate passed a resolution calling for an investigation into whether Louisiana was systemically excluding Blacks from juries followed by a report back to the Senate.[10] The mere threat of federal oversight was enough to inspire Louisiana officials to imagine clandestine approaches to jury suppression. Thus, the 1898 convention's "race-neutral" strategies–non-unanimous juries, grandfather clauses, literacy tests and the 1898 Louisiana Voter Application that had to be completed without assistance and which included a series of questions that would disqualify Blacks because they lacked "good character."[11]

As a result of this 1898 constitution, the number of Black convicts increased and the number of Black voters diminished. In short, Louisiana's decision to change its longstanding jury practice from unanimity was to: (1) obtain quick convictions that would facilitate the use of free prisoner labor (by means of Louisiana's convict leasing system) as a replacement for the recent loss of free slave labor;[12] (2) ensure Black jurors would not use their voting power to block convictions of other Blacks; and, (3) reinforce ongoing voter suppression efforts.[13]

When the 1898 law was revisited at the 1973 Constitutional Convention, the law was changed to require the vote of at least ten of twelve.[14] As in 1898, "efficiency" was a stated reason. Some mistakenly concluded that this sanitized the racial history surrounding the law. In truth, race was not completely removed from the discussion at the 1973 Convention. There was a warning that "ugly, poor, illiterate and mostly minority groups" would be impacted, as well as concerns expressed about the system undermining the reasonable doubt standard.

There was also great discussion of inequities as the codification of equality into the constitution was of up for consideration. [15] Tellingly, the 1973 delegates refused to support a clause denouncing racial discrimination despite common knowledge that prior constitutions had made such legal and customary. The non-unanimous jury system survived—not because it was studied and deemed to be in the best interest of justice—but, because of a process that mutes the voices of some and amplifies the voices of others. As one scholar observed: "the constitution of 1974 was written...by a wide and self-interested assortment of assessors, sheriffs, legislators, judges, lackeys and anyone who could get elected or appointed."[16] This isn't the only reason this system remained intact. As one Louisiana court observed, "[R]acial tension was still present in the community in 1974."[17]

It was only two years prior that Angola stopped practicing segregation. Also in 1972, Baton Rouge law enforcement was engaged in a public confrontation with Black Muslims that continued through court battles for some years. Only a few years prior, in 1970, Governor John McKeithen, in expressing his opposition to federal plans to force school desegregation by busing students into different schools for purposes of achieving a racial balance, remarked that a Louisiana parish that had 3000 Blacks and 390 whites would "be turned into a ghetto" if the federal plans were implemented.[18] That same month, McKeithen referred to the Congress of Racial Equality (CORE) as "an organization with a reputation for militancy."

In 1974, the state of Louisiana was still in court insisting that Students United, Black student leaders on Southern University's (SU) Baton Rouge campus remain enjoined from entering campus and/or participating in campus activities (discussed in greater detail at the end of chapter one).[19] There is further evidence that Louisiana had not entered its post-racial days in 1974, the year that Gary Tyler's forty-two-year nightmare started. A brick throwing mob surrounded Tyler's bus carrying Black students who were forced to integrate a formally all-white school in Destrehan, Louisiana.

13-year-old Timothy Weber, who was standing across the schoolyard with his mother, was fatally shot. Sixteen-year-old Tyler would pay the price. He was initially charged with disturbing the peace. A gun that wasn't located on the bus during an initial search mysteriously appeared later. The absence of Tyler's fingerprints was inconsequential to the all-white jury. They didn't care about the absence of ballistics either. Tyler was convicted and sentenced to death.[20]

The long life of jury suppression can't be attributed to inattention or a lack of persistence. Martinet holds a place in a long line of jury justice crusaders. A 1864 N.O. Tribune editorial writer called for a "complete reform...[of] laws relating to the formation of the jury."[21] In a 1876 Colored Tribune editorial, a writer complained about Black juror exclusion, noting that "[t]he same midnight marauders who kill a colored man, hold the inquest upon his body, and sit upon the juries whenever any of their number is arrested, to the exclusion of all colored men."[22] And nameless Southern citizens sent letters to Congress in the 1870's reporting that Blacks were being excluded from Southern juries.[23] The 1886 "Justice, Protective, Educational, and Social Club" also advocated for jury justice. Their purpose was to make sure Louisiana protected and respected the rights of Black citizens.

The organization produced the newspaper *The New Orleans Crusader*.[24] The newspaper informed the Black public on local and national issues like racial injustice, inequality, and segregation. It advocated extensively for Blacks to be included on juries.[25] And complained that anything less would continue to render Blacks as a man "who is of age for his faults, but a minor for his rights."[26] Through seasons, the identity of even more members of this nameless society of jury crusaders became known to me. In a 1895 meeting of the Citizens Committee, the group announced that the "The Jim Crow jury should be fought to death" then the group agreed to sell subscriptions to raise the proceeds to fight a legal battle against Black juror exclusion.[27]

I would discover that Booker T. Washington, the formerly enslaved person who founded Tuskegee Normal and Industrial Institute (Now Tuskegee University) in 1881 and became an influential intellectual, held membership also.[28] Washington composed a February 19, 1898, open letter to the Louisiana Constitutional Convention. In it, he urged Louisiana officials to seize their unique moment in history. He began, "Since the war, no state has had such an opportunity to settle for all time the race question...as is now given Louisiana."[29] He rather prophetically indicated that his concern "affects the civilization of two races, not for a day alone, but for a very long time to come..."[30] I would discover that

Thurgood Marshall was amongst the ranks of those who fought for jury justice.

In the 1940's, he challenged the deliberate exclusion of Blacks from Mississippi juries.[31] In the 1960s and 1970s, Louisiana attorneys Richard Sobol and Ernest Jones stood knee deep in the murky waters of jury justice battles in state and federal court. In the 1990s, Thaddeus Edmonson, a Black Louisiana construction worker, was inducted into the society of jury crusaders. He challenged the exclusion of Black jurors by private litigants in civil cases and won.[32] W. E. B. DuBois expressed bitter discontent over the "very few Negro members of juries."[33]

A year prior, the NAACP included claims of jury suppression in the South in its human rights petition to the United Nations, noting they are either excluded from the lists of potential jurors or removed though peremptory challenges or challenges for cause.[34] By 1961, The United States Commission on Civil Rights joined the growing chorus of voices, finding that the practice of excluding Blacks from juries persisted.[35] Unaware of much of this history, in 2016, I anxiously penned a letter to over one hundred Louisiana legislators, criminal justice stakeholders and other change agents asking for their joined hand in my crusade to end the use of non-unanimous juries in Louisiana state courts.

At a fleeting pace, my lone plea turned into a collaboration that became a campaign, which morphed into a movement. On November 6, 2018, I joined supporters at a watch party to await the results of the historic ballot initiative. This Jim Crow Era law was read its last rights. With no big marquee candidates on the statewide ballot and in an off-year election, sixty-four percent of Louisiana voters cast a vote to end the use of non-unanimous juries.[36]

Jonathan Wallick, Marjorie Esman, Vera Lynn Dampeer,

Malik Rahim & Angela A. Allen-Bell. Photo credit Will Snowden

In true New Orleans style, an impromptu second line funeral preceded a spirited repast after the results were announced that night. Cheers, whistles, horns, rhythmic moves and chants competed with the sounds and images coming from the newscast that blared on the stage. Caged emotions were released. The smell of victory was in the air that night.

Not long after, in *Ramos v. Louisiana* (2020), the SCOTUS ruled that the Sixth Amendment right to a jury trial—as incorporated against the states by way of the Fourteenth Amendment—requires a unanimous verdict to convict a defendant of a serious offense. Years later, I became stilled by some realizations that time had safely held in its care. The first was that what I witnessed that November 2018 was actually a win and never the victory we excitedly declared that night. Second came clarity about the fact that juries can't be addressed singularly because of the way they are situated in a contaminated system.

Lastly, came clarity about all those letters I had mailed. The thought crystalized with time. When I sealed those letters years earlier, I bound far more than my personal plea. As I secured those letters, I had unknowingly fastened myself to a perpetual struggle. In so doing, I inadvertently became installed as a member of a recondite society of jury justice crusaders. The membership scrolls included members of the Citizens Committee, Louis A. Martinet, Booker T. Washington, W. E.

B. DuBois, Thurgood Marshall, Richard Sobol, Ernest Jones, Thaddeus Edmonson and the advocates referenced throughout this book.

With this composite view of the breadth and depth of the jury justice struggle came an awareness that the efforts of those of us who worked to end non-unanimous juries was neither a start or a finish; they were a continuation. With these insights, it became clear that pausing my efforts would be an insult to my other members who never paused theirs. I strategized on the best next steps and realized that this story of a fight for jury justice held within its womb a new life–a means to transformation. In these pages, I unveil the first of a three-part strategy for transformative change.

Specifically, this book seeks to: (1) aid the reader in viewing Louisiana's unanimous jury campaign in its racial and historical context; (2) examine the historical connection between Black juror suppression and how it is bound up in the creation and perpetuation of race and supremacy; (3) situate the jury at the center of a carceral state polluted with bias, supremacy and racism, as well as an urge to respond punitively to the most basic of human transgressions; (4) help readers achieve a holistic and comprehensive view of Louisiana's legal system and the competing factors and interests that have shaped it and led to it becoming harmful to most who come in contact with it; and, (5) to awaken a desire for transformation.

The opportunity that this moment holds is too great to measure. I rely heavily on the beloved church father John Chrysostom in doing this phase of my jury work. Chrysostom's recipe calls for a rather unique blending of ingredients. Chrysostom suggests generous portions of empathy and compassion and maybe a dose of pain. He explained, "if you behave too leniently to one who needs deep surgery, and do not make a deep incision in one who requires it, you mutilate yet miss the cancer.

But if you make the needed incision without mercy, often the patient, in despair at his sufferings, throws all aside . . . and promptly throws himself over a cliff." The pain produced by the revelations in this book are necessary because I want to remove all the side effects produced by the maladies of supremacy, racial hierarchies, bias and racism, but I don't want to cause the despair that leaves one hopeless enough to jump off a cliff. My prayer is that I will perform this maneuver mercifully and with precision.

CHAPTER 1

A HISTORICAL AND SOCIAL AUDIT: AN EXPOSITORY INTO SYSTEMIC INEQUITIES IN LOUISIANA

History is not the past. It is the present. We carry our history with us. We are our history.[1]

— JAMES BALDWIN

Louisiana boasts of alluring natural resources, the world's most exuberant football fans, rousing linguistic variances, savory cuisine, celebrated architecture, world-class hunting and fishing options, euphonious music and intriguing art and entertainment, including a rivaled Mardi Gras experience. This elusive narrative of a tourist paradise negates the experiences of many of Louisiana's Black residents. Many of them, through interactions with Louisiana's legal system, are reduced to twenty-first century free people of color existing in a state of neo-slavery.[2]

This chapter examines the historical connection between Black juror suppression and how it is bound up in the creation and perpetuation of race and supremacy. This census is taken in an effort to advance an understanding of how non-unanimous juries and Black juror suppression lie within an ozone where race and supremacy, through the evolution of time, came to intersect with: labor; law, policy and custom; religion; education; justice; medicine; data; and, policing.

Successful transition of Louisiana's legal system is contingent on the ability to establish truth then reconcile "what is" with "why" it is. Through this audit, an effort is made to understand not only events, but their causes and impacts. This audit will answer "what is." The chapter also gives the "why"–individual acts of racism mutated and led to systemic racism, which provides the infrastructure for the carceral state. Because of this, Black juror suppression cannot be viewed in isolation. The jury must be analyzed for how it overlaps and intersects with other systems to maintain and rationalize white power and privilege. In this spirit, a social audit of the Black experience in Louisiana, from arrival through the establishment of what we now recognize as legal and penal systems, follows.

The Start of Black Life & the Origins of Race and Law in Louisiana

In 1682, French explorers arrived at the American coast of the Gulf of Mexico. By 1699, their flag was planted and they had declared thousands of acres in Louisiana theirs, despite the fact that various Native American tribes were already occupying that land.[3] France was insolvent from years of war. It was struggling to operate, but it seized upon the opportunity to undermine the interests of the Spanish, English and the Dutch. Sieur de la Salle secured a contract for the colonization of Louisiana from Louis XIV. Thereafter, he left France with 100 soldiers, a year's worth of supplies and 280 men, women and children. To France, Louisiana offered some attractive natural benefits, such as the Mississippi River. It also offered rich mixtures of soils and a variety of terrains, including marshes and swamps. There was a plenitude of native species, which indigenous populations had survived on, such as whitetail deer, opossum, rabbit, armadillo, raccoon, squirrel, otter, muskrat, bobcat, birds, snakes, alligator, fish and crustaceans. But there were challenges.

Diseases plagued the place. Additionally, Louisiana had long seasons of heat and humidity. It rained and flooded a lot and hurricanes were a real threat. The French knew nothing about surviving in Louisiana conditions. While French colonists were new to the area, they were seasoned when it came to slavery. The gained much experience from enslaving Africans in the Caribbean colonies of French Antilles, Martinique and Guadeloupe. The initial colonists and military that occupied Louisiana often went unpaid. Shipments of food from France regularly arrived spoiled due to the harsh conditions. They became dependent on the Native Americans who were skilled at navigating the land. Some of the Native American people generously shared their acquired survival skills.[4] Abhorrently, the French began enslaving the Native Americans, officially introducing the practice of chattel slavery in 1706.

This strategy was short-lived, partly because of the introduction of diseases that killed the natives who lacked an immunity, partly because the natives knew escape routes and elected to use them too often and partly because many of the natives practiced direct action, such as combat. The 1729 Natchez Revolt is one such example. French administrators made the fatal mistake of taking the kindness of the Natchez tribe for weakness. The tribe responded to attempts to take their land with a massacre, resulting in over two hundred deaths. At this juncture, the rule of law was shaped by French and Spanish rulers who were in command at different times.[5]

Challenged to find settlers for Louisiana, France contracted with Antoine Crozat, financial secretary to Louis XIV. In 1712, he and his company received a fifteen-year commercial monopoly over Louisiana. By 1712, a definable rule of law was in place. Antoine Crozat's charter stipulated that royal proclamations and the Customs of Paris constituted law in the territory. Under this scheme, military men exercised the functions of civil government, with no courts in operation at this point. Individual freedoms were great; political rights were virtually non-existent. The French Superior Council, modeled after the Parliament of Paris, was introduced. The Superior Council had both judicial and legislative functions. It functioned as a governing body and a high court. In general, the white Creoles had power and social standing and great influence with the Superior Council.

Crozat failed, ending his contract in 1717. John Law, who operated the Company of the Indies (initially called Company of the West), saw great potential in the colony. He managed to populate it with servants, criminals and other undesirables from France, German immigrants and slaves from Africa who, unlike the Native Americans, would not know an escape route. Under John Law's rein, some land grants were given. This helped usher in non-military, white settlers. The first cargo of enslaved Africans arrived in Louisiana in 1719 with superior artisan, craftsman and boatmen skills, as well as knowledge of cotton, rice, tobacco, indigo and corn cultivation.[6]

By 1724, chattel slavery of Africans was well underway and the *Code Noir*, which was introduced to regulate race relations and slavery, existed as a source of law that governed them.[7] This created an intersection between race and law that has, tragically, become a recurring theme for Blacks in Louisiana.[8] The *Code Noir* had a unique history. It was the offspring of the code that the French used to govern the enslaved in the Caribbean, suggesting the origins of law in Louisiana for Blacks involve an approach to lawmaking that normalized different and separate rules for Blacks.[9] Under this *Code Noir*, Blacks couldn't be players in the legal process because they weren't, in the eyes of the law, qualified for civic or social life.

"By 1732, enslaved Africans accounted for approximately 65 percent of the total population in Louisiana."[10] The stage was set for Black life in colonial Louisiana. In 1751, sugar cane was first introduced into Louisiana. During this era, the enslaved worked on farms and plantations (the plantation system had not yet come to dominate Louisiana society) for long hours and under brutal conditions. Others dug drainage canals, laid streets or worked on levees. With the change to Spanish rule in 1763 came a new legal and governmental structure.[11] In 1769, the Spanish replaced the French Superior Council with the Cabildo, which operated like a judicial system and city council combined. Louisiana was divided into parishes at this time. For its rule of law, the Spanish used codes, custom and Spanish colonial law.[12] This transition afforded shallow dignities to Blacks.

The French system focused more on the interests of owners of the enslaved. The Spanish system created new options for the enslaved. For example, it was under the Spanish system that manumission, the practice of allowing slaves to purchase their freedom, came to be. Also, the Spanish code allowed abused slaves to make formal complaints against their masters. The Spanish promoted the concept of keeping the enslaved content, which, in turn, minimized the risk of flight. By way of illustration, they awarded the enslaved a barrel of corn monthly; personal fields on the plantation to cultivate and use; Sunday's off; and, more mobility. During the carnival season, the enslaved masked, mixed with the people in the streets and attended dances.[13] This approach to governing Louisiana's Black residents survived the era. As these local developments unfolded, important national developments were taking place.

In 1776, the Declaration of Independence, the founding document of the country, was adopted. It presents grievances against King George IV and gives an account of why the colonies became sovereign and ended British rule. Life under a British dictator with unchecked power produced a yearning for equality once independence from Brittan was achieved. To memorialize its ambitions for the new society, the Declaration reads: "all men are created equal, that they are endowed by their Creator with certain unalienable Rights, that among these are Life, Liberty and the pursuit of Happiness." Slavery, a system that deprived Blacks of all three, was thriving as the ink on the Declaration dried. For Blacks, the rule of law would become as catastrophic as the constant duress of intense heat, calamitous floods, destructive storms and hurricanes and captivity. Law would remain hypocritical to Blacks. The federal constitution is afflicted with the same birth defects as the Declaration. It was ratified in 1789, at the height of chattel slavery. Similarly, the promise of liberty and justice is enshrined in it.

The Founders who framed our Constitution were men who commanded great respect, but "they were disciples of thinkers who believed in the inherent inequity of humankind" and they believed "that those who did not belong to their ranks were less than human."[14] In 1791, the Sixth Amendment to the United States Constitution, written by James

Madison, was ratified. It provided for, amongst other things, trial by an impartial jury. Enslaved Blacks in Louisiana had no liberty, no justice and no jury trial rights, but the country had written these rights into sacred legal doctrines. For Blacks, this hypocrisy conveyed several lessons about law. It taught them that law could be drafted in such a way that it could protect and harm simultaneously. Its verbiage could conceal the worst of intentions. Law could formalize and legitimize their exclusion. Law could assume the appearance of legitimacy. At this point, exclusion of Blacks and positioning them on the margins went mainstream.

By the mid-1790s, a plantation economy and culture had been realized and the population had grown impressively. "When the Spanish first acquired Louisiana, forty-nine Natchitoches planters harvested eighty thousand pounds of tobacco per year; by 1791 eighty-three plantations there yielded more than seven hundred thousand pounds."[15] Law kept expanding too, but not in an organized, linear pattern. At the time of the Louisiana Purchase in 1803, Louisiana was being governed by the laws of Spain. They were voluminous, confusing and included conflicting provisions that few could decipher.[16] On the local level, jury trial rights were introduced in 1804 while Louisiana was still a territory. The Crimes Act of 1805, setting forth the punishment of crimes and misdemeanors, was intended to bring order and reform to the territorial period.[17] It was ordered by sections and the sections listed punishable offenses, provided definitions of crimes and gave sentence ranges. The act gave the appearance of a uniform system taking form, but this wasn't so. It did not apply to Blacks.

In 1806, the legislature passed a Black Code, which repealed many Spanish laws and imposed new, stricter regulations on the affairs of the enslaved and free people of color. Beyond imposing harsher penalties, it criminalized things that the Crimes Act of 1805 did not. For whites, a new legal system, in the form of a Civil Code, was adopted in 1808.[18] In 1812, the year Louisiana became a state, Edward Livingston was commissioned by the Louisiana legislature to prepare a plan for a system of criminal law.[19] By 1841, there was a compilation of criminal statutes.[20] And by 1855, two comprehensive criminal statutes replaced all other laws: "An Act Relative to Crimes and Offenses" and "An Act to Regulate the Mode of Procedure in Criminal Prosecutions." The first defined 127 wrongs and gave the punishment for each. The second established the first procedural rules to be used. The appearance of progress did not extend to Blacks. For them, law would still not equate with justice in Louisiana. It continued to be synonymous with power, domination, inequity and hypocrisy.

<u>The Introduction & Use of Racial Hierarchies</u>

"Racial classifications can be traced back some 400 years ago to European scientists who sought to classify human beings under the false belief that European civilization at the time was 'civilized' and 'advanced,' contributing to the perpetuated belief that white and European ideals and modes of operating are better and should dominate."[21] In the 1700s, "Swedish botanist Carl Linnaeus's taxonomy reduced all people perceived as being different from Europeans to the status of 'less than' and 'other.'"[22] Despite him never having visited Africa, Asia or America, his views about the inferiority of people of color gained traction. Before his "science," superiority of white Europeans had been substantiated by religious arguments.

The racial hierarchies that presently govern life in Louisiana were conceived during this period and imposed through law.[23] "By the time Louisiana changed hands from the French to the Spanish in 1763, racial distinctions had been firmly in the colony through regulations that limited the reach of manumission, created distinct rules for 'negros' and 'freed or free-born negros,' and blurred the lines between 'negros' and slaves."[24] "Legal race making became a distinctive feature of Atlantic slave societies, reducing Africans and their descendants to....subjects without history, honor or genealogy."[25] "Blackness obliterated and flattened a multitude of cultures, languages, histories, and experiences into a single legally defined, socially constituted category of degradation."[26]

In this same period, the nation's first census was taken. Racial hierarchies presented themselves there. At that time in 1790, there were only three racial categories: free white people, "all other free persons," and the enslaved.[27] Three-fifths of the slave count went towards a state's population figures used to determine apportionment of congressional seats. Through the census, race dictated if you were recognized in a democracy or excluded from it. By the mid 1800's, the census categories of race changed, seemingly with the South in mind. The 1850 and 1860 censuses used separate forms for enslaved people and counted the enslaved under the name of their owners. In so doing, the experience of Blacks could never be centered, reflected or even considered in a democracy. This practice entered the jury box.

Race dictated social privileges and opportunities and was a "key category of difference, stratification, and social worth...."[28] Through law, race became an impenetrable wall. Confusion over racial identity prompted extreme reactions, such as when, in the late 1800s, a prominent white man found himself accused of being Black. The courthouse that housed the vital records was immediately burned.[29] Racial identity litigation was not uncommon. In 1910, a white family sued a railcar company because their two white daughters were removed from the seating area reserved for whites and instructed to occupy seats in the section that was reserved for Blacks. [30] The linchpin of the case was racial identity. If the girls were white, the railcar company was liable for the "mortification and humiliation" these white parents complained of. If they were Black, the railcar company followed the law and could not be held liable.

Because of testimony that the white father was of mixed blood, the court deemed the girls less than pure white and, as such, concluded the railcar company was not liable to the parents. Mixed blood disqualified them from being white. Susie Guillory Phipps, the wife of a well-to-do white businessman in Sulphur, Louisiana, tried to change a piece a paper that said she was Black. In her mind, having her birth certificate pronounce her white could remove her social and political stain. She engaged in a costly and lengthy legal battle that death could not even end.[31] The litigation consumed the court's time for years.[32] That's how valuable being white is under the racial hierarchies. Jury service conveyed a loud and clear message during racial identity trials. Often, the most compelling evidence was that a man had voted, sat on juries, held office, mustered in the militia, or married a white woman—all acts of citizenship that could not be performed by Black men.

Evidence of upstanding reputation, of social reception, and of the exercise of the privileges of a white man was outcome determinative. During these racial identity trials, courts found associations with citizenship and the display of moral and civic virtues persuasive proof of white identity.[33] Blackness was "coterminous with enslavement and exclusion from the political order."[34] This thinking found its way into the jury box. By the late 1900s, the racial and social practices of the slavery era had been normalized again. Segregation was the official policy, practice and custom of the state.[35] It etched a brand of legality on a system of social degradation and, for Blacks, amounted to literal exclusion from American life. Black skin was viewed as proof of inhumanity and certification of inferiority.

Black hands could not even touch white books.[36] The jubilation of sporting celebrations was overshadowed by race.[37] Pools, circuses, schools, hospitals, court rooms, neighbourhoods, prisons and every other aspect of life in Louisiana was segregated by race.[38] The end to legal segregation did not end of the use of racial hierarchies. Race still dictates consequences, opportunities, privileges and norms. Being white conferred certain "psychological wages":

> Whites were given public deference and titles of courtesy because they were white. They were admitted freely with all classes of white people to public functions, public parks, and the best schools. The police were drawn from their ranks, and the courts, dependent upon their votes, treated them with such leniency as to encourage lawlessness. Their vote selected public officials, and....had great effect upon the deference shown to them.[39]

Contrarily, being Black meant being "subject to public insult; [being]... afraid of mobs; [being] liable to the jibes of children and the unreasoning fears of white women;...[being] compelled almost continuously to submit to various badges of inferiority...[and having] wages kept low...."[40] Racial hierarchies gained national acceptance with little to no understanding of this history or of the way these baseless rankings unjustifiably elevated "white" to the superior rank. Law offered no protection for Blacks. If fact, it was the source of their greatest harm at this juncture. Even before a formal system of racial hierarchies took effect, supremacy existed. The practice of associating entitlement to experience citizenship with complexion entered the jury box as did the practice of using color as a pretext for assigning adverse consequences.

Replacing Chattel Slavery With Slavery by Law

In 1793, the cotton gin, which increased cotton production, was invented, shoring up even greater profits for Southern slaveholders. Breeding of the enslaved replaced the importation of African captives, adding an additional dimension of sexual violence and exploitation to plantation life. Around this time, enslaved Africans in France decided that their freedom could no longer be someone else's possession. This uprising prompted the Haitian Revolution, which interrupted sugar production in Haiti; thereby, increasing demand for sugar production in Louisiana. By 1860, nearly one-third of cotton exported from the United States was grown in Louisiana. Plantation commerce, by this point, was a part of global intercourse. Trade and credit connections were steadily increasing. However, ownership of agricultural land, resources and enslaved people was concentrated to a minority and not a majority of whites in Louisiana.

"Into the hands of the slaveholders the political power of the South was concentrated, by their social prestige, by property ownership and also by their extraordinary rule of the counting of all or at least three-fifths of the Negros as part of the basis of representation in the legislature.[41] This "slavocracy" controlled every dimension of life.[42] "They formulated the theory of white supremacy and made it the *sine qua non* of Southern life."[43] For them, Louisiana was an economic and commercial windfall. A surge in African slaves resulted at the behest of the plantation owners and/or Creole elites who were prospering greatly. Other whites were beneficiaries of the system, such as dealers and overseers. But, the majority of whites in Louisiana were "economic outcasts."[44] Notwithstanding that, no "Black man, according to the white supremacy doctrine, was ever to attain a position as high as that of the lowest white."[45] Efforts to disrupt this system would not be greeted politely.

As prosperity visited some whites, doom dwelled within Louisiana's enslaved population. "The experience of slavery in America was an institutionalized affront that was multiple in its modes of operation and unimaginable in the harm that it caused."[46] Its impacts are difficult to identify and even harder to quantify. Prolific historian and sociologist W. E. B. DuBois describes the cataclysmic nature of chattel slavery:

> [The enslaved]...had no right of petition....They could own nothing; they could make no contracts; they could hold no property...they could not hire out; they could not legally marry nor constitute families; they could not control their children; they could not appeal from their master; they could be punished at will. They could not testify in court; they could be imprisoned by their owners, and the criminal offense of assault and battery could not be committed on the person of a slave... The slave owed to his master and all his family a respect 'without bounds, and an absolute obedience'....A slave could not sue his master; had no right of redemption; nor right of education or religion; a promise made to a slave by his master had no force of validity. Children followed the condition of the slave mother. The slave could have no access to the judiciary. A slave might be condemned to death for striking a white person.[47]

As would be observed in the halls of Congress, the enslaved were not persons; they were chattels or things.[48] Once enslaved, one's fate was sealed and the escape routes were few. Suicide was one of the limited options.[49] Running away was another, but then the brutal realities of capture would have to be contemplated. Under the 1724 *Code Noir*, a runaway who abandoned his post for up to a month would have his ears cut off and a fleur-de-lis branded on one shoulder; a second offense would result in one being hamstrung and a fleur-de-lis branded on his other shoulder; and, death followed a third attempt. Choucoura's story is convincing proof that the *Code Noir* did not house an idle threat. The official report of him being captured as a runaway states that he was put in irons until his owner claimed him. Tellingly, the document is captioned: "In re: maimed negro."[50]

Neither death of an owner, infirmity or old age of the enslaved would assure freedom from servitude. The July 19, 1739, succession of a slave owner illuminates this point. It contains a notice of auction for "an old, infirm and half-blind Black female slave....."[51] Reducing slavery to its least common denominator suggests that the enslaved existed under "a hereditary system of marginalization."[52] Slavery was a life of exclusion that offered few escape routes from subjugation and oppression. These themes found their way into the jury box. By the late 1800's, when emancipation became a conversation, Louisiana's first system of mass incarceration–chattel slavery–was successfully operational. "Legislatures, courts, executives, almost every person holding political or social power and position in the southern states, were all arrayed on the side of slavery...."[53] Churches in the South were even tolerant of it or advocates for it.[54] The federal government had also given its full backing and support.[55]

"The plantation system came to dominate every aspect of southern life, including settlement patterns, transportation, and location of towns and cities."[56] Attempts to dismantle this system were assailed. This lesson was potently imparted by Democratic Congressman Preston Brooks through the paralyzing blows of a cane. In 1856, Mr. Brooks used his cane to beat Charles Sumner, an abolitionist and advocate for equal rights, to a pulp on the floor in the United States Congress, requiring him to take leave of his Senate duties for three years in order to recuperate. The beating was viewed as a fitting response to a champion for the "cause of niggerism."[57] The House's response was a shortage of the votes needed to expel representative Brooks. Beyond this tacit approval, there was public support. Mr. Brooks won reelection after this. Hindsight would prove this to be the "moment when all pretense of civility between North and South broke down and the question of civil war became a matter of when rather than if."[58]

In 1860, President Abraham Lincoln was elected (without a single popular vote from Louisiana). Fifteen of the thirty-four states were slave states and, at the time, the states had supreme authority over their affairs.

The national government could provide little to no protection to individuals inside state lines. This was a coveted reality for Southern states so they responded to Mr. Lincoln's election with subversion and treason. They withdrew from the Union and adopted a Confederate Constitution that supported slavery and states' rights.[59] This was not a rogue act by some extremists in Louisiana. The state provided fiscal and policy support.[60] During this period, two governments existed in Louisiana. The Confederates ran one and the federal government ran the other, making slavery legal in parts of the state and illegal in others. On March 4, 1861, a month after President Lincoln took the oath of office, shots fired, marking the start of the Civil War, "the bloodiest, most devastating conflict in American history."[61]

"The Civil War, a conflict between political as well as economic philosophies, divided the country by region and position on the slave issue."[62] The war lasted twenty years. The death toll has been estimated to be as high as 750,000 lost lives.[63] Black men and men of color in Louisiana would be in that count, either as Confederate soldiers, as Union soldiers or as enslaved people forced to aid their owners as they fought for the Confederacy.[64] Sketches of these proud Black fighters never made their way into the commissioned portrait of the Black man that would be displayed to the world. The institution of slavery might have come to end on the battlefield, but the beliefs and mindset surrounding it was never fought. And what isn't killed grows.

The Thirteenth Amendment, described by many as the legislation that formally ended chattel slavery in the United States, was ratified right after the Civil War. It was one of several steps in President Lincoln's plan to reconstruct the union.[65] The debates of the Amendment capture a range of conflicting concerns and sentiments raised, but rarely settled.[66] This irresoluteness proved detrimental to Louisiana's Black population. Those debates reveal a lack of unanimity as to what emancipation meant in the minds of these legislators, some of whom were supporters of the Southern cause and others of whom were opponents of it. Some legislators questioned if emancipation would confer civil rights, political rights or liberty alone.[67] Others such as Senator Trumbull, chairman of the Senate Judiciary Committee, interpreted the Amendment as a broad grant of freedom, remarking that "it is idle to say that a man is free who cannot enforce his rights .... [Congress must] give effect to the provision... making all persons free."[68]

Federalism provided an additional undercurrent as some feared that the Thirteenth Amendment's enforcement language granted Congress too much power.[69] Others concurred with ending slavery, but dissented as to whether enforcement language was needed given their view that Congress had power to act pursuant to its "necessary and proper" powers.[70] There were even those who believed the Thirteenth Amendment suffered a constitutional shortcoming because, as they saw it, ending slavery amounted to an unconstitutional takings (in the form of Congress taking property from a state or individual in a state). There were also concerns about Southern underrepresentation in Congress. This ambivalence claimed a seat on the Southern jury. The verbiage proved to be yet another source of contention.[71] The Representatives ultimately settled upon existing language and avoided the challenges that an entirely new piece of legislation could prompt.[72]

The Thirteenth Amendment of the United States Constitution is brief, but broad in its scope. It reads:

> Section 1. Neither slavery nor involuntary servitude, except as a punishment for crime whereof the party shall have been duly convicted, shall exist within the United States, or any place subject to their jurisdiction.

> Section 2. Congress shall have power to enforce this article by appropriate legislation.

President Lincoln was alive when the legislature adopted the Thirteenth Amendment, but he did not live to witness final ratification.[73] He was assassinated on April 14, 1865. The next day, his efforts to reconstruct the South was read its last rights. Successor Andrew Johnson became President. He hastily vetoed an extension to the Freedmen's Bureau Act[74] then he pardoned and granted amnesty to numerous Confederate officials and former slaveowners.[75]

Democrats and the people of the South collectively exhaled about the tide change that was underfoot. Even without Presidential support, a partial federal commitment to fully transitioning the formerly enslaved remained. Those federal officials viewed legal protections, such as citizenship status, equal protection and due process of law, as an essential part of this process. Towards these ends, there was a push to adopt the Fourteenth Amendment to the United States Constitution.

In 1866, William Windom stressed the urgency of action: "They have demonstrated...by the reenactment of vagrant laws and slave codes for freedmen, with how much sincerity they agreed to the abolition of slavery, and how readily that institution, abolished in name, may be reestablished in fact and with increased cruelty."[76] His appeal roused apprehension. Representative Robert S. Hale questioned the meaning and implications of the words "equal protection." Would this make Black men equal to Black men or would it make Black men equal to white men?[77] There was an added concern that this amendment could inadvertently render women equal to men and children equal to parents. Federalism concerns were raised again, with some expressing that the Amendment would "take away the power of the states" and "centralize a consolidated power" in the federal government.[78]

There were also concerns about whether passage of the Fourteenth Amendment would confer voting rights and, if so, there were attempts to understand who would hold power over voting. The Fourteenth Amendment was ultimately adopted a year *after* slavery ended. At this juncture, the notion of treating Blacks as citizens–equal to whites–was viewed as "radical" and not fully embraced.[79] By this point, governments in Confederate states had been declared illegal by Congress.[80] Federal military administrations were existing in their place. Congress refused to seat representatives from Confederate states until they: adopted constitutions guaranteeing the vote to the newly emancipated population; ratified the Fourteenth Amendment; repudiate ordinances of secession as well as their war debt; and, ratify the Thirteenth Amendment. Toward these ends, constitutional conventions were called in 1868.

The opening remarks of Louisiana's 1868 Constitutional Convention offer an unintended glimpse into the buoyancy of Louisiana's Confederates. Representative G.M. Wickliffe begins the proceedings placatingly: "The delegates to this Convention, as the direct and legal representatives of the Radical Republican party, and as the true friends of the colored race, do hereby utterly repudiate all desire for class legislation, and all desire to Africanize the state of Louisiana, and that we do not...desire...nor will we countenance bloodshed or revenge."[81] Unlike the 1864 Convention, this was not a gathering of all-white men. A perplexing portrait of Black life is on display. Forty-nine Black delegates participated, inspiring hope that the Civil War had changed the South.[82]

For Blacks, tangible signs of social progress were realized at the 1868 convention, such as: the right of Black men to vote and hold office;[83] the nullification of the 1861 ordinance of secession; disfranchisement of all persons who participated directly or indirectly in the war on the Confederate side (until receipt of an acknowledgement that the war was morally and politically wrong); adoption of the state's first bill of rights; the express prohibition against racial discrimination in schools and public transportation; abolishment of Black Code laws and the literacy test; and, racially proportional representation. Promise should not be confused with achievement. The 1868 Constitutional Convention created appearances that masked reality.

Cotton and free labor were still matters of governmental import. Official conversations revealed that Southern planters were being devastated by the production costs associated with cotton and were no longer realizing a profit (like they did during the days of chattel slavery), demonstrating a desire for a replacement free labor system. At the convention, there were references to Blacks being "best fitted" to grow cotton[84] and discussion of the need for federal loans to "restore the production of [cotton] in the South....,"[85] revealing that the industry had outlived the Civil War and would not be rendered obsolete by some Blacks attaining elected offices. At Louisiana's 1868 Constitutional Convention, there was a vote on adoption of the Fourteenth Amendment to the United States Constitution. Forty-four votes were cast in support.

The opposition was not scarce. There were seventeen votes in opposition, translating into a significant percentage of delegates opposing citizenship and due process for Blacks and deeming them unworthy of equal protection of the law.[86] The venue should not go unnoticed. This opposition walked the corridors of law and the halls of policy, directly or through posterity. Through the opposition, Blacks were taught yet another lesson about law. They learned that many lawmakers did not see them as equals or deserving a process before their liberty could be lost. Several matters that go to the heart of Southern juries and justice were conceived at this convention, the first being the union between race, voting and jury service (which is discussed in greater detail in Chapter 2).

In 1868, registered voters became eligible for jury service.[87] This was a tremendous departure from the 1864 Constitution, a document drafted by all white men, to simultaneously outlaw slavery and deny political rights to Blacks, leaving them with no voting power and, thereby, no way of playing a meaningful role in the government they had just entered.[88] The delegates limited criminal jurisdiction of appellate courts to a review of the law only, thereby creating a challenge to undoing criminal convictions imposed by a Southern judge or jury.[89] The delegates at Louisiana's 1868 Constitutional Convention also included the exceptions clause allowing for slavery and involuntary servitude in the state constitution (that mirrors the one in the Thirteenth Amendment to the United States Constitution) and this remains in the state constitution today.[90] This exceptions clause served as a trap door.

Around this time, there was an uptick in the number of Blacks convicted of crimes (as discussed in further detail later in this chapter). Before the convention ended, some delegates made a foreshadowing observation. They observed that the emancipated population was not receiving "justice under state laws in state courts, or under the civil rights bill in the tribunals designated in that bill...."[91] For Blacks in Louisiana, the hopes born of the 1868 convention would die a sudden death. Confederates and their sympathizers were holding key leadership and governmental positions and "the deep-seated racism of Confederate stalwarts was accompanied by newfound resentment."[92] If only their power were contained.

The situation was complicated by the fact that the South amassed great political power nationally because of the way the enslaved were counted and because of how the South successfully disenfranchised poor whites. Southern power brokers used that power to influence federal elections and laws and to protect its interests. A Reconstruction era report on the condition of the South exposes the fidelity of some Southern leaders to the aims of Reconstruction and accurately forecasts the inevitable:

> [T]here appears to be a popular notion prevalent in the South...It is that the negro exists for the special object of raising cotton, rice and sugar for the whites and that it is illegitimate for him to indulge...in the pursuit of his own happiness in his own way. Although...he has ceased to be the property of a master, it is not admitted that he has a right to become his own master...The whites esteem the Blacks their property by natural right...they still have an ingrained feeling that the Blacks at large belong to the whites at large, and whenever opportunity serves, they treat the colored people just as their profit, caprice, or passion may dictate...An ingrained feeling like this is apt to bring forth that sort of class legislation which produces laws to govern one class with no other view than to benefit another.[93]

United States Representative Henry Wilson shared the concerns outlined in that report. He correctly predicted that law would assume the role of slave master:

> After the surrender of Lee,...the rebels were absolutely under the control of the military authorities of the government. They were then ready to accept any terms the nation chose to give. But to-day the rebels have possession of Virginia, of its government, of North Carolina, South Carolina, Georgia, Florida, Alabama, Mississippi, Louisiana; and on Thursday next they will take possession of the government of Texas... These states want admission into Congress...for what purpose? ...not only to govern these states, but to direct and control the policy of the nation...They are not sorry for their revolt against the country....[94]

The collision between the grand ambitions of the Union and the steadfastness of the Confederates was politely concealed by what was conveniently marketed as a crime problem. The Black Codes became the start of an uninterrupted pattern of laws written with a racial animus in post-Civil War Louisiana. The Black Codes were enacted shortly after the Civil War ended to recreate the conditions of slavery by restoring white control over the autonomy, mobility and employment of the emancipated people.[95] By way of illustration, the Black Codes prevented the formerly enslaved from securing employment other than as sharecroppers or tenant farmers, imposed travel, housing and jury restrictions; limited property rights; and, criminalized vagrancy and disorderly conduct.

The Black Codes were a part of a much larger pattern of enslavement by law. Immediately after emancipation, a bill requiring newly emancipated people to have a home and a means of support within twenty days was filed in the Louisiana legislature.[96] The penalty was immediate arrest, allowing offenders to be hired out to the highest bidder by operation of law.[97] Opelousas, Louisiana banned Blacks from the town unless they were in service to a "white person or former owner."[98] Violation of this ordinance resulted in the imposition of a fine, a penalty or corporal punishment. The accused were not afforded trials. Instead, there was a summary proceeding, which prompted some Blacks to experience flashbacks to those votes in opposition to the Fourteenth Amendment. Through the use of peonage, vagrancy and curfew laws, the Thirteenth Amendment's exceptions clause acted as a legislative slave catcher dispatched by Democratic and Confederate lawmakers.

The exceptions clause served as a means of building a new labor force (which is explored further in the forthcoming discussion of "The Collision of Race, Profits and Incarceration"). In other words, the people who were freed by one part of the Thirteenth Amendment were enslaved by another part of it.[99] Through this, critical lessons about law were imparted. Blacks in Louisiana learned well that the same law could liberate and oppress. The law told them they were no longer slaves. However, six years *after* passage of the Thirteenth Amendment, courts were still referring to Blacks as "property,"[100] eighty-five years *after* passage, courts were interpreting the amendment as having never attempted to endow Blacks with "social rights,"[101] and they were finding themselves subject to a new form of mass incarceration. The Civil Rights Act of 1875 was the last civil rights law that the Reconstruction Congress passed.

In a few short years, it was declared unconstitutional by a SCOTUS committed to diminishing the role of the federal government in Reconstruction. The Freedmen's Bureau had been closed for nearly three years and federal troops had withdrawn from the South.[102] The will of Congress was not strong enough to defeat the South's commitment to white supremacy. Census data reinforced all the perverse notions about Blackness that had been introduced during the 1700s and 1800s.[103] "After the Civil War, the 'crime problem' had become in all Southern states confused with the 'Negro problem,' in so far as Black convicts began greatly to outnumber white convicts in all penitentiaries."[104]

There are a few ways to explain the increase in Black convicts. One is to believe that, by osmosis, white people suddenly became law abiding, and Blacks suddenly became lawless. Another is to acknowledge that convict leasing was taking form as a replacement for the free labor system that was lost by way of emancipation (which is explored further in the forthcoming discussion of race and labor). At the time, the public saw this data in the abstract. And they viewed the portrait it painted with fear and emotion. Many Blacks in Louisiana, at the hands of the law, were experiencing the same anguish that chattel slavery had produced. Law was one system of oppression that had replaced another.

The WHO World Report on Violence and Health (WRVH) defines violence as the "intentional use of physical force or power, threatened or actual, against oneself, another person, or against a group or community that either results in or has a high likelihood of resulting in injury, death, psychological harm, mal-development or deprivation." Many Blacks saw law as the use of power against a group that results in an injury. It became a form of structural violence, a form of violence wherein social or cultural structures or institutions harm people by preventing them from meeting their basic needs. Slavery by law entered the Southern jury box.

<u>The Confederate Battle that *Followed* the Civil War</u>

A matter of months after the abolishment of slavery and the seeming Civil War defeat of the Confederates, there were signs that death of the Confederacy had been prematurely announced. After the Civil War ended, Confederates were viewed as "patriots" and those who supported the Union were "objects of prejudice, dislike, and often persecution...."[105] At the Louisiana Democratic Convention that year, the party expressed the official position that the "government was made and is to be perpetuated for the exclusive political benefit of the white race."[106] Louisiana's Confederates assumed official government roles "as a reward for their service to the rebellion."[107]

The Confederates avoided consequences and accountability. They continued their commitment to their cause of supremacy, this time without battle gear. The future of the state would be shaped by these incorrigible men. For too long, change agents have failed to contemplate the consequences of this and to appreciate how the imprint of these former Confederates remain on today's legal system. Apprehension about what was underfoot was expressed both near and far.

At the end of Louisiana's 1867 Constitutional Convention, Representative Belden observed:

> Every man of this state knows the guilty men to be the politicians and office-holders who had the control and management of the Government of Louisiana in 1860 and 1861, and who were in concert with men of like character in other Southern states, and not the men who were driven into the rebellion by the result of the powerful combinations concocted and consummated by these politicians and office holders. [108]

Similar sentiments echoed from the halls of Congress when Senator Henry Wilson memorialized his concerns about the seeming ambitions of the post-Civil War South:

> [T]his is not a struggle for the re-admission of the rebel states into the
> Union, but a struggle for the admission of rebels into the legislative
> branches of the government; not a struggle to put rebels under the laws
> of the country, but a struggle to enable rebels to frame the laws of the
> country. A loyal people see that the Confederate States, reconstructed
> since the surrender of the rebel armies, are as completely in the hands
> of rebels now as on the day Jeff Davis was incarcerated at Fortress
> Monroe.[109]

After the Civil War, the Confederacy remained organized and committed to its ideals. Four years *after* the Civil War, Confederate veterans created the Southern Historical Society. Eleven years *after* the war, this society published the *Southern Historical Society Papers*, a collection of essays defending the Southern war effort. In 1886, over twenty years *after* the war, the former Confederate President Jefferson Davis emerged from his plantation exile to the likes of a crowd awaiting a rock star. He remarked: "Your demonstration now exceeds that which welcomed me then. This shows the spirit of southern liberty is not dead."[110] Former Confederate soldiers gathered for reunions that were formally organized twenty-four years *after* the Civil War ended. Thirty-five years *after* the Civil War, 80,000 people attended.[111]

Eighty-eight years *after* the Civil War, bonds secured by surpluses from the Confederate veterans' and widows' pension fund were used to create a new Shreveport hospital that would bear the name Confederate Memorial Medical Center until 1978. The hospital was dedicated to the memory of the Confederate soldiers on Confederate Memorial Day in 1953. To date, Confederate efforts continue surrounding specialty license plates, monuments, school curriculum, flag displays and more. There was a modified Civil War that was fought off the field. It was fought in legislative chambers, in academic settings, in the judiciary and in other official spaces. Henry Plauché Dart, Edward Douglas white, Jr., Paul Tulane and Dr. Standford E. Chaille (discussed in chapter two) are poster children for this mutated Civil War battle. Men like these former Confederates would do more to shape post-Civil War life than Reconstruction did.

Henry Plauché Dart was a member of the white League, a statewide, domestic terrorist group that advocated white supremacy. It organized militarily and closely mimicked the Ku Klux Klan.[112] Dart despised Republicans and Blacks. In his lifetime, he became an accomplished litigator, making frequent appearances before the state supreme court. He later became an instructor of law, a historian and author. Through his writings, Dart contributed extensively to a version of Southern history that was friendly to the Confederacy. Pursuant to his Lost Cause reasoning, Confederates were heroes and the Civil War was never about slavery, but, instead, about states'rights.

The Lost Cause reasoning also celebrated the Confederacy for defending a way of life that it characterizes as "happy." It also claims the South never lost the war, but was, instead, overwhelmed by the Union's resources. Dart's contribution to this reasoning resulted in these false teachings entering Southern history books for generations upon generations. But that's not the only damage done by him. Dart was an active member of the New Orleans Law Association and the American Bar Association. Dart organized the Louisiana Bar Association in 1898 and was its president until 1901. He was chairman of the Louisiana supreme court committee on bar admission and disbarment from 1898 – 1908. He shaped bar admissions practices during his day and they were not inclusive. He was also a charter member of the American Law Institute and of the New Orleans courthouse commission. This one man had influence over historical narratives, policy, bar licensing and discipline and none of what he did in his fifty year career was done with a vision of inclusiveness. He did not see Blacks as equals and with the broad powers he had, he battled on his modified playing field.

E.D. White, Jr. was a man of both physical and intellectual prowess. He was the son of a slaveholder and former Louisiana governor who fought on the Confederate side of the Civil War.[113] E. D. White, Jr. was a lawyer and a Louisiana legislator before claiming a seat on the Supreme Court of the United States (SCOTUS). As a member of the legislature, he was instrumental in fashioning unsuspecting legislative schemes and even better at convincing the public of their appeal. He spoke of some of his mischievous machinations in an 1878 speech where he shared details of "reform legislation"[114] that: revised election laws; purified the jury system to facilitate the administration of justice; improved the criminal appeals process; ensured the longevity of convict labor; and, implemented work schemes for convicts.[115]He described efforts to place power in the hands of local police juries, a body that would be used to carry out the wishes of the White League. One instance was levee repairs, a job that would often be performed with convict labor.

He spoke of costs and corrections conjointly. For example, he favored levying taxes "for criminal proceedings in such a manner as to secure the lowest rate of expense possible" or letting officials "regulate the price to be paid for keeping prisoners."[116] He was able to present an estimate of savings to the state due to convict labor, changes to criminal appeals and the regulation of fees for keeping prisoners. He termed this a "remodeled judicial department."[117] If only this were the end to the harm to result from this one man's presence in places of import. While at the SCOTUS, he, in the *Plessy v. Ferguson* case, voted against Homer Plessy, a Black man who challenged segregated seating aboard Louisiana's railcars, and he consistently voted to uphold laws that were oppressive to Southern Blacks. He fought alongside the Crescent City White League in the 1874 Battle of Liberty Place, an armed insurrection that aimed to overthrow the state government and re-establish white rule.

Placing his imprint on voting, criminal justice and social norms was not enough for E.D. White, Jr.'s appetite. He also impacted higher educational opportunities for Blacks by using Article 230 of the Constitution of 1879 as a means of covertly transforming a public college supported by state dollars to one that would be designated private and, through the use of those same state dollars, exclude Blacks.[118] The legislation did not disclose Tulane University of Louisiana as the beneficiary of the expansion that was referenced in Article 230. In 1881, diehard Confederate Paul Tulane conveniently made a conditional, million-dollar donation for educational purposes. More than gratuity was at work.

Tulane's intent was to continue the social hierarchy that the federal government had just attempted to destroy. The condition of this donation was that it be used to educate young whites for leadership roles in society. By 1884, a corporation had been formed towards these ends. The corporation, the Tulane Education Fund (TEF), attached these desires to the University of Louisiana. Under the arrangement, the state was relieved of its obligation to make annual appropriations and Tulane would accomplish his goal of educating whites so they could maintain the power and control that whites had exclusively held in the South.

Randall Lee Gibson, a former slaveowner and a member of the Confederate army who descended from one of the largest slaveholding families in Louisiana, was another key player in the modified Civil War effort in Louisiana that Blacks with civil rights would exist under. He joined the effort to use education as a weapon. Mr. Gibson, founding president of the board of administrators of Tulane University and "the architect of the Tulane University endowment..."[119] viewed Reconstruction as a "fall from honor, virtue and patriotism."[120] He successfully lobbied the legislature to transfer control of the public university to the TEF. William Preston Johnson, a lawyer and former Confederate soldier, served as the first president of Tulane University. E. D. White, a graduate of Tulane University Law School, served as one of Tulane's original administrators.

Tulane University of Louisiana enjoyed exemption from taxation. This deal was blessed by the governor, the superintendent of education, the legislature, the mayor of New Orleans and many in power who served as administrators of the TEF. The weight of this much power and influence behind this plot speaks to the degree to which an educated Black population in Louisiana could have disrupted the entire social order. By this juncture, "the race question was not whether...[Blacks] would be equal to white[s]...It was...how far beneath white people Black people were to be."[121] This became the aim of the reinvigorated Civil War.

Louisiana's 1879 Constitution would see to that being done. It undid many of the positive gains achieved by the 1868 Constitution, such as the guarantee of equal rights and integrated schools.[122] And it made no apologies for its actions. In the opening minutes of the convention, it assigns as its right and duty the business of reversing the 1868 enactments. The resolution reads:

> *Be if further resolved*, That the Convention of 1868, in exercising the power over the right of suffrage, which is now vested in this Convention, transferred the government...to the negro race, without any regard to intelligence, property or interest in the government or patriotism to the state, and that it now becomes the duty of this Convention to re-transfer the government, by establishing a qualified right of suffrage to the white race, to whom the government belongs, as an inheritance and birthright....[123]

This exiled Confederate mission claimed a seat in the jury box.

The Collision of Race and Medicine in Louisiana

Racial medicine joined forces with law to further the oppression of Blacks in Louisiana. It pathologized "the slave system as specifically fit for African Americans."[124] Colonial powers used the now-discredited 'scientific' theories of biological races to justify laws prohibiting non-whites from enjoying the most fundamental of human rights...."[125] Phrenology, which supposedly used measurements of the human skull to determine mental ability and personality, was one. "Like planters during this period, physicians used their knowledge of Black bodies to discuss key social and political questions....as to position the medical profession as a cure for many of these ills."[126] Dr. Samuel Adolphus Cartwright was one of the South's most noted examples. This slaveowner, medical writer and physician to Confederate soldiers, rose in ranks, claiming local, national and international notoriety.

Dr. Cartwright supposedly reached a medical finding to explain why those submitted to chattel slavery might try to escape. Drapetomania would be the name assigned to the mental illness he concluded they had. Rascality was his theory to explain the disease that made the enslaved commit petty offenses. Pursuant to his "science," the enslaved were indifferent to punishment and genetically inferior. He termed this condition, dysaesthesia ethiopica. His recommended treatment was often corporal punishment. He offered prescriptions for planters seeking ways of extracting the most labor from the enslaved.[127] Dr. Cartwright's "ideas existed as a part of a national medical curriculum that promoted the idea that Black bodies were biologically different and required alternative treatment practices"[128] and were "psychologically and physiologically fit for slavery."[129] "Cartwright and other early proponents of racial medicine were key players in the long process of embedding racial thinking into medical knowledge and education."[130]

During one of his New Orleans lectures, physician and scientist Josiah Nott told the audience that the enslaved in the South were content and biologically designed for servitude over freedom.[131] Another Louisiana doctor spoke of slavery as a "system of ethics."[132] In the South, racial medicine "confirmed Black inferiority and placed it on different, nearly unassailable ground."[133] The acceptance of this "science" influenced Black life in Louisiana in the most nuanced of ways. In the 1842 case of *Bank of U.S. v Merle*, the plaintiff's counsel argued that notice of a legal claim was defective because it was left with a Black servant, presumed to be an enslaved person. Counsel contended that service upon a table or desk in the house would have been valid, but not upon a Black slave, suggesting that the enslaved person's capabilities were less than that of an inanimate object, such as a table or desk.[134] For purposes of this audit, it is noteworthy that the state never took this position when it came to prosecuting Blacks. In that one instance, they were not viewed as property or things. They were viewed as beings who could be held accountable.[135] These deposits were made into Louisiana's legal system. They have yet to be withdrawn.

By the late 1800's, racial medicine became justification for segregation. A May 7, 1867, editorial in the *Daily Picayune* denounced efforts by Blacks to end segregated railcars. The writer retorted, "the only reason that a distinction was ever made as to color, was...the inferiority...of the Black race on a social scale."[136] Racial medicine should not be dismissed as a relic of the past. In 1997, a Black defendant received a life sentence after psychologist Dr. Walter Quijano testified that Hispanic and Black men were more likely to be dangerous than the average person.[137] Racial medicine continues to influence systems, laws and policies in the state and country. It both causes and justifies Black exclusion. It entered the jury box.

Using Policy, Procedure and Systems as the New Strategy for Racial Control

By the early 1900's, the modified Civil War was producing undeniable results insofar as whether Blacks would live the written words of the Reconstruction era amendments (and be included in the American democracy) or be denied these protections (and be excluded from the American democracy). At this point, 100% of political officials in the South were white. In Louisiana, convictions had been swift and steady between post-emancipation and 1928 when Louisiana enacted its first Code of Criminal Procedure.[138] Despite its heavy reliance on a justice system, "the criminal law…remained in disorder, tangled, contradictory, and uncodified until 1942."[139] The process, before and after a code, would, too often, produce Black criminals instead of punish them as the public had been led to believe.

A look at two laws aid in this understanding. Vagrancy was a misdemeanor at a time when there was no right to a jury trial for misdemeanors in Louisiana. There was also no right to appointed counsel for misdemeanors.[140] In instances where an attorney could be retained, the appellate process proved an obstacle as judicial review was limited.[141] Louisiana's vagrancy laws were not invalidated until 2020. The second consideration is the way criminal cases are reviewed on appeal. After a person is convicted by the trial court, they can take an appeal questioning the sufficiency of evidence to convict, but the appellate court can't reverse a conviction just because, as a panel of judges, they feel another outcome is better. By force of law, those appellate judges, many of whom are former prosecutors, must review a criminal appeal in the light most favorable to the prosecution.[142] After doing so, they can only reverse a conviction if the evidence was insufficient to convince a rational trier of fact that all of the elements of the crime were not proven beyond a reasonable doubt.[143]

During this process, they are not allowed to review facts related to guilt or innocence, only the law (due to previously referenced changes made during the 1868 constitutional convention). Over the years, the state has maintained its commitment to limiting the scope of appellate review of criminal cases. For all these years, individuals were convicted as vagrants, not necessarily because they were harming the public, but because of a race-based, automated process akin to a legal assembly line. They weren't criminals. Their Blackness was criminalized vis-a-via an intentionally designed legal "process" that robbed them of an ability to effectively mount a challenge to their oppression. There was a parasitism between this social construct of race and the way this group would interface with the law. This entered the jury box. The criminal legal system became central to new strategies of racial control.

The criminalization of Blackness became part of the fabric of the state. It makes an appearance in *Plessy v. Ferguson* where Homer Plessy was criminally charged due to his Black skin and no other legitimate public safety concern. It presented itself again when college students and citizens became intolerant of segregation. It had only been a ninety-two year wait since the promise of equal protection had been granted by way of the Fourteenth Amendment. The state responded to their peaceful presence at segregated lunch counters,[144] on college campuses,[145] outside courthouses[146] or in public libraries[147] with criminal charges (for attempting to experience the very equality that the United States Constitution told them to enjoy). This practice of using law to create Black criminals, as opposed to as a response to criminal behavior, continues.

Obstacles to Blacks dissociating themselves with criminality were weaved into the system at every seam. "The Rules of evidence— rules fashioned to control juries and lawyers—were also constructed to assure the property interests of slave-owners, and the domination of whites over Blacks."[148] Lawyers who championed the causes of the oppressed were regularly arrested for offenses associated with their representation, such as contempt or sedition. Race even limited one's ability to give testimony in a court of law, sometimes rendering absent testimony that could exonerate an accused Black person.

In 1987, it appeared Louisiana was doing cutting edge work when it acted ahead of most of the nation in formulating a way to protect the public from the spread of AIDS and/or HIV. The legislature made it a felony for a person who knows of their positive HIV status to expose another through any means of contact without the knowledge of the other person. The law criminalizes non-sexual behaviors that don't transmit the virus, such as biting or spitting. It imposes a maximum penalty of ten years in prison and a $5,000 fine, with an additional year and thousand dollars tacked on if a police officer is involved. According to a report by NOLA.Com, Black men make up 15% of the population in this state and 44% of those living with HIV and 91% under this law. HIV is no longer a guaranteed death sentence. The law hasn't evolved in light of the increased treatment options for person infected with the virus.

Other states have made modifications, such as requiring transmission or intent for a conviction and reducing the penalty from a felony to a misdemeanor. Louisiana is also in the minority of states in the nation that require a person convicted under this law to register as a sex offender for fifteen years so, as is now predictable, punishment is amplified. This causes life-long harm, such as preventing parents from entering libraries or schools with their own children or not being available for employment opportunities that they are otherwise qualified for due to them being on the sex offender registry and/or convicted felons. The 2018 reform efforts proved fruitless.

The strategies for ensuring racial control have been divergent. By 1954, the state legislature created a Segregation Committee whose purpose was to "provide ways and means whereby…[the] existing social order shall be preserved…."[149] There would also be an Association of Citizens Councils of Louisiana, incorporated by many members of the Segregation Committee, that was created to "'protect and preserve by all legal means…Southern Social Institutions in all of their aspects."[150] Advising registrars throughout the state of voter suppression tactics was one.[151] Efforts expanded by the 1960s. Louisiana added a sovereignty commission to its arsenal. Its purpose was to "perform any and all acts and things deemed necessary and proper to protect the sovereignty of the state of Louisiana from encroachment thereon by the Federal Government, or by any branch, department or agency thereof, and to resist by all legal means, the usurpation by any agency of the Federal Government or by any organization of rights and powers reserved to the states by the Constitution....").[152]

These local efforts were reinforced by simultaneous national efforts, such as the Southern Manifesto of 1956, a formal declaration against integration, signed by nineteen United States Senators and eighty-two United States Representatives.[153] Louisiana's longest serving United States Representative, F. Edward Hebert, joined this effort. Mr. Hebert represented Louisiana in the United States Congress from 1940 through 1976. He was repeatedly reelected despite his known support for segregation and states rights' and his known opposition to lynching legislation, civil rights and racial equality. Louisiana paid homage beyond votes. The campus of Tulane University named a building in his honor.[154] The inclination to use policy, procedure and systems as a form of racial control entered the jury box.

The Union of Race and Education

Before and during chattel slavery, free people of color could be educated (at their own expense), but education was never an option for the enslaved. After emancipation, education was highly desired by the newly emancipated people. The army forced the process of educating them. In Louisiana, the army appointed a Board of Education and granted it power to erect and operate schools for Black children. The schools they operated were to be funded through real and personal taxes paid by Louisiana citizens. Nothing about this was well received by whites. Confederates returned to power and swiftly ended the practice. "When the collection of the general tax for Negro schools was suspended in Louisiana by military order, the colored people were greatly aroused and sent in petitions."[155] "One of these petitions, thirty feet in length, represented ten thousand Negros, who signed mostly with marks. They offered to pay a special tax, if the schools could be kept going."[156]

Blacks persisted as they have done in every aspect of life. In the South, Blacks are to be credited for leading the effort to achieve the general education system, funded through taxes, that we have all come to know.

There was never buy in. Consistent with the previously referenced 1868 Constitutional Convention efforts, a public education system for students of all races was put in place in 1869. That year, Louisiana passed a law providing a system of public education without distinction of race or color.[157] But schools remained segregated. And, where Blacks attended, funding was often stolen or misappropriated.[158] There was always a disparity in the distribution of funds so the majority Black schools received less. Black students were most harmed by this.

By the early 1900's, progress still hadn't been realized on the education front. "[A]ppropriations for teacher salaries in Louisiana on a per capita basis for white students were $13.73, and $1.31 per Black student."[159] "The school term for Black students was typically half that of white students, with Black students receiving three to four months of instruction in a year."[160] "School buildings for Black students in the South were rare and primitive in both condition and educational instruction."[161] The quality of equipment and facilities was another variance, with the majority Black school on the lesser end of the distribution. As one man recalled, when it came to hiring Black teachers for the Black students, the trend was to select "the less competent."[162] Another challenge to Black education during this period was labor contracts. They regularly prevented Black children from attending school because their labor was needed to make ends meet in the household. By the civil rights era, the South was no longer the sole decision maker when it came to Blacks having access to education. At least, that's what the Constitution's Supremacy Clause would have one think.

Louisiana's response to the 1954 *Brown v Board of Education* decision that declared segregated schools unconstitutional was swift and intense. The Louisiana legislature passed a resolution condemning the SCOTUS's "usurpation of power."[163] In November 1954, the voters of Louisiana approved an amendment to the state constitution that required school segregation in an effort "to promote and protect public health, morals, better education and the peace and good order in the state, and not because of race."[164] State officials used a series of legislative maneuvers to defy federal court orders. For example, the

Louisiana legislature declared that anyone who contested state control over public education in Louisiana was subject to fines and jail time. Moreover, the governor could close any school where a riot or mob threatened to form and deny accreditation, material resources, and official recognition to any state school that integrated.

A law authorizing the state legislature to determine the racial composition of schools in large cities, such as New Orleans, was enacted in 1955. In November 1956, the voters of Louisiana approved a state constitutional amendment that barred all lawsuits against school boards.[165] In 1960, the legislature enacted legislation that imposed mandatory jail time and a fine on any federal judge or other federal officer who attempted to impose school desegregation. Louisiana officials also used baseless litigation[166] and tuition vouchers as a means of maintaining segregated schools.[167] It also approved a joint resolution, urging all white parents to boycott the two desegregated schools. The resolution appeared as a paid notice in all New Orleans newspapers.

A decade after the *Brown v. Board of Education* decision officially ended legal segregation in schools, "just 2.3 percent of the nearly 3 million school-aged Black children living in the former Confederate states attended racially integrated schools."[168] In 2024, racial disparities in K-12 academic achievement still exist at every stage of the education pipeline and Louisiana still has a school desegregation suit pending.[169] In that *Moore v. Tangipahoa Parish Schools* case, a Black candidate for principal successfully demonstrated a racially discriminatory hiring process. The resolution was removal of the selected white principal and installment of the Black applicant. This occurred in May 2024, suggesting that the racism that caused the filing of the fifty-nine-year-old court case has maintained its grip on the public education process for children in Louisiana.

In 2023, the legislative auditor issued a report at the request of the Louisiana legislature. According to *Student Racial Demographics Louisiana Elementary and Secondary Public and Private Schools*, "Black public-school students were more than five times as likely to attend 'D' or 'F' rated schools as compared to white public-school students." The report also indicates that "Black public-school students, attending both traditional public schools and charter schools, made up the majority of the students enrolled in schools rated 'D' and 'F'." It continued, "About 41% of Black public-school students attended a school rated 'D' and 'F', while only 8% of white students did." Further, according to a 2024 Axios review of federal data, "Louisiana's public schools have become more racially segregated in the past 30 years."

In Louisiana, Black higher education is not as manifest as it appears. One should not be misled by the high number of Historically Black Colleges and Universities (HBCUs) for a single state. S U is the only one of Louisiana's HBCU's that was birth by the state. The other HBCU's were conceived through other means.[170] S U was brought into existence at the 1879 Convention, leading some to entertain optimism about Reconstruction.[171] These observers interpreted a higher education option for Blacks as an indication that Black elected officials had garnered some political muscle by this point in time. To them, it also suggests Louisiana's white power structure had been forced to concede to at least this much equality for Blacks. Others see the creation of SU, a segregated educational option endorsed by some white segregationists who did not want Blacks at other institutions, as a mechanism by which Democrats and former Confederates would usher Blacks into a more subtle form of servitude. Holders of this view cite to the Southern Democratic education model.[172] This model advocated that one should be educated for the position they would occupy in life.[173]

In 1880, SU was chartered and incorporated "for the education of persons of color." A 1912 legislative act seeking to "enlarge the scope" of SU's usefulness establishes the "Industrial and Agricultural Normal School" as a department.[174] Its purpose was to supply teachers to teach agricultural and industrial subjects to Black students.[175] A 1932 newspaper story, in discussing SUs import to the state, described it as a training ground for Black teachers who would instruct Black pupils and an instructional site for a workforce skilled in agriculture, home economics and industrial and mechanical work.[176] The story showcased one illustration of that industrial training–the construction of several campus buildings by students. The story referred to Dr. Joseph Samuel

Clark, the President, as a "safe" leader. The state's seeming support of higher education for Blacks must be considered in light of these details.

These efforts on the educational battlefront continued and expanded in the years to come for a few reasons. Lack of education: rendered Blacks available for farming and labor; removed the threat of revolt or civil disobedience that education could inspire; left Blacks ill-equipped to successfully mount a challenge; and, ensured their inability to pass literacy tests that could qualify them to vote or to detect other cleverly disguised schemes to deprive them of civil, social or political rights. This virulence entered the Southern jury box.

<u>The Intersection of Race and Policing</u>

The narrative of law enforcement as a community of devoted civil servants who risk their lives because of a greater calling to protect and serve everyone, equally, irresponsibly divorces a system from its sinister roots. It is true that many men and women gravitate toward a career in law enforcement because they feel called to ensure public safety. It is also true that many of these men and women pursue their calling in an equitable manner, as well as respect the enormous powers of the badge. But this audit is not about individual actors. It seeks to expose patterns, history and customs and the outcomes produced by them.

It is patently false to speak of the system of policing as a system created for the equal protection of all people. Many members of the law enforcement community, as well as many members of the general public lack an awareness of this fact. As a result, there has been a lifetime of avoidable tension between many people of color and many members of the law enforcement community, as well as internally amongst the ranks of white and Black officers.

The origins of policing differ in the North and South. In the North, policing began when business owners became uncomfortable with an influx of immigrants. They were new and different and fear became the response. Immigrants gathering on public streets after work made white business owners uncomfortable, so they organized and came up with the idea of a police force, not to protect and serve all, but to protect and serve some. The police did what they were paid to do. They walked the street and made white business owners feel safe. They surveilled the immigrants and made the immigrants feel uncomfortable. Before you knew it, there became a crime problem. Business owners used this to convince the government they should accept responsibility for public safety. Government officials did just that. In the North, policing evolved from this starting point.

When it comes to Blacks in the South, policing had been underway many years before the word became associated with the practice. The Fugitive Slave Acts of 1793 and 1850, passed by the United States Congress, allowed for the arrest of Blacks *suspected* of being runaway slaves. Also, by force of Louisiana law, Blacks were human prey sought by slave patrols. Laying the groundwork for policing in the South, these slave patrols were cloaked with authority to search, seize, confront, question, brutalize and terrorize the enslaved.[177] They existed to watch, demean and control the enslaved population. Arrest was the consequence of not having documentation justifying movement or proving freedom or for simply being out of place (in the view of the white patroller).

Many free Blacks were caught in these dragnets and criminalized because of their skin color and because they were deprived of the right to jury trials.[178] Local jurisdictions forced white males to assume the role of patrollers or searchers so they too were coerced into a monogamous relationship with suspicion based on skin color. No matter the nomenclature, these public patrols formed from this template and existed in all states where chattel slavery existed. The hurts and presumptions of these relationships outlived chattel slavery. They found their way into the jury box.

During the Civil War, the military became the primary form of law enforcement in the South. During Reconstruction, many local sheriffs functioned much like the earlier slave patrols, enforcing segregation and the disenfranchisement of freed slaves. During the Reconstruction era, surveilling Blacks continued through state associations or through the actions of private vigilante or militia groups, such as the Ku Klux Klan (KKK), rifle clubs or The White League, Democratic Party members who were often former Confederates. Those doing surveillance in Louisiana during Reconstruction were often Confederate trained and were most certainly not amongst the ranks of the formally enslaved. To many Confederates, it was a natural progression to use their military training after the Civil War to maintain control over Blacks in Louisiana. Nathan Bedford Forrest, a slave owner who fought as a calvary officer in the Civil War, is one example.

Forrest is famously known for leading the massacre that killed countless Black Union soldiers. After the Civil War, he proudly joined the KKK. Not only did these private and state-sanctioned enterprises accomplish social control, they served as a ready response to Black organizing, as a rapid mobilization response when Blacks needed to be whipped into submission or when a reminder that the Confederacy remained alive was needed. These forces were never about protecting and serving all people. A look at the lynching history and the Battle of Liberty Place solidifies this point.

The Economic Policy Institute reports that, between the 1870s and the 1950s, about 75% of lynchings were done with the assistance of law enforcement. As British journalist Aatish Taseer explains, "A lynching is much more than just a murder...A lynching is a public spectacle; it demands an audience... A lynching is a majority's way of telling a minority population that the law cannot protect it."

In 1874, there was a hotly contested election in the state. The winner would hold political power in the state. When Governor Kellogg refused to relinquish the governorship, the White League galvanized into action. They attempted to oust Governor Kellogg from office and eliminate the Metropolitan Police force. On September 14, 1874, The Battle of Liberty Place ensued. Police, Black citizens and Republicans were slaughtered in mass numbers and Kellogg was forcefully removed from office.

Change agents must understand that, in general, police in the South, at this hour, protected and served the Southern caste and supremacy systems and nothing beyond that. It's difficult to reconcile, but there were some Black police at this point.

In 1867, New Orleans was the first Southern city to integrate its police force, which was a municipal police force similar to a militia. In 1870, New Orleans, Louisiana had 177 Black officers and three of five Police Board members were Black. Many were free men of color, not formally enslaved people, however. Importantly, their presence was not sufficient to disrupt the system of policing that had developed. This was so because they were given positions, but not power. They had access, but not opportunity, seemingly a recurring theme in this audit. One scholar describes what policing while Black looked like in 1804 Louisiana:

> [The] police force showed a distinct preference for white men to serve as rank and file, and stipulated that its commanders be white. When in 1816, the city council sought to prevent looting in a flooded portion of the city by deploying a patrol boat, it insisted that all rowers be white. The double standard of the city council led to occasional ironies: it allowed free Black militiamen to bear arms when they participated in police patrols, but prevented Blacks from giving or receiving instruction in fencing.[179]

In 1868, the legislature created a state-controlled police force. Blacks were amongst the ranks of this metropolitan force. Most whites in Louisiana didn't look to any of them for public safety. They still preferred the militarily trained Confederates who operated private vigilante groups. Integration of state-wide forces did not result in equality. Blacks were usually hired because of external pressure. They were often assigned to segregated details and to segregated units because they were never seen as qualified to watch, which is a superior position, over those who are watched. It would also put them on par with white colleagues, something the South has been unwilling to accept.

This supremacist ideology has governed the way a number of white officers view Black officers and Black citizens. It has also shaped the way Black officers view white officers, Black officers, white citizens and Black citizens. Anti-Blackness affects Black people, too. Many Black police officers exhibit more anti-Black bias than the Black population as a whole.

Black officers are also victim of anti-Black bias. In 1954, Shreveport hired William Hines as its first Black police officer. He recalled being routinely called the N-word by other officers and by superiors. He also said he was never treated as an equal. For example, while white officers had patrol cars, he had to walk the streets and call a white officer if an arrest needed to be made. By 1973, Hines could no longer contend with the daily indignities. He filed suit. Hines is no anomaly. Albert Burns, Sr. and William Duplessis Alcorn, Jr., are two Black officers who worked for the Baton Rouge Police Department during an entirely different era.

Burns was hired in 1972. Alcorn was hired in 1973. Most would describe the period as the civil rights era, which would make much of this talk about chattel slavery and Reconstruction policing ancient history by this point. Yet, they got the same as their predecessors. By the 1990's Burns and Alcorn couldn't endure anymore. In *Alcorn v. City of Baton Rouge* (2004), the men claimed they were victims of race-based harassment that created a hostile work environment continually throughout their careers. Both men reported a history of racial epithets, slurs and derogatory remarks as early as their police academy days.

In that litigation, Burns and Alcorn testified to hearing the N-word and other racially derogatory references on the patrol radio regularly over the years and they both described superiors using the words "honky" and the N-word and making unfavorable comments about race on a consistent basis. After a 2002 trial, the jury entered a verdict in favor of Burns and Alcorn. The trial court rendered judgment in accordance with that verdict, awarding Alcorn $300,000.00 for race-based harassment, $200,000.00 for racial discrimination, and $50,000.00 for unlawful retaliation. It further rendered judgment in favor of Burns in the sums of $300,000.00 for race-based harassment and $200,000.00 for racial discrimination.

What the city did not do speaks volumes. The City did not call Burns and Alcorn liars. The City also never confessed how well acquainted it was being caught in the act of sidestepping the rule of law. In *Garner v. Louisiana* (1961), students from SU participated in a sit-in to protest segregation as allowed by the First Amendment. Although peaceful, the students were arrested and charged under Louisiana's disturbing the peace statue. The case was litigated up to SCOTUS who found in favor of the students.

In 1961, the First Amendment abuses in Baton Rouge continued. In *Cox v. Louisiana* (1965), Elton Cox led a peaceful march in Baton Rouge, but was later arrested for disturbing the peace and obstruction of a passageway. The SCOTUS held that Louisiana's disturbing the peace statute was unconstitutionally vague and noted that the City of Baton Rouge exercised its assembly policy in an arbitrary way.

In 1972, students protested the lack of resources at SU and the failure of university officials to respond to their legitimate grievances. On November 16, 1972, peace officers arrived on campus with full military-grade equipment, including tear gas. Not long after, two innocent students – Denver Smith and Leonard Brown – lay dead at the hands of law enforcement. Countless other people were also shot or injured. That day and days leading up to this, law enforcement arrested members of Students United (who were later enjoined from returning to campus in separate civil proceedings).

History records the events of the day as overkill, unnecessary and preventable. As was the case with previous constitutional gatherings, peace officers responded with excessive force and displayed disregard for the First Amendment. Despite all of this unfavorable history, the city followed the age-old formula: hide behind the procedural rules. It appealed. Instead of seizing the moment to implement needed changes, the city would spend years more in court claiming that Burns and Alcorn waited too long to mount their challenge. It stands to reason that an officer who is incapable of accepting a trained Black as an equal is undoubtedly challenged to approach a Black civilian as an equal. Federal policy helped turn the likes of this loose in Black communities.

By March 8, 1965, President Lyndon B. Johnson's 1965 Law Enforcement Assistance Act, inserted the federal government into local police operations, court systems, and state prisons, starting the United States' first "War on Crime." "President Johnson saw the urban policeman as the 'frontline soldier' of this mission, and, as a result, the administration focused on building the weapons arsenal of local law enforcement."[180] A seismic shift in law enforcement practices, priorities, budgets and power was underway.

"The 1965 legislation created a grant-making agency within the Department of Justice, which—with $30 million at its disposal, or $223 million in today's dollars—purchased bulletproof vests, helicopters, tanks, rifles, gas masks and other military-grade hardware for police departments."[181] One result was the Omnibus Crime Control and Safe Streets Act of 1968, the last major piece of domestic legislation Johnson passed, which gave the Department of Justice a new degree of influence over social policy by enlarging the grantmaking agency into the Law Enforcement Assistance Administration (LEAA).[182] President Johnson created a Commission on Law Enforcement and Administration of Justice. Their 1967 final report called for sweeping changes in policing, the courts, and corrections.[183] Their call did not fall upon deaf ears.

In 1968, Richard Nixon's campaign for the Presidency emphasized the rising crime rate throughout the country and presented demands for "law and order." In 1970, President Nixon ordered Attorney General John Mitchell to devise a ten-year "Long-Range Master Plan" for American corrections with the idea of it serving as a model to the states.[184] "The Crime Commission—which was started by [President] Johnson—start[ed] making projections of prison populations based on what the Black youth population would be, and prison construction [was] planned accordingly."[185] By the 1970's, with law enforcement having license to engage in more direct contact with citizens vis-a-via stops justified by only reasonable suspicion, arrests and incarceration rates increased. The response from the federal government was fiscal support to states for prison construction.[186]

By 1975, the racial dynamics of incarceration in the country had transitioned from majority white to majority Black and Latino.[187] Between 1969 and 1973, the federal government's law enforcement budget tripled; federal aid to state and local law enforcement grew from $60 million to almost $800 million.[188] The LEAA was one of the principal conduits for these funds. The War on Crime of the 1970s was premised upon the belief "that crime is really a problem of a specific population, so policymakers and officials thought: if we can identify that population and put them in prison for petty crimes before they go on to commit more violent crime, we will deal with the problem."[189]

Sting operations metastasized. At the height of the crack era in the 1980s, mass arrests was the country's trademark. Contrary to popular lore suggesting that the Reagan administration "spearheaded the rise of urban surveillance and mass incarceration, federal policymakers had already dedicated a total of $7 billion in taxpayer dollars (roughly $20 billion today) to crime-control programs before Reagan took office in 1981."[190] Many years later, President Nixon's domestic policy adviser and Watergate co-conspirator confessed that this supposed war was never really about drugs; instead, he described it as attempt to silence Blacks and the antiwar left.

According to John Ehrlichman, "We knew we couldn't make it illegal to be against the war or Blacks, but by getting the public to associate the hippies with marijuana and Blacks with heroin, and then criminalizing both heavily, we could disrupt those communities. We could arrest their leaders, raid their homes, break up their meetings, and vilify them night after night on the evening news."[191] Despite this admission, surveilling Black bodies remains a legitimate method of policing. Federal funds in the form of LEAA grants became available to states at a time when an increase in global oil prices resulted in an increase in state oil revenue.

The national "tough on crime" politics took wings locally. And, for once, money was not an object. One such example was New Orleans D.A. Harry Connick, Sr. who, in the 1970s, was building his career as a "tough on crime" politician. He used the LEAA grants and eagerly obtained convictions. He also assisted in drafting legislation that instituted mandatory sentencing and reduced good time and parole eligibility. "Tough on crime" became the love language of many Louisiana voters. Connick won five elections and served as district attorney (DA) between 1973 and 2003.

He alone is to be credited with adding an enormously high number of bodies to Louisiana's prison landscape. But there were many more "tough on crime" DAs doing the same throughout the state. And there was also a "tough on crime" legislature eager to enact laws that were consistent with this agenda. Racialized policing made these dreams come true. As incarceration grew and expanded, findings from criminologists indicated that incarceration did not reduce recidivism more than non-custodial sanctions did. Data-driven or research-based responses to crime were ignored. Incarceration became a near automated response. And police were the group who could breathe life into these policies.

By the 1990s, Louisiana had the distinction of being the state that led the nation in mass incarceration. Racialized policing was one contributor. Federal law was another. Then-Senator Joe Biden proposed the Violent Crime Control and Law Enforcement Act of 1994. It significantly increased funding for police departments and prisons. Louisiana's taste buds began to water. Policing became more aggressive and more targeted. To accommodate more bodies, private, for-profit facilities were added as an additional housing option and rural parishes began building facilities that could provide more bed space. Attempts to reverse these patterns have been undermined.

During the 2019 legislative session, the "Data Collection Task Force" was created in Louisiana. The task force was designed to collect data in a wide range of areas, such as: traffic stops, pedestrian stops, clearance rates, use of special weapons and the use of special force. Law enforcement agencies who have adopted a written policy against racial profiling are exempt from compliance. Exactly what qualifies as an anti-racial profiling policy? The current law does not offer guidance, leaving each department to its own devices when it comes to making this determination.

According to the Southern Poverty Law Center (SPLC), one third of 331 Louisiana law enforcement agencies have reported that they do not have an anti-racial profiling policy in place. This means that a third of the agencies should be reporting statistical data. The remaining two-thirds of the agencies reported having an anti-racial profiling policy. As such, they have availed themselves to the exemption. In doing so, they seize upon a legislative escape route that rarely exists for people of color. This drafting technique entered the jury box.

Data about stops is of great importance. Absent reliable data on traffic stops, it is impossible to know if policing has a disproportionate impact on certain populations, such as people of color, people with disabilities or people who identify as lesbian, gay, bisexual, transgender or queer. Perhaps that's the motivation for not collecting it. The data is also a tool that law enforcement agencies can use to improve their performance or refute criticisms that their practices unfairly target certain groups or that misconduct persists across an entire department. Additionally, the data can help law enforcement agencies identify crime trends, allocate resources, and assess the effectiveness of training and operational planning.

And, public access to data increases transparency and helps build trust with the community. These stops or other law enforcement encounters often come with terrible consequences. There's a documented problem of police brutality and improprieties around the state. In 2005, when officers came to Baton Rouge to provide reinforcements after Hurricane Katrina, one state trooper from Michigan said Baton Rouge police attempted to thank him for his help by letting him beat a prisoner. A trooper from New Mexico wrote a letter to the Baton Rouge police expressing the concerns of seven New Mexico troopers and five Michigan troopers that Baton Rouge police were engaging in racially motivated enforcement, that they were physically abusing prisoners and the public and that they were stopping, questioning and searching people without any legal justification. Many visiting officers abandoned the state because of these practices.

There also appears to be a culture of impunity, protection and a lack of accountability. For example, in 2020, an Associated Press records review revealed a pattern of racially charged text messages and emails exchanged between white officers and Black colleagues and an internal environment that excused the behaviors and failed to hold anyone accountable. A second example occurred in the immediate aftermath of George Floyd's murder as protests were ongoing. Officer Edenfield, a white man, admitted to making this post: "This 'S_ _ _ _' has moved on from being about George Floyd.

These idiots want to act like animals, block the road and start a checkpoint asking people if they are police officers? I am running them over, and shooting if lethal force were my only way out. The 'A _ _ _ _ _ _' under the truck got what he deserved." He also referred to a female as a "trash B_ _ _ _ _" and called protesters "savage animals."

Officer Edenfield was terminated from his job as a sergeant with the New Orleans Police Department (NOPD) after his personal social media post came to light. The police chief expressed concerns about future court testimony being tainted by this conduct and officials claimed he violated the department's social media policy. In 2023, the Louisiana Supreme Court reversed the termination and found, as did the Civil Service, that an 80-day suspension was the appropriate response.[192] Perhaps this is a case of the students following the lessons taught by the teacher. Attorney C. Scott Courrege is a law enforcement officer turned lawyer who, through his consulting business, provides instruction to many Louisiana officers.

In 2024, Courrege submitted an affidavit in the case of *Ternell L. Brown v. Baton Rouge Police Department*. In it, he set forth what he represented as credentials that would qualify him as an expert in a case involving constitutional criminal procedure and civil rights issues. In addition to law enforcement experience and teaching law enforcement classes when invited to do so, he cited only one law journal article or academic journal, which is underwhelming in the world of experts. While under oath, Courrege described that law review article, written while he was a law student, as a "peer-reviewed" publication, a term that suggests scholarly works have been vetted for rigor by experts in the field. Courrege also described himself as an adjunct member of a law faculty.

During his deposition, opposing counsel revealed that that school's administration said Courrege was not a member of the faculty, had never been interviewed by the faculty or hired by the faculty. The administrator explained that Courrege was instead contracted to grade student writing submissions when needed, a seasonal, part time gig at best. Courrege maintained that he was a member of the faculty. After contentious questioning, he agreed to remove the reference after he sought clarity about the nature of his employment. Those left to witness this couldn't help but question why a city with a history of lawlessness within its ranks would hitch its defense of a serious case of constitutional proportions upon the testimony of a man who was experiencing challenges understanding something as simple as the terms of his employment.

A representative from the city attorney's office watched his expert reveal that he lacked the capacity to decipher the terms of his employment. In that same deposition, Courrege was questioned about the misleading nature of describing his student-written, student-selected and student-edited law review article as "peer reviewed." After, he maintained that his lone law review article was peer reviewed. Courrege replied: "I don't know all the parameters of peer reviewed....I don't know all the details of all the law reviews. ***I am not a professor***." A representative from the city attorney's office watched this too.

When later asked if the city had decided to abandon this "expert," continued support was communicated. When asked if the city defended the Baton Rouge Police Department's use of the "Brave Cave," a Black site where some law enforcement officers clandestinely took women, men and children to be tortured, brutalized and/or strip searched, the practice was never denounced. Beyond Brown, the other known victims of the Brave Cave are disproportionately Black. There is one explanation for this and it is date stamped. Those slave patrols were cloaked with authority to search, seize, confront, question, brutalize, terrorize and control.

In 2023, the DOJ opened an investigation into the Louisiana State Police after receiving a volume of claims of racial discrimination both internally and with the public. That came after officers beat Ronald Greene, an unarmed, forty-nine-year-old Black man, then concocted a story to conceal the truth. The cover up even included hiding the video that captured the murder. Greene's family was initially told that his death resulted from injuries that he sustained in a high-speed chase crash. In May 2021, a body camera video was published by The Associated Press that showed officers tasing Greene, then beating and dragging him by his ankles while facedown and shackled. In a state as committed to criminal accountability as Louisiana is, surely these officers are in shackles.

Not one was ever charged with murder. Kory York, a man who arrests others for breaking the law, responded to his indictment for negligent homicide and malfeasance with a court challenge and insistence that he should not get the same accountability he gave. Others had charges dropped. Some faced short suspensions. A few received reprimands or counseling letters. Others were able to resign with pensions intact and with the potential for future employment elsewhere. Some received no discipline and remained employed. The grace, mercy and leniency that these officers received ran out before Trooper Carl Cavalier could get any.

Cavalier became an outspoken critic of the state police in the aftermath of Green's death. Many describe Cavalier as a whistleblower. Cavalier wasn't on the scene when Green was murdered and he wasn't engaged in the coverup. Yet, Cavalier was terminated following a 200-hour suspension. Cavalier's termination letter mentioned that he was "criticizing the department," "being unloyal," "making public statements," and "seeking publicity." Cavalier is a Black officer, a point that merits discussion because one could easily make the case that there is a disparity amongst the ranks insofar as the level of protection extended after transgressions. Cavalier received the ultimate and he did the least of all cases discussed. Cavalier was terminated.

Derrick Stafford, a Marksville, Louisiana police lieutenant, and city marshal Norris Greenhouse, both Black, were on duty when the pair fired eighteen shots at a vehicle. Stafford insisted that he felt threatened and responded accordingly. Both said they were not aware that a child was in the vehicle at the time. They also denied seeing the father's hands up inside the vehicle. Stafford repeatedly expressed remorse and regret for the loss of the child and the resulting harm. Both occupants of the vehicle were white. In 2017, Stafford was convicted of manslaughter and sentenced to forty years in prison.

Greenhouse pleaded guilty to negligent homicide and malfeasance in office to avoid trial in the shooting death of Jeremy Mardis. He too received jail time and the added condition that he surrender his certification so he can never again perform law enforcement functions. Consistent with national norms, whites compose the entire leadership structure of Louisiana's police unions and associations. These unions traditionally defend officers and aid them in circumventing consequences. They ghosted when it came to Cavalier, Stafford and Greenhouse.

There are those who, by now, have deemed me irreverent and anti-police, which I am neither. I respond only to say the DOJ must be even more so. Before this federal intervention, the DOJ investigated the NOPD and found a pattern and practice of misconduct and unlawful actions in 2011, including discriminatory practices. The DOJ determined that NOPD failed to ensure that its officers routinely respect the Constitution. They also concluded that the deficiencies inside NOPD were both individual and structural.

In 2021, ACLU of Louisiana's *Justice Lab: Putting Racist Policing on Trial* campaign collected more than 400 complaints of police misconduct statewide, filed upwards of 30 cases against law enforcement officers, and documented countless stories from survivors and family members impacted by police violence throughout the state.

This historical dynamic where Blacks are subject to twenty-four-hour suspicion by law enforcement combined with the codified subjectivity of modern laws has resulted in a culture of racial profiling that leads to greater rates of police encounters, arrests and deaths in the Black community.[193] Current statistics offer support. Data from the Bureau of Justice Statistics' 2018 Police-Public Contact Survey shows that, during police-initiated stops, Blacks and Hispanics experience greater use of force or threats of force than whites and are placed in handcuffs more often.

In 2020, the Economic Policy Institute studied the relationship between lynchings and Black deaths at the hands of law enforcement. Their findings illuminated a statistically significant relationship between historical lynchings and the difference in the share of officer-involved shootings of Blacks compared with whites. The Institute concluded that

Blacks who live in areas that had fewer historical lynchings make up a lower share of officer-involved shootings compared with whites. Yet, Blacks who live in areas that had high levels of historical lynchings make up a larger share of officer-involved shootings compared with whites. This research was undertaken in an effort to understand how historical imbalances in relationships remain a factor in modern policing. The state's lynching history compels attention to these findings.[194]

A recent survey from the Reilly Center for Media & Public Affairs at Louisiana State University's Manship School of Mass Communication, reported that a majority (55%) of the state's residents believe Black people are treated less fairly than white people in dealing with the police. The Police Scorecard provides another perspective. It assigns a score ranging from 0-100% based on the performance of law enforcement in each state. States with higher scores spend less on policing, use less force, are more likely to hold officers accountable and make fewer arrests for low-level offenses. In 2023, Louisiana's score is a dismal 43%.

Blacks have no reason to feel hopeful about future reforms. To the contrary, law, policy and custom have served as an impediment to progress. Officers must be certified to work in law enforcement. To prevent officers with histories of misconduct from "wandering" to other jurisdictions, the legislature created a database. It was supposed to track police certifications. The problem is that many officers who transgress are never decertified. The law requires the employing agency to initiate decertification. Many don't. The law also allows for an officer to be decertified if they resign or are fired due to excessive force (only). The result is a culture of "wandering" officers who break the law or commit misconduct then go to another jurisdiction and secure employment with impunity.

This database is available to the public in many states. Louisiana does not allow public access to its database. The reference to Louisiana as a "sportsman's paradise" resonates in a special way with Blacks. When it comes to communities of color, policing too often feels like a social control system that runs counter to the country's advertised values of liberty, freedom and privacy. Race and policing converged in such a way that, for Blacks, there is often an element of risk, danger, trauma and anxiety in law enforcement encounters and, for members of law enforcement, there is often an element of fear or distrust when they have encounters with Blacks. These dueling sentiments entered the jury box.

The Amalgamation of Race & Labor

The slavery era's physical and financial exploitation of Black bodies immersed itself into post-slavery labor schemes.[195] A glimpse into some of the experiences of the enslaved are foreshadowing. During chattel slavery, Ignace's owners wanted him to perform physical labor despite him having an enlarged heart and pressure in his lungs. When he succumbed to these maladies, a court decided his latest buyer should recover the money spent to purchase him. The justification was that Ignace was defective since he could not perform labor, the sole purpose of a slave.[196] The concept of Blacks existing solely as instruments of service took wings.

Eulaie's story exposes another dimension of this labor dynamic. Eulaie, an over-sixty-five-year-old formerly enslaved woman who had lived as a free person for over forty-five years, sought her release after she and her sixteen children and grandchildren were forcibly taken and claimed as slaves by the defendants. The defendants successfully argued to the trial court that the plaintiffs had no right to experience freedom. On appeal, the court discussed the ways emancipation could be achieved. In that context, the court told of Louisiana's "interest... in *disposing of* such persons after they have acquired their right to freedom....," making it clear that there was no use for a Black person if their body or labor could no longer be subject to exploitation.[197]

Thereafter, the Court explained, as a step in perfecting the process of emancipation, that the judge must appoint an agent to hire out such slaves until they have earned a sufficient sum to defray the expense of their removal to Liberia. As that process unfolds, the person, according to the court, is the property of the state. Beyond the open acknowledgement of the freedom to exploit the labor of a Black person, there are also subliminal messages about the commodification of Black bodies. In addition to the reality of what would come of the fruits of that exploitation, there is a storyline in the making concerning Black people bearing the cost of their own oppression. This theme grows in epic proportions as this story matures.

Through Mange and the unnamed female slave victim of overseer Hendricks, we gain an understanding of how Black bodies became transactional commodities. Mange's owner described him as a "well-behaved skilled cooper" who was left blind at the hands of another enslaved man.[198] His owner complained, not of the harm done to Mange, but of *her* loss. She explained that, prior to the accident, he was worth $1800 and the additional $45 per month *she* earned for hiring him out to others. According to her, *she* was injured because, as a result of the accident, "not only can Mange no longer work and earn money but expenses have to be incurred to feed him and pay physicians to attend to him."[199] To Southern whites, Blacks had worth to the extent they could be transacted. An extension of this presents itself in the case of the injured enslaved female left in the care of Overseer Hendricks who treated the slaves in his care in an "utterly indefensible" manner.[200]

The injuries he inflicted upon the enslaved caused medical bills and losses due to the enslaved being physically unable to work. The plantation owner reduced the overseer's monthly salary, prompting litigation. The court agreed with the jury's decision that a salary reduction was warranted and the court even awarded a greater damage award because, according to the court, more than the loss of labor was at issue with one female slave. The court found that her value was permanently impaired by the bodily injuries she sustained. In the end, the infliction of permanent injuries upon a Black woman was cause for a damage award, reducing a Black body to nothing more than a transactional instrument.

Even the clergy had a hand in shaping racial labor customs in Louisiana. In his 1860 Thanksgiving Sermon to his New Orleans congregation, Reverend Benjamin M. Palmer, a minister to Confederate soldiers, proclaimed the abundant benefits that awaited Southern whites who insisted on the maintenance of a labor regime like Louisiana's:

> Need I pause to show how this system of servitude underlies and supports our material interests? That our wealth consists in our lands, and in the serfs who till them? That from the nature of our products they can only be cultivated by labor which must be controlled in order to be certain?.... every attribute of their character fits them for dependence and servitude..... As [slavery's] constituted guardian, [we] can demand nothing less than that it should be left open to expansion, subject to no limitations....[201]

"Tens of thousands of copies of the speech were quickly printed and circulated throughout the South, while regional newspapers published Palmer's words, often alongside enthusiastic commentary."[202]

As W.E.B. Du Bois explains, the iniquitous post-Civil desires for the emancipated people were far reaching: "The North d[id] not especially want free Negros; it want[ed] trade and wealth. The South d[id] not want a particular interpretation of the Constitution. It want[ed] cheap Negro labor and the political and social power based on it."[203] Many of the emancipated people entered the world as free people of very limited skills and without awareness of these things. More than what they did not know was what they did not have. Key to their transition was ownership of land since they largely relied on the agricultural and labor skills they utilized during slavery for their survival after emancipation. Having the land that was intended for them–the land abandoned and seized during the Civil War–would have amounted to self-sufficiency for many of them.

After President Lincoln's death, President Andrew Johnson swiftly reversed this law and ordered the land returned to the original owners, forcing the formerly enslaved into tenant status. "The share of Louisiana farmers classified as tenants expanded from one-third in 1880 to two-thirds in 1930."[204] For Blacks who remained in the South after emancipation, freedom looked and felt a lot like enslavement. Leaving land ownership in the hands of whites left them in control of the economy and the wealth because, in large part, if Blacks did not work for them, they did not work at all. It also left the economic and social hierarchies from the slavery era in place. The post-emancipation law required that Black workers be paid for their labor so Southern farmers complied by extending housing to the newly emancipated in the slave cabins on the same plantations they were freed from.

Under this peonage system, a labor contract that favored the property owner and disadvantaged the worker governed. These contracts often advanced money or supplies, based on the laborer's expected share of the future crop, in exchange for payments after crops were sold. Later, laborers often discovered their share of the crop did not cover what they owed the landowner, a deliberate aspect of these contractual relationships. In turn, the worker would be forced into more work in an effort to resolve this balance. Many landowners required the laborer to remain on the property until the debt was paid in full. The terms of these *civil* contracts often included *criminal* penalties for the worker. There was often no due process for the worker so, the word of the white property owner, was usually enough to prompt an arrest of the Black worker and usher a person attempting to work and live free into slavery (behind bars).

If the allegation of breach did not place a worker in penal custody, a response to an unsuspecting person in their home in the middle of the night would often do it. That's exactly what scheduled the death date of Pink Franklin, who received the death penalty for shooting at an unknown man who entered his home at 3:00 am. He believed the man to be an intruder. It was later determined that the victim was a law enforcement officer there to take him into custody after the property owner filed a labor complaint with the magistrate. Hidden within the pages of this case is a loud message that the life of this Black man no longer mattered since he could not, like Ignace, fulfill his ordained role.

In this death penalty case, the court said it had no interest in evaluating his claim that the warrant used to set the events of the evening in motion was null and void. The court continued its dismissive reply, noting that it "would not be competent,"[205] under any circumstances, to rule for the accused Black man. This type of labor exploitation continued into the early 1900s when the head of the Tabasco family pleaded guilty to forced labor on Avery Island, Louisiana. He admitted to the U.S. Civil Service Commissioner that he chained one of his tenants to a tree, observing that the methods he used in retaining help were common practice. These unwritten labor norms resulted in labor schemes that placed white workers in positions of greater pay, greater power and greater authority. Black workers experienced the margins. Exclusion prevailed in this space too. This mindset entered the jury box.

Considerable effort went into maintaining this system of labor exploitation. The Louisiana State Constitution of 1879 moved the seat of government from New Orleans to Baton Rouge. "New Orleans was the 'citadel of commerce,' protected by a chain of fortresses near the mouth of the Mississippi, including Fort Jackson and Fort St. Philip."[206] "The city was a center of international trade for the agricultural and commercial goods—particularly cotton—that were produced in the Mississippi River valley and exported to Europe."[207] New Orleans offered labor opportunities to Blacks that Baton Rouge did not. Blacks in New Orleans were not limited to agricultural work. They could work in urban settings or could become successful entrepreneurs, such as formerly enslaved Rose Nicaud who purchased her freedom and started a coffee business in the French Quarters in the 1800s. She sold cafe-au-lait to French Market vendors from a pushcart, making her the first New Orleans street vendor to offer fresh coffee.

She saved the proceeds of her sales and later opened a permanent location in the French Market. Entrepreneurship and access can lead to wealth and power. That risk became a factor in moving the capital where white political domination would not be threatened. As with chattel slavery, there would be great resistance to efforts to equalize labor terms. Louisiana's Black sugar cane workers found that out when they planned "a second emancipation."[208] "Sensing they were in a strong bargaining position, workers banded together in several sugar parishes, including St. Mary, Iberia, Terrebonne, and Lafourche, demanding cash wages of $1.25 per day, or $1.00 if meals were included."[209] They opposed other Black workers not joining their efforts. They secured the help of the Knights of Labor, an experienced union who presented a list of demands to the Louisiana Sugar Producer's Association, including the elimination of scrip, a small increase in wages and biweekly payments.

After their demands were ignored, a month-long strike ensued. This adversely impacted the entire region. Property owners, such as future Supreme Court Chief Justice E.D. White, Jr., responded with evictions or arrests. The local judge in Thibodaux, Lafourche Parish District Judge Taylor Beattie, who was also an ex-Confederate and White League member, declared martial law. On November 22, 1887, there was an onslaught. The 1887 Thibodaux Massacre ended in the loss of at least three hundred Black cane workers. Official accounts underreported the number of casualties, present the actions of the white murderers as necessary and defensible and the actions of Black strikers as a "regrettable...indiscretion"[210] on the part of "simple and...ignorant [negros who] allowed themselves to be led by bad advisors."[211]

None of the attackers were held accountable in state or federal court. Sugar planter Andrew Price was among the attackers that morning. He won a seat in Congress the next year. The massacre accomplished a few noteworthy things. It kept labor unions out of the South. It kept Southern whites in a position of power in the Southern labor dynamic. It reinforced stereotypes about Blacks being created to be servants, being unworthy of and unsuited for personal autonomy and not deserving of equality. It reminded southern Blacks that Reconstruction had been little more than a failed experiment. And, in the words of plantation mistress Mary Pugh, the massacre would "settle the question of who is to rule, the n[_ _ _ _ _] or the white man, for the next fifty years...."[212]

By the 1960s, some Blacks had escaped the fields and entered workplaces only to discover the plantation hierarchy there too. Despite federal laws forbidding segregated workplaces, Crown Zellerbach Corporation, the largest paper manufacturer in the U.S. at the time, maintained a segregated workplace (as did many other local employers).[213] After legal challenges forced an end to segregation, the company attempted to pay Black workers who sought transfers to what was once white departments less money than they were earning in their former jobs.[214] This was done to deter the transfers and maintain segregation.

The company also implemented an irrelevant testing system that conveniently produced scores that favored white test takers and disadvantaged Black test takers.[215] The ultimate motivation was to relegate Black workers to low paying jobs and jobs that would ensure they remained unskilled laborers. This ensured that white workers earned greater pay, controlled the knowledge and power base in the employment setting while simultaneously maintaining Black workers in a position of financial dependency and financial inferiority and limited to servant class roles that would reinforce a system of social and political inferiority. [216]

Louisiana created an impenetrable system of oppression. Some sought escape through military service. Congressman John Rankin, a southerner and a known segregationist, got his way when he insisted that the 1944 GI Bill be administered by state officials and not the federal government. This legislative maneuver laid the groundwork for a wealth and opportunity building program to disproportionately benefit whites who served in World War II. The free college tuition, low-cost home loans and unemployment benefits disproportionately went to them.

Obstacles, such as higher rates of dishonorable discharges, placement in underfunded vocational programs that lead to unskilled labor opportunities, denial of mortgage loans and application of restrictive covenants, all reinforced the placement of Blacks in a social structure that, over time, made their suitability for the carceral state justifiable to many. Despite the failures of the GI Bill, W.E.B. DuBois, the respected Black author, intellectual, statesman and activist of the day, observed, in his 1948 progress report, a notable shift to more skilled Black laborers (from a history of mostly unskilled Black laborers).[217]

For Blacks, labor unions have been another obstacle. By 1869, Blacks began making appearances at Nation Labor Union meetings in New York. Their presence seemingly inspired a strategy of dividing labor by racial and social lines while branding the effort one labor movement.[218] "Through this separate union, Negro labor would be restrained from competition and yet kept out of the white unions where power and discussion lay."[219] Beyond this, the Southern states formed a commitment to wage slavery through the advent of right-to-work laws and anti-union measures. The average union worker earned substantially more per week than the average non-union worker. This labor initiative was sought to fulfill a few aims, such as the prevention of interracial organizing that could result in fair wages for all workers and the absence of union representation to advocate for fair wages for Black workers.

Racial division and discord amongst workers was more valuable to a system committed to relegating Blacks to low wages and a lack of power or wealth. One would not be wrong for deeming it a success. For many years, the only labor unions available to Blacks in Louisiana were segregated. As of 2021, "No Southern state with the exception of West Virginia has a union membership rate over 10%...."[220] According to data released from the Bureau of Labor Statistics in 2023, only 4.5 percent of Southern workers belong to labor unions, which is eight percentage points below the non-South average.

Transition requires an understanding of how, at the critical time of reconstructing the country, national industrial labor desires collided with the labor demands of the emancipated people which collided with the labor demands of former plantation owners which collided the labor demands of poor whites in the South and elsewhere. Accordingly, W. E. B. Du Bois encourages a view of Reconstruction as an "economic revolution" and not just a race war:

> Reconstruction [must be viewed] slowly and broadly as a tremendous series of efforts to earn a living in new and untried ways, to achieve economic security and to restore fatal losses of capital and investment. It was a vast labor movement of ignorant, earnest, and bewildered Black men whose faces had been ground in the mud by their three awful centuries of degradation and who now staggered forward blindly in blood and tears amid petty division, hate and hurt, and surrounded by every disaster of war and industrial upheaval. Reconstruction was a vast labor movement of ignorant, muddled and bewildered white men who had been disinherited of land and labor and fought a long battle with sheer subsistence, hanging on the edge of poverty, eating clay and chasing slaves and now lurching up to manhood. Reconstruction was the turn of white Northern migration southward to new and sudden economic opportunity which followed the disaster and dislocation of

war, and an attempt to organize capital and labor on a new pattern and build a new economy. Finally Reconstruction was a desperate effort to dislodge, maimed, impoverished and ruined oligarchy and monopoly to restore an anachronism in organization by force, fraud, and slander... with a new capitalism and a new political framework.[221]

For too long, change agents have failed to consider the way slavery and Reconstruction served as incubators for Louisiana's racial labor norms and how they shape the contours of Louisiana's criminal legal system. These views on labor and race entered the jury box.

The Collision of Race, Profits & Incarceration

Without dispute, there is a race and a capitalist arch to Louisiana's prison system. Neither started with the end of slavery. This infection formed long before emancipation. Construction began on Louisiana's earliest incarceration facility in 1729. This two-building facility was in New Orleans. It contained a civil courtroom in one area and cells and a dungeon in another area. Louisiana's colonial jails typically held soldiers, immigrants, laborers or sailors in custody. Blacks were needed to meet the market demands of the chattel slavery system so the preferred approach was to administer justice to the enslaved on plantations so production would not be disrupted. This isn't to suggest Blacks were never incarcerated before emancipation. They were on occasion, but the preferred sentence was corporal punishment so they could be returned to their chattel slavery duty station.

During this pre-emancipation period, Black bodies were presumed to be in their proper place when they were performing labor under the chattel slavery system so there were limited reasons for a Black person to be elsewhere. When Blacks were found in jail, it was most often due to: a court order involving insolvency of the owner (so his property was taken to secure his debts); being caught and held as a suspected runaway; at the request of the owner (for discipline or safekeeping or because they couldn't perform);[222] because of criminal charges or a conviction; or, due to a sale. The other noteworthy connection between Blacks and jails during the chattel slavery era is that jails were often sites for slave auctions.

During the pre-emancipation period, penal philosophy was greatly impacted by the 1764 treatise *On Crimes and Punishments*. This treatise endorsed time in silence and reflection and the rest of the time performing labor, as a deterrent and rehabilitation. Louisiana heard the labor part of this philosophy loud and clear. In the late 1700s, there was public resistance to increasing the number of jails because of the cost of maintaining them. As population increased, the resistance to incarceration being a burden on citizens increased. It didn't take long for this to translate into a policy of making incarceration profitable.

By the early 1800's, incarceration was becoming a more structured affair in Louisiana. A 1814 act established the provisions due those in custody. Convicts were entitled to two sets of seasonally appropriate clothing each year and a per diem allowance consisting of one pound of beef or three-quarters of a pound of pork, one pound of vegetables, one pound of potatoes or a comparable portion of rice, four quarts of vinegar, and a small salt allowance. By 1817, the law required that medical care be provided to persons in custody and it allowed for jailers to be reimbursed the cost of enslaved people held in custody (at a rate of twelve and a half cents per day).

"The 1820s and 1830s were the years of great penitentiary debate in the United States (and Europe)...." [223] Two opposing systems were advocated. The first, considered the more economical of the two, was modeled after the penitentiary in Auburn, New York. It employed convicts "together during the day, but under the rule of absolute silence enforced by the whip."[224] The second, considered the more philosophical, was modeled after the Philadelphia penitentiary, which "confined convicts to a strict 24-hour solitary existence, including work alone during the day."[225] Both plans recognized that "the free association of criminals only confirmed them in their antisocial habits."[226] Economics dictated Louisiana's position in this debate.

The state ignored Edward Livingston's call, the author of the first criminal code, for "reconditioning" and rehabilitation (instead of retribution).[227] In 1826, Governor Henry Johnson was openly advocating for the use of penal labor on public works projects or hard labor in general.[228] The 1831 Governor incorporated a like message, making it clear what the state's policy would be. Governor Jacques Dupré told the legislature that incorrigible offenders would pay the expense of their conviction and punishment.[229] Pursuant to this policy aim, the first penitentiary was established in 1832.[230] It was followed by the creation of a 1833 Board of Public Works, a state agency tasked with overseeing penal labor projects.

By 1835, Louisiana had added a penitentiary complex on the outskirts of Baton Rouge, complete with living quarters for staff, over two hundred cells, a prison hospital, a foundry and other shops for inmates to work. Inmate labor built this new facility. In 1837, the country was in its first great depression. By 1839, there were legislative concerns being expressed in the state about the cost of corrections. Louisiana needed money, and the penitentiary was thought to be a solution. Inmate labor was being heavily used. A 1840 newspaper advertisement told buyers the prison-made shoes and boots, were "as good if not better than those imported from the North."[231] It seems the anticipated profits weren't being realized and the penitentiary was becoming a burden on the state.

With the 1842 election of Democratic Governor Alexandre Mouton came an end to state funded efforts to house, manage or reform convicts. What little enlightenment philosophy that had been embraced was abandoned in favor of an industry approach to corrections. One of several cost savings measures was leasing the state penitentiary to a private manager. The facilities and its inmates were handed over to private companies like McHatton, Pratt and Company who, in 1844, obtained a five-year lease agreement. The agreement allowed the company to keep all profits. The business plan was built around inmate labor. Around this time, there was an increase in migrants who entered the country through the port of New Orleans. A number of them remained. They became good for business.

The law even allowed for the exploitation of children. In 1848, the state legislature passed a law making all children born in the penitentiary to Black women serving life sentences property of the state. The women would raise the children (often born of rapes by other inmates or staff) inside the prison until the age of ten then the child would be auctioned on the courthouse steps. The prison was remodeled into a textile mill that would produce cloth and clothing. Immigrants were being disproportionately incarcerated (with Irish born inmates showing a high representation). The venture proved successful and a second lease was signed. With each lease and every demonstration of profit, the state got further and further away from an ideal of reform and closer and closer to view of corrections as a source of profits.

A judicial opinion describes the prison conditions of the era. It tells that the Black man who perished within days of leaving was "in a very cold room, without a bed, couch, or chair, with nothing but a single blanket to lie upon, and so emaciated and feeble as then to be unable to get up on his knees without the assistance of another man."[232] The court noted that a doctor was not called until two and a half months of his arrival at the jail and opined that a deadly disease was contracted in the prison. In it's conclusion, the court remarked that "the circumstances in which the patient was found...were neither fit nor decent for a human being of any color."[233]

By the time the third lease was presented in 1855, the state suddenly got interested in placing the penitentiary under state control. Not long after the penitentiary was placed under state control, a 1856 fire destroyed it. By 1857, it was back in the private hands of McHatton, but this time, they could only claim half of the profits. The state would claim the other half of the profits under this new lease, making corrections a lucrative industry for the state and private parties alike. Work assignments expanded over the years. Profits were consistently realized, but they fluctuated. Samuel Lawrence James set his sights on the possibilities this new human trafficking system offered.

James, a former Confederate major, is the brainchild of Louisiana's post-Civil War convict leasing system.[234] Through profitable leases with the state, James took custody of Louisiana's convicts. He housed them on his former plantations then leased them out to employers who often housed them in dilapidated, travelling camps. James was paid handsomely for that work. The inmates worked on levees and railroads and also performed agricultural, mining and road construction work. Because many of the enslaved were highly skilled, they even worked as blacksmiths, brick masons, coopers, seamstresses and more.

Around this same time, railway expansion in the country was underway and labor force for this backbreaking work was always a high demand.[235] There was no oversight and no health and safety requirements. Abuses were incalculable. "In Louisiana, Negro convicts were furnished in large numbers...."[236] "[C]onvicts, unlike antebellum chattels, cost lessees nothing."[237] Blacks had "entered into a relationship with the state unmediated by a master."[238] "They were divested of their status as slaves in order to be accorded a new status as criminals."[239] James' enterprise lasted from 1867-1884. Success was measured through profits. In the South, the number of imprisoned Blacks increased "from less than one percent before 1861 to as much as 90 percent in certain counties and states after 1865...."[240]

State audit records show steady increases on the state penitentiary leases immediately after emancipation: $2,228.63 in 1869; $15,159.77 in 1870; and, $31, 913.80 in 1871.[241] Five years after emancipation in Louisiana (in the year 1870), there were 400 white persons convicted and 359 Blacks convicted. Fifteen years post-emancipation (in the year 1880), Louisiana reported 230 white convicts and 847 Black convicts. In 1900, Louisiana created a Board of Control to oversee state penitentiaries.[242] By 1901, over ninety percent of Louisiana's inmates were Black.[243] Around this time, Black female change agents were using their platform to call attention to this. Selena Sloan Butler submitted *The Chain-Gang System* paper to be read at the National Association of Colored Women meeting.[244]

Ida B. Wells published a chapter entitled, *"The Convict Lease System,"* wherein she spoke of the harms of the system and the racial dimensions of it.[245] Mary Church Terrell wrote *"Peonage in the United States: The Convict Lease System and the Chain Gang."*[246] "In her essay, Terrell showed that the chain gang system in the South was a continuation of slavery."[247] "Damningly, she also revealed how the courts and lawmakers rendered the Constitution meaningless by supporting such system."[248] The "identity between Blacks and criminals in the minds of many Louisianians not only helped to perpetuate the lease system but survived long afterward as an impediment to penal reform."[249]

Questionable "expert" opinion became the basis for official policy. Frederick H. Wines, a northern penologist, provided the rationale for the continued exploitation of Black workers behind bars. In 1906, Mr. Hines spoke to the annual congress of the National Prison Association about his tour of Louisiana prisons where he observed mostly Black men performing agricultural work. He opined: "[T]he negro is not fitted for indoor life. He is not wanted as an industrial rival to the white man...I cannot imagine, except for the question of reformation (and they are not reformatory), anything more ideally suited to the conditions on which the convicted population is assembled, properly cared for, and governed."[250]

By 1910, Louisiana had 1642 white convicts and 3382 Black convicts. Louisiana's children were not exempt. Upon a declaration of a judge that service was in the best interest of the child, the child was placed in the custody of a landowner and apprenticed until the age of eighteen if female or twenty-one if male. Many of these children were the very children who were freed by the Thirteenth Amendment or the offspring of those who were. Parental consent often was not required. These adult landowners were frequently former slave owners. The judges were compensated by the landowners who were awarded these children.

By the mid-1900's, profits, speed, race and incarceration had become indelibly woven into the fabric of life in Louisiana. This did not begin with chattel slavery. In 1718, Britain passed the Transportation Act, providing that people convicted of certain crimes could avoid hanging by going to America.[251] Merchants, many of whom were experienced in the slave holding, were paid to take custody of this "property" and given permission to work them until they completed their sentences.[252] Many of these immigrants ended up on tobacco plantations as indentured servants.[253] Approximately one quarter of all British immigrants to America in the 18th century were convicts.[254]

In current publications, the Louisiana Department of Corrections boasts that Angola "consists of 18,000 acres of the finest farm land in the south" and it intimates that the layout of the grounds reflect the priority farming has on its operations.[255] This makes sense given the fact that the prison was built on the site of former plantations.[256] This was a post-

Civil War strategy used by many former Confederate states. For example, in 1901, Mississippi State Penitentiary, Parchman Farm, was opened on the site of a former plantation and, like Louisiana, their prison system became the closest thing to slavery that survived the war.[257] One is left to decide which is worse–the former or the current, which is to construct prisons near Superfund sites or on nuclear test sites, toxic waste sites or old mines.

Much like the chattel slavery days, Angola's agricultural work is performed under the supervision of horse-riding, shotgun-toting guards. This is an upgrade from days gone by when white inmates served as guards. [258] What has not changed is the racial composition of the justice-impacted laborers. Blacks remain the majority of the laborers in the fields and whites remain the majority of the "overseers." According to Marianne Fisher-Giorlando, Grambling State University Criminal Justice Professor Emerita, "census records document the fact that prison employees engaged in racially disparate practices through prison job assignments in the early 1900s."

She continued, "These records illustrated that policy makers and corrections' officials of the time used Jim Crow assumptions that Black men were more suited to manual work in the fields and on the levees than were white men, because, presumably, white men were more intelligent than Black men." "Accordingly, if any white men appeared on the census records at the levee camps, they were assigned to white collar jobs such as clerks, said Fisher-Giorlando. "Currently, Prison Enterprises [the business arm of the Louisiana Department of Public Safety and Corrections that uses inmate labor to produce goods and provide services] plants, grows and harvests wheat, corn, soybeans, cotton and milo...."[259]

"The penitentiary...produces many crops for consumption by the justice-impacted population such as tomatoes, cabbage, okra, watermelon, strawberries, onions, beans and peppers."[260] "Some of the crops that are harvested and used to support the livestock and flight bird operations...but the majority are sold on the open market."[261] A 2024 Associated Press forced labor investigative report described unmarked cattle trucks leaving Angola for sales and then ending up in supply chains that led to supermarkets and restaurants across the country. Agricultural work is not the only option. Louisiana inmates also make office furniture and metal structures, bedding and clothing. And they sew and weld.

Angola's Prison Enterprises industrial operations "include a license tag manufacturing plant, a silk screen shop, print shop, metal fabrication shop, and a mattress, broom, and mop factory."[262] Under Louisiana law, persons in custody can experience forced labor that is unpaid for the initial three years of incarceration.[263] Thereafter, persons in custody are eligible to earn certain wages in exchange for their labor. As in the case of peonage, said wages are notoriously low, with the introductory pay level being $0.02. Typical Louisiana wages are about four cent per hour, amounting to thirty-two cents a day, resulting in nine days of work to earn $3.00. Inmates must work at least eight hours daily, five days per week.

The sales generated a handsome source of income, which, in the 2018-2019 years, included $9,787,583.00 from manufacturing products and $2,702,114.00 from agricultural products.[264] Reminiscent of the slavery era, corn, cotton and soybeans were amongst the agricultural products sold in 2018-2019.[265] Louisiana inmates also work in private settings, sometimes without pay, performing carpentry, waste removal, welding, cooking and other jobs as needed. The reasoning is to give them training and work skills that can be used upon release. Sometimes, these private employers reap the simultaneous benefit of a free labor base, avoidance of injury claims and handsome tax breaks. This is said to have been the reason British Petroleum embraced the idea of using inmate labor to clean up after the Deepwater Horizon oil spill. These mostly Black laborers are said to have gotten more than a visit from the brutal Louisiana heat. Toxins likely visited them as well.

A governor can also benefit from this fusion of incarceration, race and labor. During slavery, "[b]ody servants or valets were enslaved men assigned to closely attend to their masters."[266] "Elite planters directed valets and body servants to serve them with intimate tasks such as dressing and bathing."[267] "Valets also labored closely with elite men when they were ill."[268] Governors in Louisiana can avail themselves to this historical bounty. They are allowed inmate butlers to handle mansion duties in the same way slave masters or Confederate soldiers used Blacks as butlers or body servants.[269] By 1951, the justice-impacted resisted. That year, more than thirty inmates slashed their Achilles tendons to avoid grueling labor in the fields.[270]

A spirit of reform emerged in the 1950s, but budget cuts in the 1960s rendered concern for the justice-impacted an afterthought. A 1967 news story reported that the "legislature felt that the penitentiary should become self-supporting and that the Board of Institutions believed their main function was to produce a profit rather than rehabilitate prisoners."[271] In its 1975 report, the Louisiana Advisory Committee to the United States Commission of Civil Rights found that the "educational and vocational programs in the three institutions that comprise the adult penal system in Louisiana...,for the most part, failed to adequately equip offenders with the skills and experiences necessary for successful reintegration into society."[272] That's likely due to the fact that Angola was consumed with sugar production well into the 1970s in the same way sugar was the object of desires during chattel slavery.[273]

<u>Audit Findings</u>

This audit offers four significant findings. It first finds that, when slavery ended, a mistake of generational portions occurred. The mistake was the failure of the Reconstruction Congress to achieve a meeting of the minds about the vision for and an exact understanding of what freedom was to be once they ended chattel slavery. Some representatives viewed post-emancipation freedom as simply movement. Others saw freedom as an exemption from external control or regulation, the power to determine action without restraint and/or the absence of constraint in choice or action.

Without a clear vision, there could never be a sound strategy. The lack of a sound strategy emerged during this discussion. This should not be confused with not having a strategy at all. The Reconstruction Congress did ultimately adopt a strategy. The strategy was to separate civil rights protections from political rights protections. This created a pathway for malicious state officials to make post-emancipation mirror pre-emancipation. Senator Carpenter explains: "[T]hose political rights of voting, of holding office, of serving as a juror...may be taken away at the pleasure of a state even under the Constitution as now amended."[274] Louisiana would not be accused of being modest. It took in heaping portions from the newly emancipated people who entered this next phase of life not fully appreciating the impact of what had just been done under the cover of law.

This audit reveals the consequences of these failures. At one point, the failure was solely on the part of government. Today, the failure is assigned to people. Do we even understand what post-emancipation freedom should look like? The result of this failure is a population of Black people who today live much of what they lived during chattel slavery—a life of hereditary marginalization. A natural outgrowth of this is the failure of many Blacks to truly experience life in a democracy. Jury service and judgement by jury are some of the classic ways people experience or partake in democracy,

This is why this audit is necessary and non-negotiable. It's a form of truth-seeking. Truth-seeking work helps identify victims, quantify and acknowledge harms and traumas, assess fault and responsibility, pursue accountability and fashion remedies so healing and reconciliation can begin. This quest for truth is motivated by not only a desire to correctly memorialize events, but, more importantly, their causes and impacts. This is the proper and only starting point for understanding the unique racial history surrounding Blacks in the jury box or for studying criminal justice transformation in general.

Secondarily, the audit finds that racism and systemic inequities are deeply ingrained in the fabric of Louisiana's legal system. "Racism is not some great omnipotent evil in the sky that rains down disadvantage on poor Black folk."[275] Racism is "racial prejudice combined with power, creating the structural racial oppression and inequitable outcomes we see across US society."[276] Racism "includes attitudes, practices and beliefs rooted in ideas or theories of superiority, as a complex of factors, which produce discrimination and exclusion."[277] Racism focuses on concentrating power.[278] Malice is not required for racism to occur. Racism, a legacy of slavery, has permeated American culture in two ways: (1) through the structural inequality that mitigates against the equitable inclusion of Black people in the society; and, (2) through beliefs about Black inferiority."[279]

Initially, Blacks were on the receiving end of racism by single racists, such as an individual slave owner. By the end of the evolution, systemic racism, a phrase coined by political activist Stokely Carmichael and sociologist Charles Hamilton in the late 1960's, had become the obstacle.[280] Systemic or institutionalized racism involves the cumulative and compounding effects of an array of societal factors, including the history, culture, ideology and interactions of institutions and policies that systematically privilege a dominant group and disadvantage individuals of a marginalized group.[281] Systemic racism is composed of intersecting, overlapping, and codependent racist institutions, policies, practices, ideas, and behaviors that give an unjust amount of resources, rights, and power to white people while denying them to people of color.

One example of institutionalized racism was brought into existence by the Mississippi legislature when it created the 1956 Mississippi State Sovereignty Commission (Commission) in response to the May 1954 *Brown v. Board of Education* ruling. The Commission's objective was to do and perform any and all acts deemed necessary and proper to protect the sovereignty of the state of Mississippi, and her sister states from perceived encroachment thereon by the federal government or any branch, department or agency thereof. With the use of government funds, the Commission investigated, oppressed and harmed individuals and organizations that challenged the racial status quo.[282]

On the federal level, COINTELPRO–short for Counterintelligence Program–worked comparably. COINTELPRO started in 1956 to disrupt the activities of the Communist Party of the United States. In the 1960s, it was expanded to include a number of other domestic groups, such as the Ku Klux Klan, the Socialist Workers Party, the Black Panther Party and others. J. Edgar Hoover used his power as director of the Federal Bureau of Investigations to neutralize many activists, advocacy groups, dissident voices, artists and innocent citizens.[283] His tactics were often unconstitutional and largely illegal.[284] False arrests, harassment, assassinations and torture were some of the practices he employed under the ruse of COINTELPRO.[285] For over forty-seven long years, J. Edgar Hoover acted as a "political pervert" as he declared war on free expression, chilled speech, intimidated and bullied dissenters, meted out private punishments, invaded privacy rights and engaged in discriminatory law enforcement practices.[286]

What happed to Black farmers at the hands of the government is yet another example of institutional racism. Litigation confirmed that the U.S. Department of Agriculture ("USDA") systematically discriminated against Black farmers on the basis of race–in violation of the Fifth Amendment to the United States Constitution, the Equal Credit Opportunity Act, Title VI of the Civil Rights Act, and the Administrative Procedure Act–when they resolved farm loan or assistance requests made by Black farmers.[287] When there is institutional racism, there are "policies, procedures and practices of institutions that produce patterns of inequitable outcomes for staff and personnel based on their race, color, descent, or national or ethnic origin." [288]

Law Professor Khiara M. Bridges posits that institutional racism, no matter how elaborately defined, can always be recognized by these four elements: (1) laws or policies drafted with the intent of achieving hierarchical results; (2) an official action that involves mundane, routine decisions of daily life; (3) an official action that appears race-neutral; and, (4) a scenario where the actions of a single actor is irrelevant (in comparison to the scheme or system itself).[289]

The four elements of Professor Bridges' analysis are present in all these scenarios. Each of these examples presents an intentional practice that has the appearance of race-neutral actions. Each arises in ordinary acts of American life, such as voting, jury service or self-expression. In each instance, there is a power dynamic that places people of color in a position of disadvantage.

Thirdly, this audit finds that Louisiana's legal system suffers from structural inequities, which are a component of a larger and darker carceral state. The carceral state enables formal institutions and economies of the criminal legal system—police, lawyers, correction officers, the incarcerated, and those paid to house their bodies—to exert their bias and power over people of color. But this, alone, is not all it is. The carceral state encompasses "logics, ideologies, practices and structures that invest in . . . punitive orientations to difference, to poverty, to struggles for social justice and to the crossers of constructive borders."[290]

Through its examination of–labor; law, policy and custom; religion; education; justice; medicine; data; and, policing–this audit illuminates how all the formal institutions of Louisiana's carceral state have worked together to exert bias, supremacy and power over Blacks. Non-unanimous juries and Black juror suppression lie at the center of this universe.

Professor Ruby Tapia explains the breadth and depth of carcerality with rare precision:

> Carcerality captures the many ways in which the carceral state shapes and organizes society and culture through policies and logic of control, surveillance, criminalization, and un-freedom . . . 'punitive orientation' that revolve around the 'promise and threat of criminalization' and the 'possibility/solution of incarceration.' The carceral state, operating through these punitive orientations, functions as an obstacle and a substitute for 'humane solutions to social problems' such as poverty, racism, citizenship status, and other forms of inequality and discrimination. The carceral state, and its punitive processes of criminalization and control, operate in highly discriminatory ways and have both produced and reinforced massive inequalities along lines of race, class, gender, sexuality, and other identity categories. [291]

The groundwork for today's carceral state was laid generations and administrations ago. "Large crime policy projects, like the War on Drugs and the War on Crime that were mounted in the 1980s and 1990s, involved thousands of agencies including state legislatures, police departments, prosecutors, and prison authorities."[292] The result was structural inequities, which were not produced by any one stage of the system but are the combined product of each stage in the sequence. [293]

Finally, this audit finds that non-unanimous juries and the suppression of Black juror participation is representative of the larger pathology described in this chapter. Thus, juries cannot be viewed in isolation, but, instead, must be analyzed for how they overlap and intersect with other aspects of the legal process to maintain and rationalize white power and privilege and ensure punitive responses to human transgressions.

Political rights–voting, office holding and jury service–are potent weapons for use in a counterattack against the things detailed in this chapter. It is through the exercise of political rights that Blacks experience something greater than mere freedom. Political rights equip one with power. For example, jury service divests the Black juror of the badge of inferiority because, for that limited time, the juror can directly determine an outcome in the democracy. For the accused, a proper process guards against an unwarranted governmental intrusion. Because of the unique way political rights allow Blacks to experience power through democratic participation, a separate inquest into political rights is undertaken. Chapter two builds on chapter one's audit by examining the way political rights have been used to bound Blacks in matrimony to a life of exclusion–to a state of neo-slavery.

CHAPTER 2

AN INQUEST INTO THE JURY BOX: HOW POLITICAL RIGHTS HAVE BEEN USED TO EXTEND THE LIFE SPAN OF SYSTEMIC INEQUITIES

There is no crime known among men which it has not committed under the sanction of law. It has bound men and women in chains...and sold them...like a beast....It so constituted its courts that the complaints and appeals of these people could not be heard....It has for many years....trampled upon the national Constitution....No nation could adopt a code of laws that would sanction such enormities and live.[1]

— JAMES ASHLEY

The NAACP came out of the womb championing the cause of political rights.[2] From 1915 to 1948, the NAACP brought twenty-seven cases before the SCOTUS. They prevailed twenty-four of those times. Those victories included outlawing the exclusion of Black jurors and ending the use of grandfather clauses and white primaries in Southern states. Louisiana officials responded by removing the state's welcome mat.[3] In order to appreciate the intersection between race and the three political rights—voting, office holding and jury service—there must be a reckoning with this official response. W.E.B. Du Bois designated emancipation as the starting point for that reckoning. He elucidated:

> The four million people who had suddenly been released...while falling within the category of *'free persons,'* were not yet political persons. This emancipated multitude has no political *status*. Emancipation vitalizes only natural rights, not political rights. Enfranchisement alone carries with it political rights, and these emancipated millions are no more enfranchised now than when they were slaves. They never had political power.[4]

The lack of political power that Du Bois speaks of persists, but in more subtle ways so it is often overlooked. To understand Black jury suppression and/or the state's refusal to address the vestiges of non-unanimous juries, one must see, feel, hear, taste and breathe these insights about political rights. The ability to discern when political rights are being deprived is as essential to transformation as an understanding of the harm that results from the deprivation of political rights.

Of greater importance than both is the ability to understand the will to divest a people of these rights. When one exercises political rights, they possess power because they become players in a democracy—not just present in one. They possess the ability to change things that they don't like. In short, they experience something greater than freedom. Tangentially, supremacy, marginalization, oppression and racism are best sustained by the deprivation of political rights.

For too long, change agents have overlooked the way juries are locked in an embrace with the remaining two political rights. By way of example, consider the way juries and voting intersect. The purpose of a jury is to cast a vote so that is one obvious way. The connection between juries and voting runs deeper. In Louisiana, the default way of selecting prospective jurors is through voter registration lists. If Blacks are underrepresented as voters, they run the risk of being underrepresented as jurors.

This demonstrates how the suppression of one political right inspires and necessitates efforts to suppress other political rights. It also illustrates why granting a single political right causes angst over potential power shifts where others are concerned. For this reason, the work of ending non-unanimous juries must be contextualized and change agents must understand that fights involving any of the political rights are never singular.

The non-unanimous jury effort involved more than a single law about the number of people who decide a criminal case. It involved the system that housed that law, the mindset that enacted it and the power imbalance that produced and sustained. In short, ending non-unanimous juries involved an unexpected confrontation with the systemic racism that pumps throughout the veins of Louisiana's legal system and the punitive ideology that keeps its heart beating. There is hope that this discussion will illuminate the shortcomings of reforms and the rewards of transformative change when the desired change involves longstanding ideologies and systemic practices, such as juries in Louisiana.

The First Political Right: The Vote

In the post-slavery South, casting a vote was not an inconsequential act. Voting was viewed as a privilege[5] and looked upon as a "shield" or weapon "for defense or for aggressive warfare."[6] There was a sanctity to casting a vote. It was considered a form of public service.[7] A voter was seen as exercising the "functions of an office conferred for the purpose of administering and maintaining" government.[8] Abraham Lincoln captured the potency of the vote when he expressed that, "the ballot is stronger than the bullet."[9]

The failure of the Framers of the Constitution to incorporate the right to vote when they drafted the Constitution and the Bill of Rights stabilized the political marginalization of the emancipated population. Subsequent amendments sustained this. The amendments only tell states what they cannot do when it comes to voting rights; they don't tell states what they have to do to ensure voting rights. This framework has nourished local and national voter suppression efforts.

As society was being reconstructed after the Civil War, the design of the renovated world was carefully considered by some key players. Striking a balance between enough, but not too much freedom and equality consumed discussions of the day. Southern leaders well understood that "voters chose the sheriffs and prosecutors who ignored the rights of Black citizens."[10] A careful line of demarcation between civil and political rights became the solution. This architectural design has not sufficiently been considered by change agents.

This blueprint is still in use. In 1850, Senator Stephen Douglas placated fellow Congressmen with the observation that free Blacks in Illinois were protected in the enjoyment of all their *civil rights* but were not upon an equality with whites. He continued, "they are not permitted to serve on juries, or in the militia, or to vote at elections; or to exercise any other *political rights*."[11] On another occasion, Representative John D. Stiles questioned the "right of negros to become voters, jurors, and in all respects equal with the white man"....[12] In 1866, a member of the United States Congress expressed his concern about courts mistakenly interpreting the words civil rights in legislation to mean "that the right of suffrage was included."[13]

Senator Augustus Merrimon posited: "To sit upon a jury is not a civil right...any more than to hold office is a civil right...the rights of life, liberty, and property...are civil rights." [14] The debates on the Civil Rights Act of 1866 capture this same concern about ensuring a distinction between political and civil rights.[15] Representative Russell Thayer reasoned:

> The words themselves are 'civil rights and immunities,' not political privileges; and nobody can successfully contend that a bill guaranteeing simply civil rights and immunities is a bill under which you could extend the right of suffrage, which is a political privilege and not a civil right.[16]

Representative Wilson expressed:

> Do they mean that in all things civil, social, political, all citizens, without distinction of race or color, shall be equal? By no means can they be so construed. Do they mean that all citizens shall vote in the several states? No; for suffrage is a political right which has been left under the control of the several states, subject to the action of Congress

only when it becomes necessary to enforce the guarantee of a republican form of government. Nor do they mean that all citizens shall sit on juries, or that their children shall attend the same schools. These are not civil rights....I understand civil rights to be simply absolute rights of individuals, such as...the right to personal liberty and the right to acquire and enjoy property. [17]

Representative Lawrence further asserted that the Civil Rights Act of 1866 "does not affect any political right, as that of suffrage, the right to sit on juries, hold office, etc." [18]

The Fourteenth Amendment was later adopted with the same aims under the surface. Representative John Bingham, co-author of the Fourteenth Amendment was clear in his position that "[t]he [proposed] amendment does not give...the power to Congress of regulating suffrage in the several states."[19] In his introduction of the Fourteenth Amendment in the Senate, Senator Jacob Howard reassured his fellow legislators that "the first section [which includes the Equal Protection Clause as well as the Privileges and Immunities and Due Process Clauses] of the proposed amendment does not give to either of these classes [Blacks or whites] the right of voting."[20] Years later, Senator Matthew Carper reiterated: "[A] broad distinction is made between the privileges which belong to every citizen...and those political rights as to which the Constitution recognizes the right of a state to discriminate between its citizens."[21]

A renewed understanding is also in order when it comes to the vote being viewed as a singular action. In official chambers, voting has never been approached singularly. In these protected spaces, voting has always been understood as being interconnected with office holding and jury service.[22] In 1869, Representative Wilson opposed a proposed version of the Fifteenth Amendment that would do nothing more than protect the vote. He declared it "imperfect" to "have the right to vote, but ...not have the right to sit upon a jury or the right to hold office...."[23] Further into that same debate appears the suggestion that granting Blacks the right to vote "will take care of the right to hold office."[24] The tedious effort to carefully craft laws that would grant civil rights and limit political rights was undertaken for less than complex reasons.

In his report on the condition of the South, Major General Carl Schurz warned that the grant of political rights to Blacks would turn the South on its axis:

> [T]he rights of a man of some political power are far less exposed to violation than those of one who is, in matters of public interest, completely subject to the will of others. A voter is a man of influence; small as that influence may be in the single individual, it becomes larger when that individual belongs to a numerous class of voters who are ready to make common cause with him for the protection of his rights.[25]

In 1875, ten years after Emancipation, Congress trumpeted: "[W]e have established the grand doctrine of universal freedom, universal civil equality–not political equality, but civil equality....," making its aims and intentions clear when it came to the question of how free it intended to make the emancipated people.[26] Emboldened by this, the state, given the way political rights are intertwined, endeavored to achieve simultaneous and overlapping efforts to suppress one in the interest of preventing another.[27] Louisiana officials weaponzized political rights, starting with the vote.

From the *Code Noir* of 1724 until 1864, the political right of suffrage was reserved for white males by operation of law.[28] Before the end of chattel slavery, Blacks were making demands for political inclusion.[29] They grasped that voting is the "essence of a democratic society"[30] and one of the "defining elements of citizenship."[31] In February 1864, two free men of color traveled from New Orleans to Washington, DC as the chosen "Delegates of the Free Colored Population of Louisiana." Former Union Army Captain E. Arnold Bertonneau and newspaper publisher Jean-Baptiste Roudanez arrived armed with a petition, including over 1,000 signatures, demanding free Black participation "in establishing a civil government in our beloved state of Louisiana."[32] They directed it to President Abraham Lincoln and Congress.

In January 1865, a Convention of Colored Men of Louisiana convened.[33] It was the first time in the history of the state that there would be an organized, state-wide effort to mobilize Blacks, politically. A demand for suffrage was made and subsequently communicated to President Lincoln, the Secretary of state, the Secretary of War and members of the state legislature.[34] Then President Lincoln did not need much convincing. Unbeknownst to them, Lincoln had already penned a confidential 1864 letter to Louisiana Governor Michael Hahn, expressing support for extending the franchise "to some of the colored people...as, for instance, the very intelligent, and...those who...fought gallantly in our ranks."[35]

President Lincoln also spoke these intentions in an April 11, 1865 address, which would become his last. The prospect of Black voting infuriated audience member John Wilkes Booth to a murderous degree. This attempt to grant political rights cost President Lincoln his life. Tragically, his assassination would not be an anomaly. Violence and repercussions in response to voting demands became as much a local tradition as Mardi Gras, fishing and hunting. After the Civil War, as "the economic power of the planter waned, his political power became more and more indispensable to the maintenance of his income and profits."[36] For too long, change agents have dodged the blunt force blows of this era.

Only a surface understanding of the efforts taken to silence the Black vote is needed to appreciate the matrimony its shares with the suppression of Black presence on juries. The Mechanics' Institute Massacre (MIM) is an effective teacher. The Constitution of 1864 did not give Blacks the right to vote.[37] The MIM followed an effort to both recall delegates who wrote the Constitution of 1864 and to reconvene the constitutional convention in an effort to rewrite the 1864 constitution to provide for voting rights for all Black men over the age of twenty-one and to protest a rewritten *Code Noir* that forced Blacks, including free men of color, into labor.

On July 27, 1866, a constitutional convention was held at the Mechanics Institute in New Orleans. A sampling of the resolutions before the body hint to the enormity of the moment:

> Resolved, That the 75,000 citizens of Louisiana qualified to vote, but disfranchised on account of color, 20,000 of whom risked their lives in her behalf in the war against the Rebellion may claim from her as a right that participation in the Government which citizenship confers.

* * *

> Resolved, That until the doctrine of the political equality of citizens irrespective of color is recognized in this state there will be no permanent peace.[38]

That day, intense debate on the issue of the Black vote occurred.[39] On July 30, 1866, over two hundred Blacks, many former Union soldiers, beating drums to announce their presence, gathered outside the assembly. Their demonstration was attacked by an angry white mob, many of them Confederates, that included police and firemen. Mass numbers of unarmed Black men were beaten and shot at what would later be remembered as one of the bloodiest massacres of the Reconstruction era.[40]

This sounded a siren to Congress who responded by setting up military districts so the federal government could force Reconstruction on the South. The MIM also led to swift passage of the Fifteenth Amendment (in 1870), which prevented states from depriving citizens of their right to vote. Confederacy supporters were removed from office and, because of federal presence, Black men cast votes for the first time in 1867.[41] If they were lucky, Blacks who voted were only terminated from employment, removed from housing on plantations where many Blacks worked as sharecroppers or beaten.[42]

Around 1868, planters were finally seeing a post-Civil War financial recovery period. A politically active Black population was bad for business.[43] Law became the weapon of choice once again. The state passed a new election law in early 1870 that created a Returning Board responsible for counting ballots cast within the state. If that Board was of the opinion that fraud, violence, intimidation, or corruption had occurred, it had the authority to invalidate votes from the returns. The new laws gave the governor authority over all sheriffs, constables, and police officers on election day.

It allowed the governor to appoint a state registrar of voters and a supervisor of registration for each parish and they controlled local elections. Time has blurred the count on Black lives loss over the desire to exercise the vote. The onslaught of Blacks attempting to exercise the vote had become ritualistic. There would be a Bossier Parish Massacre (1868),[44] the Opelousas Massacre (1868),[45] the St. Bernard Parish Massacre (1868),[46] the Donaldsonville Massacre (1870),[47] and the Coushatta Massacre (1873).[48]

The Colfax Massacre of 1873 would be the game changer. At the time of the Colfax Massacre, Blacks had attained a written form of political rights when the Fifteenth Amendment was adopted in 1870.[49] They cast votes in an emotionally charged 1872 gubernatorial election and in local elections.[50] Angry over the role Black voters played in shaping the outcome, a white mob, led by the White League determined to take control of Grant Parish, surrounded the courthouse (where many Blacks were inside) on Easter Sunday 1873.[51] An exchange of gunfire followed then the roof was ablaze, prompting the Black occupants to surrender. They exited the burning building peacefully. Peace was not reciprocated.

Some Blacks were shot and killed instantly. The others were lynched or tortured before being murdered. More Blacks were murdered indiscriminately about the town throughout the day. In the end, about three white men and nearly two hundred Black men perished that dreadful day. Prior to this massacre, in 1870, Congress had enacted legislation, that made it a felony for two or more people to conspire to deprive anyone of federal civil rights.[52] A federal remedy was thought to be the answer to the domestic terrorism that Black voters were met with. The ruling handed down in *United States v. Cruikshank*,[53] emasculated Congress's attempt to act as a legislative bodyguard to the newly emancipated and pronounced the terms of Black freedom and citizenship that had, before, been ambiguous.

In *United States v. Cruikshank,* close to one hundred people were indicted.[54] Seventeen were tried for sixteen violations of the 1870 law. Consistent with trends, there were no murder charges (as murder was a state offense and not a federal offense and state officials did not pursue state charges against the white transgressors). The "right and privilege to peaceably assemble together" was the most serious of the charges prosecuted by federal officials. The trial court found the defendants guilty. On appeal, they argued that Congress exceeded its authority in enacting the federal legislation used to obtain these convictions.

They furthered that the Fourteenth Amendment gave the federal government authority to act only against state government violations of civil rights, but not against one citizen's violation of another's civil rights. The highest court in the land agreed, ruling that local offenses should be resolved by local tribunals and with local laws. There is genuine debate over which is worse—the holding or the reasoning. As reasoning, the *Cruikshank* court explained:

> To constitute an offense...of which congress and the courts of the United States have a right to take cognizance under this amendment, there must be a design to injure a person, or deprive him of his equal right of enjoying the protection of the laws, by reason of his race, color, or previous condition of servitude. Otherwise it is a case exclusively within the jurisdiction of the state and its courts.[55]

This ruling rendered political rights sterile and justice unattainable to the newly emancipated people whose rights were just placed under the custodial watch of Southern state courts where the Democrats who committed these murders were hailed heroes, the KKK often had seats on the bench, Jim Crow juries ruled the jury box and Black criminality and deviance was a presumption. This case had further impacts. Congress failed to enact any major civil rights legislation in the period between 1875 and 1964. When Congress finally succeeded in doing so, the approach shifted from enforcement pursuant to the Reconstruction Amendments to the expanded powers of Congress under the Commerce Clause. The town of Colfax still hasn't recovered from this occurrence.[56]

By this juncture, Southern courts had become "instruments of vengeance"[57] that would soon close the coffin on the hopes of Blacks.[58] In particular, "Criminal courts were part of a continuation of a white-dominated socioracial hierarchy established during slavery."[59] In interpreting the Reconstruction Amendments narrowly, the courts dimmed the light on any hope the Reconstruction Amendments had created. Congress was less than a friend at this point too. In 1894, after the Democrats regained control of Congress and the White House, Congress repealed many of the Reconstruction era provisions the Supreme Court had left standing. Incidentally, Randall Lee Gibson was a member of the U.S. Congress at this time.

Violence continued.[60] And, as was the case with deprivation of civil rights, "experts" were used to conceal misdeeds. Dr. Stanford E. Chaille, a man with a pedigree like the other architects of Southern oppression, was a highly regarded medical doctor during the Reconstruction era who maintained the vital records used by the Register of Voters for many purposes, including the census. He was also a professor of medicine at Tulane Medical Center where he worked for over forty years until his retirement in 1908. Prior to this post, he served as surgeon in the Confederate Army during the Civil War. Dr. Chaille had a great affinity for public policy and statistics. He was regularly called upon to apply his statistical knowledge to politics. This led to his 1876 invitation as one of ten physicians selected from the entire U.S. to address Congress on the issue of voter intimidation.

His "data" laced testimony convinced Congress that allegations of race-based voter intimidation was overstated and nearly non-existent. His 1876 testimony followed countless lynchings and massacres to suppress the Black vote. The words of a white man proved more credible than the irrefutable facts documenting the loss of Black life. This pattern claimed a seat in the jury box. Dr. Chaille was not the only former Confederate still in battle mode, armed and ready to maim political rights.

In the late 1800s, E. D. White released some of his post-Civil War bullets as a sitting SCOTUS justice when he cast a vote against a Mississippi citizen whose liberty rested in the hands of an all-white grand jury that was selected from a limited list of registered voters as a result of a Mississippi law that subject voters to poll taxes, literacy tests and grandfather clauses.[61] The SCOTUS recognized that the law had the potential to disenfranchise Black voters and, therefore, impact the pool of potential jurors, but, with the help of E. D. White, refused to declare the scheme illegal or otherwise grant relief in this capital murder case.

During Reconstruction, Democrats claimed political control, electing a Democratic Governor and winning a majority of the legislative seats by 1878. But Blacks made up the majority of registered voters. The situation was so bad, Louisiana found itself the subject of an 1879 investigation by a United State Senate Committee tasked with looking into the election of 1878. "The committee found that, in Concordia and Tensas Parishes, an orchestrated move by former Confederate officers and Klansmen resulted in a violent purge of Black officeholders and Black voters."[62]

Additionally, testimony before the committee documented a state-wide pattern of Black voter intimidation, suppression or outright murder.[63] Miraculously, Blacks were not dissuaded. By 1882, the Secretary of state reported 85,451 registered white voters and 88,024 registered Black voters in Louisiana. "In 1888[,] there were 127,923 [Black] voters and 126,884 white voters on the registration rolls in Louisiana; the population of the state was about fifty per cent [Black]."[64]

By the late 1890s, the Democratic party had "resorted to bribery, intimidation, and vote-stealing" to win elections because of the number of Blacks in Louisiana and because of their active participation as voters.[65] The disfranchisement movement became the more reliable and permanent solution.[66] E.D. White was an active player in it. In 1903, over 5000 of Alabama's Black citizens, as a result of Alabama's 1901 constitution, were subject to a test that white citizens were not and, as a result, were disenfranchised. The disenfranchised Blacks sued to force Alabama officials to enroll them as eligible voters. E.D. White, Jr. joined the majority in denying them relief under a scheme set up by the all-white state legislature.[67] This Confederate general disabled people with law in a way that he could not do on the battlefield and perhaps more potently since this one shot killed the vote, jury service and future legal challenges.

Through the use of various suppression methods–violence, termination from employment, damage to personal property, or arrest–the Black vote all but vanished. In Louisiana, Black voter registration fell from 95.6 percent before the adoption in 1896 of a new registration law to 1.1 percent in 1904....By 1910, less than 0.5 percent of adult, Black males were registered. By 1918, thirty-seven of sixty-four parishes had no Blacks registered to vote. Blacks "constituted as much as 44 per cent of the electorate prior to this movement to restrict suffrage; by 1920 Negro voting had been reduced to less than 1 per cent."[68] Between 1921 and 1944, the percentage of Black voters never exceeded one percent.[69]

Incidentally, in many democracies, citizens are automatically registered to vote. The requirement that citizens register to vote is both atypical and costly.[70] Registration is embraced by Louisiana officials. Over the years, Louisiana has used a smorgasbord of voter suppression tactics. Felony disenfranchisement laws is one. Many of the most disabling felony disenfranchisement laws in the United States were enacted after the Civil War so the power lost by Confederates during Reconstruction could be regained.[71] Louisiana's post-Civil War actions are in sync with this. Before the Civil War, when Blacks were enslaved, Louisiana disenfranchised voters for committing felonies that related to election integrity. After slavery, Louisiana conveniently began disenfranchising persons with felony convictions.[72]

With Louisiana's 1974 constitution came a slight change that would disqualify persons under an order of imprisonment for a felony.[73] When Louisiana's justice-impacted citizens challenged the constitutionality of this voter suppression tactic in court, Secretary of State Tom Schedler tried to separate Louisiana's justice-impacted citizens from an important source of sustenance–seventeen Louisiana constitutional law and history professors. He shamelessly filed an opposition to their amicus curiae brief. The court followed with a ruling indicating that there was nothing unconstitutional about the state's legislative scheme.[74] Not long after, in 2019, the legislature slightly modified the law to qualify as voters justice-impacted people who had been out of custody for at least five years.[75] In addition to continuing the suppression of votes (because any probationer or parolee incarcerated within the last five years will still not be allowed to vote), the process is anxiety producing.

It requires the justice-impacted person to first obtain a voting rights certification form from their probation and parole officer. After, the justice-impacted person presents that letter to their parish's voter registration office along with a valid ID. Incidentally, many states that disenfranchise justice-impacted citizens also bar them from jury service, effectuating two forms of exclusion for the price of one.[76] Blacks challenged one tactic only to see the state respond with a new one. The ploys have ranged from poll taxes to grandfather clauses[77] to white primaries[78] to good character clauses[79] to political corruption and fraud to intelligence tests (making the vote contingent on intellectual fitness) to interpretation tests or understanding clauses (requiring prospective voters to explain or interpret challenging constitutional or legal provisions as a condition for registration)[80] to the use of police juries[81] to in person signing of a poll book in the local sheriff's office.[82]

In 1965, The Voting Rights Act (VRA) was passed. It "put the responsibility for adhering to the Constitution onto state and local governments."[83] The VRA "thrust the federal government into the role of supervising voting in large parts of the country to protect African Americans' right to vote, a duty it had not assumed since Reconstruction."[84] Louisiana resisted what it viewed as more federal meddling. And Louisiana was not alone in its resistance. The South continued to insist on the withholding of political rights. Louisiana's actions were part of a larger Southern trend, meaning what remained when non-unanimous juries were confronted was even more deeply entrenched than what may have initially appeared.

South Carolina immediately sued, arguing the VRA infringed upon the state's sovereignty. After this legal challenge failed, other Southern states persisted in legal challenges, all because they did not want Blacks to vote, hold office, serve on juries and become political equals. The VRA caused a dramatic increase in Black voter registration and participation. For example, "In Mississippi, Black registration went from less than 10% in 1964 to almost 60% in 1968."[85] The fight continued with refurbished weapons, such as criminalizing citizens for efforts to register voters, encourage voting or for voting.[86]

Breka Peoples knows a little something about this. For her efforts to encourage Blacks to cast votes during a 2020 election in DeSoto Parish, she ended up looking jail time in the face. Her confrontation with the law came after she says she noticed poll workers directing whites to cast their votes using the voting machines while, according to her, young Black voters were handed paper ballots. Peoples says her reports of improprieties were ignored. Peoples, like so many Black women before her, was determined to see Blacks participate in government. She successfully galvanized Black voters, got them to the polls and stood guard as they cast their votes.

Peoples knew what (not who) she was warring with so she anticipated repercussions. The history of massacres to silence the Black vote assured her there would be a consequence for her actions despite them being legal. Local officials didn't seem to understand what (not who) they had decided to war with. Peoples was not about to cower in fear. Peoples was the embodiment of legions of Black ancestors who started what she was there to finish that day. Election officials started increasing their public presence and they began instructing the public that, if they were standing within 600 feet of the polling entrance that they would be ticketed if not voting.

There were no boundary markers for them or the public to identify the prohibited zone. As a precaution, Peoples changed locations. She crossed the street and stood there that day. Peoples came back with more voters on another occasion. As they voted, she stood at the distant location, once again. Peoples continuously repeated that pattern. In the days following, a warrant was issued for Peoples.

It ordered her arrest for wearing a mask promoting a candidate, having a bullhorn in the crowd and remaining at a polling place after failing to comply with orders to leave. She faced six months imprisonment for each misdemeanor charge. Peoples was sentenced to a suspended sentence of six months in jail and one year of supervised probation. She was ordered to a pay $65 per month as a probation fee, a fine of $300, in addition to court costs.

Another strategy was voter suppression through legislation, which continues to date. In 1901, Alabama changed its law to render persons convicted of "any crime involving moral turpitude" unqualified to vote. This was done with bad intentions, but written as if it was legislation in the interest of the greater good. The plot was orchestrated through consultation with a local justice of the peace who reported to the state's suffrage committee, based on the cases he presided over, that "such crimes as vagrancy, living in adultery, and wife beating were thought to be more commonly committed by Blacks." [87] The plan worked. From 1901 until the practice was ended in 1985, a disproportionate number of Blacks were disenfranchised. There should be no solace in the belief that these are machinations of a day gone by.

The 2013 actions of North Carolina legislators show better. As soon as the SCOTUS ruled in the 2012 *Shelby County v. Holder* opinion that Confederate states no longer needed federal permission to make changes to voting laws, North Carolina implemented a new photo identification requirement and changed early voting, same-day registration, out-of-precinct voting and preregistration practices. These changes were not happenstance. They followed inspection of racial data establishing that each of these mechanisms led to an increase in Black voter participation.

The Court later determined the legislation to be a deliberate plot to disenfranchise Black voters, which "target[ed] African Americans with almost surgical precision."[88] We dare not commit the sin of noticing the speck in our neighbor's eye as we fail to see the log in ours. Louisiana has been on the receiving end of a similar rebuke. In response to allegations by Blacks that votes were being suppressed, the highest court in the land once remarked that "discriminatory practices [were]...deeply engrained in the laws, policies, and traditions of the state of Louisiana."[89] This fell on deaf ears.

Louisiana experimented with voter suppression through the use of at-large voting districts. Under at-large voting, all voters cast their ballots for all candidates in the jurisdiction (as opposed to dividing the parish into districts that vote for only one representative candidate). Because many voters vote along racial lines, this system prevents voters of color from electing their candidates of choice where they are not the majority in the jurisdiction. The votes of voters of color often are overshadowed by the votes of a majority of white voters who often do not support the candidates preferred by Black voters.

Terrebonne Parish is a case study in the harms of this. Judge Timothy Ellender was suspended for attending a 2003 Halloween party in blackface, an orange prison jumpsuit, an afro wig, handcuffs and shackles with his wife as a police officer and his brother-in-law dressed as Buckwheat.[90] Had he stayed home that day, he might have received the missed memo about how, to perform its high function in the best way, "justice must satisfy the appearance of justice."[91] Subsequently, he was elected to office in 2008 under Terrebonne Parish's at-large system, despite the opposition of Black voters, who comprise approximately 14% of the parish.[92]

Had those Black voters not been marginalized, the Louisiana Supreme Court might have been spared from having to suspend this same judge again in 2009, this time for acting in a condescending and demeaning manner towards a lady seeking protection from domestic abuse and for failing to take the matter seriously.[93] No Black candidate who has faced opposition has ever been elected in Terrebonne Parish (or any other at-large, parish-wide position), regardless of political party affiliation. It would take a lawsuit under the VRA to end at-large elections to the state high court in 1999.[94]

In 1866, Representative Thaddeus Stevens failed in his attempts to convince Congress that the South would use law to finish fighting the Civil War. He astutely predicted the various ways the South would suppress the Black vote if Congress did not, through legislative drafting, prevent such:

> [A] state may enact that a man shall not exercise the elective franchise except he can read and write, making that law apply equally to the whites and Blacks, and then may also enact that a Black man shall not

> learn to read and write, exclude him from their schools, and make it a penal offense to instruct or to teach him, and thus prevent his qualifying to exercise the elective franchise according to state law....They may provide that no man shall exercise the elective franchise who has been guilty of a crime; and then they may denounce these men as guilty of a crime for every little...petty offense. They may declare that no man shall exercise the right of voting who has not a regular business or occupation...and then they may declare that the Black man has no settled occupation and no business....[95]

Louisiana officials read his mind well.

The Second Political Right: Office Holding

Given what is presented about the intersection between voting, elections and jury service, one might anticipate parallel suppression efforts on the election front. Blacks in Louisiana confronted deliberate plots to prevent them from office holding as well. Eliminating Black candidates by any means necessary became the understood mantra. It's unfortunate that no one warned Oscar James Dunn about this. In 1867 Dunn, a formerly enslaved person, was elected to the New Orleans City Council and, in 1868, he was elected Louisiana's first Black Lieutenant Governor, making him the first Black Lieutenant Governor in the U.S. His mother's marriage to a free man of color led to his freedom. As a free person of color, he was able to attend school. His formal training merged with his natural propensities, making him a respected commodity. Dunn actually served as governor for thirty-nine days in 1871 when Gov. Henry Clay Warmoth was recovering from injuries.

Before the Civil War and Reconstruction, he became head of the Black Masonic Lodges for Louisiana. After the Civil War and Reconstruction, Dunn gained popularity in the Black community because he drafted labor contracts that allowed for them to finally be paid for the work they performed. Soon, his popularity led to his ascension in politics. As he rose through the ranks as a Radical Republican, he took his uncompromising demand for equal rights with him. W.E.B. Du Bois referred to Dunn as "an unselfish, incorruptible, leader."[96] His demands for civil rights, integrated schools and voting rights for Blacks made him an instant enemy of Democrats (many of whom were former Confederates). In 1872, there became talks of impeaching governor, Henry Warmoth.[97] If that materialized, Dunn would become the first Black governor in both the state and country. There was also speculation that the President of the United States, Ulysses S. Grant was considering Dunn for Vice President.

After eating at a public dinner in 1871, Dunn succumbed to illness. Within two days, he was dead, leaving many to believe he was poisoned.[98] While the circumstances surrounding his death may be uncertain, one thing that is certain is the unabiding refusal by many white Louisiana citizens to be governed or led by a Black official with the intestinal fortitude of Oscar Dunn or to allow an unapologetically Black official who was not an accommodationist share power.

Before you consider discarding this as a paranoid utterance, ask why the Governor signed an act authorizing a monument to Dunn, $10,000.00 in funds were allocated for it, yet it never got built.[99] Some would argue that the presence of it might inspire more Blacks to conceive of themselves as elected officials. If it's true that you won't be what can't see, the absence of it likely became as necessary as his death.

Efforts to deny Blacks the right to hold office have persisted and spanned from school boards[100] to parish counsels[101] to police chiefs[102] to aldermen[103] to legislators[104] to marshal[105] to judges[106] and all else. Louisiana did not elect its first Black member of the House of Representatives until Ernest Morial was elected in 1967. It wasn't until 1974 that Sidney Barthelemy was elected to one term in the Louisiana State Senate, becoming the first Black to serve in that body since Reconstruction.

Despite the first enslaved person arriving in Louisiana in 1719, Louisiana did not see its first Black judge until 1969, Judge Israel Augustine. As was the case with education in the state, Blacks led the fight to expand opportunities on the bench. In 1987, Ronald Chisom and several others filed a complaint on behalf of a class of all Black persons registered to vote in Orleans Parish, alleging the method of electing justices from their district—the first supreme court district, composed of Orleans, Jefferson, St. Bernard, and Plaquemines Parishes —impermissibly diluted minority voting strength.[107]

After more years of fighting, a favorable ruling came, saying that Section 2 of the Voting Rights Act applied to the election of state judges. The matter was subsequently settled through a legislative compromise that ultimately led to Justice Revius Artique claiming the first seat as a Black justice on the Louisiana Supreme Court in 1992.[108]

Before this, in the 1980's, Janice G. Clark (who later became a judge) and numerous others challenged the manner district lines were drawn, contending they disadvantaged Black candidates.[109] When the suit was filed in 1986, the state had only elected five Black judges. The data produced by the plaintiffs was damming:

> In the twentieth century, no Black citizen has been elected to statewide office in the state of Louisiana...to the United States Congress... no Black attorney has been elected to the Louisiana Supreme Court... all of the current officers of the Louisiana Bar Association are white... None of the present Black members of the Louisiana legislature was elected from a district which was majority white in population... None of the elected district attorneys in the state of Louisiana are Black...According to 1980 Census figures, the median family income in the state of Louisiana was $20,867 for whites and $10,459 for Blacks. [110]

In *Clark*, the federal court confessed that Louisiana had "a long history of de jure and de facto restrictions on the right of Black citizens to register, to vote, and otherwise participate in the democratic process."[111] In the end, the court agreed with the plaintiffs who alleged multimember districts violated the voting strength of Black judicial candidates and, therefore, violated Section 2 of the VRA. Additional litigation became necessary.[112] Judge Sylvia Cooks is a compelling example of the way exclusion of Blacks from participation in democracy harms—not just Black people—society in general. Her story is the projectile that moves us from just noticing exclusion to actually measuring the cost of it.

Cooks was a plaintiff in the *Clark* litigation. Had this fight not been had, she would likely have never become a sitting judge in Louisiana (in 1992). On January 1, 2021, Judge Cooks began her tenure as the first female Chief Judge of the Third Circuit Court of Appeal, state of Louisiana. She was a pioneer long before then though. Retired Judge Cooks was: the first Black student to be on Law Review at LSU Law School; the first Black law clerk at the Louisiana State Supreme Court; the first Black Assistant District Attorney in the Fifteenth Judicial District, Lafayette Parish, Louisiana; and, the first Black woman to be elected to the Louisiana Third Circuit Court of Appeal. Since it is true that political rights are entangled, it must also be true that the absence of capable jurors of color, like Cooks, is equally harmful in the jury box.

Based on census figures, 2022 commenced with Blacks significantly under-represented in federal and state government.[113] According to the 2010 U.S. Census, more than 30 percent of the state's population was Black, yet in 2022, only 16.6 percent of Louisiana's congressional districts were majority-minority and approximately 25 percent of the state legislative districts were majority-minority. As of January 2022, Blacks held "a majority in only one of Louisiana's six congressional districts and just one of its seven state Supreme Court districts. The remaining districts ha[d] white Republican strongholds."[114]

Minority voters were also under-represented in the state legislature and on the state school board.[115] While there are white Louisiana legislators representing Black-majority districts, there are no Black legislators representing majority-white districts. Irrefutably, there are structural inequities in the process. As redistricting maps were considered in response to these numbers, Louisiana's Republican lawmakers resisted maps tending to give minority voters more equal representation.[116]

The tension of the debate was eased when James Henry presented a map proposal that eliminated all of Louisiana's majority-Black districts.[117] A few of the Republican lawmakers said they were impressed by his proposal.[118] On March 9, 2022, Governor John Bel Edwards declined the invitation to join the historical ranks of officials who would exclude Blacks from the democratic process in general and office holding in particular. He vetoed the exclusionary maps and, more importantly, spoke of the harms to have come from him doing anything less:

> [I]t is clear that the primary rationale behind the creation and passage of the map was to protect incumbents and to preserve the party split in the current congressional delegation. In so doing, the Legislature disregarded the shifting demographics of the state, which unquestionably call for the addition of a second majority minority district....It is my firm belief that this map violates Section 2 of the Voting Rights Act of 1965 and further is not in line with the principle of fundamental fairness that should have driven this process....[119]

In a rare move, both chambers of the Louisiana legislature voted to override the Governor's veto of the congressional maps.[120] Rep. John Stefanski, the Crowley Republican who headed the House committee in charge of redistricting, pointed to the legislature's constitutional responsibilities on redistricting. "The Voting Rights Act is federal law, not Louisiana Constitution," he said. Yet another court battle ensued. *In Robinson v. Landry*, a district court judge found that the state's 2022 map, which included only one majority-Black district, likely violated Section 2 of the VRA. In January 2024, the Louisiana Legislature enacted SB 8, which includes a second majority-Black district.

Shortly after SB8 became law, non-Blacks filed *Callais v. Landry*, challenging the newly enacted map as an unconstitutional racial gerrymander. These plaintiffs claimed that "race was the sole reason" for the passage of the map. The Black *Robinson* litigants quickly intervened in *Callais* to defend the rights of Black voters to have a fair and representative map in the 2024 election. By summer of 2024, the age-old fight was ongoing with each contender bobbing and weaving until the referee pronounces an end to the match.

That same summer, other fights were being planned. During a June 2024 press conference, Attorney William Most and Black members of the East Baton Rouge Parish Metro Council alleged that the new district map for the Baton Rouge Metropolitan Council, effective January 1, 2025, dilutes Black voting strength in violation of the VRA and the U.S.

Constitution. Most explained, "the new map does so by 'packing' large numbers of Black voters into a few majority-Black council districts. The new map packs more than 68.5% of the Parish's Black registered voters into 42% of the Parish's Metro Council districts."

The group also charged that white residents have been declining in numbers in Baton Rouge and no longer are the majority group. Yet, according to them, the new map increases white control of the Metro Council by creating an additional majority-white council district. These local tactics are part of a larger effort to protect white supremacy. According to the Brennan Center for Justice, in 2021, at least nineteen states passed thirty-four laws restricting access to voting. "More than 440 bills with provisions that restrict voting access were introduced in 49 states in the 2021 legislative sessions."[121] "Many of these laws impose limits on mail-in voting, stricter voter ID regulations or more barriers to people with disabilities."[122]

"Some of these laws include provisions that could allow interference in election administration where officials can be threatened with criminal penalties for facilitating voter access."[123] True to form, in 2024, Louisiana's legislature passed a new law that will require proof of citizenship in order to register to vote. In a 2024 report, National Public Radio looked into the difficulty a law like this could pose. Its survey found that about "one in ten adult citizens do not have or could not quickly find" proof of citizenship. Their survey also showed "disparities by race, ethnicity and political affiliation" insofar as who these laws present a challenge to.

<u>The Final Political Right: Jury Service</u>

With the breadth and depth of the state (and nation's) fight to deprive Blacks of the vote and the right to hold office, one can begin to appreciate what was at stake when efforts to end non-unanimous juries took form.[124] It involved more than a simple change in law. It required a confrontation with an unseen assailant having an unrelenting will to fasten Blacks to a position of political impotence. To appreciate the jury as a political right, one must first accurately understand the jury itself. This chapter embarks upon that educational journey. Following that discussion, this chapter, in an effort to center non-unanimous juries in their rightful place in the legal landscape, gives special attention to the unique experience of Blacks wishing to serve on a jury and Blacks wishing to be judged fairly by them.

Experiencing the Sixth Amendment as an Ideal

One underestimates a jury by viewing it as a simple gathering of people who decide the outcome of a case. Rather, a jury is a term of art–an institution, which is both multifaceted and sacred. Juries have utility beyond the aims of a trial, making them as vital to the public as they are to the accused. Juries are a significant and often overlooked part of a democracy. Sharing "in the administration of justice is a phase of civic responsibility."[125] They, according to anti-federalist thought, are the means by which citizens engage in self-government. To "the typical American citizen, participation in government is represented by voting and jury service."[126] Juries serve as "a tangible implementation of the principle that the law comes from the people."[127] This is such a cherished and universal sentiment that distant jurisdictions–such as Japan, Russia, Taiwan, South Korea, Spain and Kazakhstan–have transitioned from a no jury system to a jury system.

The "function of the jury can be a solemn one."[128] "It is the jury, not the judge, who must pronounce a man 'guilty' or 'not guilty'—an awesome responsibility."[129] When one sits on a jury, they are no longer amongst the ranks of the ordinary. Momentarily, they claim judicial powers. They are endowed with both power and control over the lives of others. They, for these moments, are also the functional equivalent of political officeholders. They give citizens the last say on the law and/or on what's tolerable in their communities. "No other institution of government rivals the jury in placing power so directly in the hands of citizens."[130] Juries are also "instruments of public justice."[131] In the eyes of the community, criminal verdicts can legitimize actions of state actors that are adverse or penal in nature. These juries serve to ensure public confidence in judicial outcomes.

The philosopher Tocqueville saw an added value to jury participation.

He saw the jury as an instrument through which the important goals of inclusion and belonging could be achieved:

> [T]he man who is judge in criminal trial is the real master of society. Now, a jury puts the people themselves or at least one class of citizen on the judge's bench. Therefore the jury as an institution really puts control of society into the hands of the people or of that class.[132]

Tocqueville was not speaking an alien voice. Mr. Cox, a Black juror who received a jury duty summons in the 1950's offered a shared perspective about the way he felt when he received his summons. Cox said, "I got a sense of really belonging to the American community...It was a very proud moment when I opened my letter and found that I had been... selected to serve on a federal jury."[133] Participation, to a citizen, is a badge of inclusion in the democracy. Exclusion of citizens casts a spell of unbelonging upon them.

Some of the Anti-Federalist saw the jury box as a site of civic education. Others espoused the belief that a more informed voting population results from scholastic sessions in the jury box. Others build on this thinking and assert that juries are sites of edification to citizens. Edward Livingston, the American jurist and statesman who influenced penal policy in the country, described the jury as "a school...where the dictates of the laws, and the consequences of disobedience to them, are practically taught."[134] He viewed the jury as a forum for educating citizens and making them better. Henry D. Gilpin, a respected lawyer and public servant shared his similar view:

> The jury is a school where the people come to learn their rights, where they come into contact with the most learned and enlightened of the upper classes, where the laws are taught in a practical way and one within the scope of their intelligence, by the most intelligent minds.[135]

The founders saw juries as bodies that made liberty something more than a platitude. John Adams described representative government and trial by jury as "the heart and lungs of liberty." Thomas Jefferson considered a trial by jury "the only anchor yet imagined by man, by which a government can be held to the principles of its constitution." The early Federalists, led by James Madison and Alexander Hamilton, saw trial by jury as "essential to secure the liberty of the people." Their rivals, the Anti-Federalists, had a completely different view of the role of government, yet they agreed on the matter of juries. According to leading Anti-Federalist Patrick Henry, "Trial by jury is the best appendage of freedom."

Southern juries have always been viewed as sites of power and prestige and access has always been guarded. Juries have never been entirely inclusive. Pursuant to Colonial practices, some whites were marginalized when exclusion laws denied them a seat in the jury box due to religious or property qualifications. Before then, under the laws of England, to be qualified for jury service, one needed to be "sensible and upright and among those in the middle rank."[136] When it comes to juries, whether it be for the accused or the juror, Blacks have had an unparalleled experience. An evaluation of Louisiana's jury practices within the contours of this unique political rights panorama is essential if transformation is to be realized.[137]

Experiencing the Sixth Amendment While Black in Louisiana

According to the Sixth Amendment, ratified in 1791, persons accused of crimes shall enjoy the right to a speedy and public trial by an impartial jury. The right to jury trial took form in Louisiana in 1804.[138] By that time, the Sixth Amendment had been in existence for thirteen years. For jurors and accused people of color, the jury has served as the surety to maintain and rationalize the white privilege and power detailed so far. The jury has been the lock that secured the other two political rights.[139] Keeping Blacks out of the jury box ensured the balance of power would never shift or be shared. Excluding Blacks from Southern juries accomplished a few things. First, it "was based...on the expectation that an all-white jury [would] return a verdict that accords with racial standards and views held by the white community."[140] Additionally, the denial of impartial courtroom justice was a cornerstone that allowed slavery to be sustained.

During chattel slavery, Blacks who were dealt with through the judicial system (and not via plantation justice), were typically brought before special courts. The "process" usually involved "three white persons–a single justice of the peace and two freeholders–who were frequently also slaveowners."[141] "There were no constitutional protections...."[142] "Confessions could be coerced by torture."[143] And, as is often the case today, the process of appealing a criminal conviction was spurious because the Black Codes prevented reversals based on "errors of form."[144] Further, violent "acts by whites against Blacks were rarely defined as criminal and then only as property crimes committed against the slave's white owner."[145] "Not only did the legal structure of slavery fail to protect Blacks against the violent acts of whites, but it denied African-Americans the right to seek legal redress, or to testify as a witness against whites."[146]

Another motivation for excluding Blacks from juries was the notion that Blacks were unfit and inept to serve as an "arbiter of the life, liberty, and property of the white man."[147] Through the natural progression of things, this dynamic found its way into future jury inclusion and suppression plots. In fact, during the Thirteenth Amendment debates, Senator Harlan identified the denial of Blacks "of a status in court" as a badge and incident of chattel slavery. Senator Harlan argued that the institution of slavery had "robbed [Blacks] of all their rights and then robbed [them] of their capacity to complain of wrong."[148]

Jury suppression and exclusion tactics have been imaginative and enduring. They impact the process at the point where citizens are called as potential jurors who might serve in a jurisdiction and at the point where prospective jurors are actually selected to serve on a particular case. Racially discriminatory procedures in either instance results in an unrepresentative jury, which violates the rights of the accused and of the prospective juror.[149] Louisiana officials currently assault the Sixth Amendment in both respects.

Not long ago, Louisiana officials weren't kind enough to disregard the Sixth Amendment in only these two ways. There was a third–no jury at all. In certain cases, the absence of a jury continued into the civil rights era in Louisiana and, without the sacrifices of eighteen-year-old Gary

Duncan and attorney Richard Sobol, would likely have lasted longer. In 1967, "Plaquemines Parish yielded grudgingly as its schools were desegregated...."[150] An unsuspecting Gary Duncan innocently found himself caught in the tensions of forced school integration when he happened upon Black and white school children engaged in a verbal exchange.[151] This chance encounter placed him in the unrelenting grips of Plaquemines Parish leader Leander Perez, Sr. a known segregationist and "one of the most powerful political bosses in American history, ruling Plaquemines Parish with absolute control for five decades, from the 1920s through the 1960s."[152]

Perez was known by some as "the third house of the Louisiana legislature."[153] During his fifty year reign, Perez served as a district judge, district attorney, and president of the Plaquemines Parish Commission Council. There were two reoccurring themes in his life: race and power. Duncan successfully defeated the initial charge of cruelty to a juvenile, only to be charged with simple battery later. The simple battery charge, a misdemeanor, was punishable by a maximum of two years imprisonment and $300 fine. Reminiscent of days gone by, under Louisiana law at that time, he was not entitled to a jury trial so his fate would be decided by a Southern judge.

At trial, white witnesses testified that Duncan slapped Herman Landry, one of the white boys, on the elbow after threatening him. The Black witnesses testified contrarily, describing a mere touch (elsewhere described as "a gesture of equal parts paternal admonition and conciliation").[154] The trial court adopted the version of the facts presented by the white witnesses and sentenced Duncan to serve sixty days in parish prison and to pay fine of $150. After Louisiana courts refused to grant relief, Duncan found himself before the SCOTUS. At issue at the SCOTUS was whether the Sixth Amendment, made applicable to the states by way of the Fourteenth Amendment, allowed for the loss of liberty without the protection of a jury.

Disgracefully, Louisiana officials insisted that it did.[155] Fortunately for Duncan and all other accused people, the SCOTUS disagreed with Louisiana officials. The SCOTUS ruled that a trial by jury in criminal cases is fundamental to the American scheme of justice. And they concluded that the Fourteenth Amendment guarantees a right of jury trial in all criminal cases. Because of this, they found that Louisiana violated Duncan's constitutional rights when they refused his demand for a jury trial.[156]

Though big, a pronouncement by the SCOTUS that assured the presence of a jury in criminal cases would do little good in the hands of Southern officials hellbent on allowing Blacks only one spot in a courtroom, that being a chair at the defense table reserved for the accused. Long before Gary Duncan's fight, Louisiana officials had been chiseling away at other aspects of the Sixth Amendment, such as eliminating Black presence in the jury box despite laws outlawing such as far back as 1866.[157] If it could be ascertained, Louisiana could hold the patent on the exclusion of Black jurors. This has been ongoing since the days of Reconstruction and has continued, without interruption, until the present.

The means and methods for doing so have varied, but the effort has been consistent. Sometimes, jury suppression was accomplished through the use of jury commissioners who had endless discretion to decide who was qualified for jury service. White jury commissioners exclusively or disproportionately qualified only or mostly white men for jury service. One Evangeline Parish jury commissioner unilaterally decided who should be entered into the pool of potential jurors based on "the way the person talk[ed]".[158] This same individual excluded ministers, attorneys and persons over seventy from the pool of possible jurors, despite the objective being to achieve a jury that reflects the community.[159]

Something similar happened to residents of a Black housing project in Orleans Parish. The jury commission discontinued service of subpoenas to the 2695 residents of the Desire Housing Project who were of age to serve.[160] During the appeals process, state officials did not deny the illegality of their actions; they requested that their illegal actions be excused. Hugh Pierre, a Black man accused of killing a white man, fell victim to this practice.[161] Pierre sought review in Louisiana courts, claiming there was a deliberate plot to exclude Black jurors from serving at trial or on grand juries in St. John the Baptist Parish.

Pierre's evidence in support of his claim that his equal protection rights were violated included proof that: from 1896 to 1936 no Black person had served on grand or petit juries in the Parish; and, there were many Blacks qualified to serve as grand or petit jurors. The state chose silence in the face of this evidence. Louisiana courts supported the state in depriving Pierre of his constitutional rights. It took the SCOTUS to conclude that Pierre made a strong prima facie showing that Blacks had been systematically excluded—because of race—from the grand jury and the venire from which it was selected and deemed this to be a denial of his equal protection rights.

Henry Montgomery's case brings the consequences of jury suppression to life. Montgomery was tried during the segregation era. At his 1963 trial, his lawyers argued that Blacks were excluded and underrepresented on his jury because, at the time, reputation and acquaintanceship was the criteria jury commissioners used for selecting potential jurors. His attorneys brought to the court's attention that "the vicissitudes of a segregated society with its social, political and economic ostracism and pressures effectively prohibit qualified Negroes from entrance into community circles wherein acquaintanceship and reputation for honesty, character and integrity could be established."[162] The court found this inconsequential.

The all-white jury convicted him. The 17-year-old mentally-challenged boy was "entombed"[163] until he was released in 2021 after serving approximately fifty-eight years in custody.[164] In 2012, the SCOTUS decided that the imposition of mandatory life without parole sentences for those convicted of crimes that occurred under the age of eighteen was unconstitutional, but the court did not state if the decision should apply retroactively.[165] Louisiana refused to give retroactive effect to that 2012 ruling.[166] A suit was brought on Montgomery's behalf.[167] In 2016, the SCOTUS ruled in his favor (stating that the decision applied to people already convicted and serving sentences).[168]

Montgomery's case was instrumental in extending the possibility of freedom to hundreds of people sentenced to life in prison without the opportunity for parole when they were juveniles. Louisiana prosecutors were then tasked with revisiting sentences for all "juvenile lifers," which meant considering if the person in custody was the rare juvenile offender whose crime reflected irreparable corruption or if the crime reflected unfortunate yet transient immaturity. As a result of that ruling, Montgomery was resentenced to life with parole in 2017. The judge who resentenced him referred to him as a model prisoner who seemed to be rehabilitated. In 2019, he was denied parole for the second time.

The opposition claimed he needed further programming.[169] As this saga unfolded, juvenile lifers across the nation were being released under Montgomery's ruling as he remained in custody. Soon, those releases began in Louisiana, but Montgomery was not the first or even near the front of the line. In 2016, Andrew Hundley, a white man, was Louisiana's first juvenile lifer to be released. The now college-educated, executive director of Parole Project eloquently spoke in support of Montgomery's release at the November 2021 parole hearing.

Hundley told the Board that, at least ninety of Louisiana's justice-impacted people had benefitted from the ruling that bore Henry's name as Henry watched helplessly. Hundley continued to the Board, "Henry is no less worthy of this opportunity than any of us....57 years and nine months have passed...it is time for Henry to come home." Montgomery was released at the age of seventy-five. Beyond demonstrating the practical consequences of these abstract jury suppression efforts, the cases of Pierre and Montgomery highlight an important ancillary issue—that being who bears the burden of remedying systemic failures or willful misconduct on the part of official actors.

Despite the duties of their respective offices, official actors and bodies rarely rise to the occasion. Instead, the very individuals who are harmed or their sympathizers are left to correct these injustices if they wish to avoid extended losses of liberty or a more prolonged period of state-inflicted trauma.[170] This happened with non-unanimous juries and is a reoccurring theme in the state.

Angela A. Allen-Bell & Henry Montgomery

a few days after his 2021 release.

Another jury suppression ploy was achieved through a matrimony with voter suppression. The union between voting and jury service is hidden in plain sight. By its most basic terms, a jury is a voting body (in that its role is to cast a vote). Additionally, voting is the paramount right upon which all other rights rest for protection, preservation and safety. Other rights, such as the right to serve on a jury or the right to be judged by a jury of one's peers, "are illusory if the right to vote is undermined."[171]

"Across the South, the exclusion of Black jurors from the jury box, in tandem with the exclusion of Black voters from the ballot box, served as a key lever for the reassertion of white supremacy."[172] This often-overlooked synergy was both seen and understood by the Reconstruction Congress, possibly explaining why voting and jury service was not included in the rights protected by the Fourteenth Amendment. To them, voting and jury service were covered by the Fifteenth Amendment as they saw the vote as a pathway to the jury and to office holding.

There were a few ways to accomplish jury suppression vis-a-via voter suppression. Sometimes jury commissioners selected potential jurors who had the qualifications of registered voters. During the era of jury commissioners, registered voters had to have a level of understanding about government functions. An additional one involves the exclusive use of voter registration records to compile the list of potential jurors to be called out for service. In 1997, Louisiana Code of Criminal Procedure article 408.1 was amended to expand the sources from which the master list for the grand jury and petit jury members are to be drawn, representing a more inclusive cross-section of the community, rather than only including registered voters.

The amendment indicated that the list shall be derived from voter registration lists, lists of actual voters, motor vehicle license and registration records, lists of individual utility customers, and other sources approved by a majority of the district judges of the particular judicial district.[173] Notwithstanding this, the practice of relying exclusively on voter registration records is championed and defended in many state and federal courts[174] and put to widespread use throughout the state.[175] These jurisdictions simply disregarded the data establishing that the use of supplemental source lists are preferred over exclusive reliance on voter registration records (as a means to combat underrepresentation).[176]

Even more troubling, they disregard the SCOTUS who has made it clear that jury wheels must not systematically exclude distinctive groups in the community and thereby fail to be reasonably representative of a cross-section of the community. Incidentally, it was the use of voter registration records that aided Louisiana officials in shaping its non-unanimous jury system. Those records helped them predict the number of jurors that would likely be Black (back in 1898, that was three so the law required nine of twelve jurors to convict). [177] Practices like these prompted the passage of The Jury Selection and Service Act (JSSA) in 1968, which states, in no uncertain terms, that it is the policy of this country that "all litigants in Federal courts are entitled to trial by jury shall have the right to...juries selected at random from a fair cross section of the community....and that all citizens shall have the opportunity to be considered for service on...juries in the district courts of the United States...."[178]

Congress sought to achieve its goals by specifying that "the names of prospective jurors shall be selected from the voter registration lists . . . [or] some other source . . . of names in addition to voter lists where necessary to foster the policy and protect the rights secured" by the JSSA. Louisiana officials displayed their usual situational commitment to law. There is respect for it only when others break it. A mere two years after passage of the JSSA, there would be accusations of Blacks being underrepresented on federal juries in Louisiana because the court elected to select its pool of potential jurors exclusively from voter registration records. With express permission from congress written into the JSSA, a federal court for the Eastern District of Louisiana refused to expand its source lists, prompting the late attorney Richard Sobol's legal challenge on behalf of Black food stamp recipients who were targeted for prosecution.

That litigation confirmed that the use of voter registration lists caused an underrepresentation of Black persons in the jury pool for the Eastern District of Louisiana federal court.[179] In a place with a commitment to making sure justice is seen and not just expressed, this revelation would have inspired a reexamination of practices. It didn't. Attorney Richard Bourke and the Louisiana Capital Assistance Center (LCAC) produced data establishing an underrepresentation of Blacks in the United States District Court for the Eastern District of Louisiana again in 2021.[180] Worse, the 2021 litigation revealed that the court's jury plan relied exclusively on voter registration records to create the master wheel.[181]

The clerk who defended the exclusive use of voter registration records retained an expert who, in my view, made a compelling case against their use. He testified that "the district's jury-selection process...gives a fair and equal opportunity for everyone *on the voter registration list*....".[182] It was downhill from this point. When the trial judge denied LCAC's fair cross-section challenge, he suggested that the problem was not the clerk's method of calling jurors, but the Black people who lacked sufficient concern for government to register to vote or to actually vote.[183]

When the LCAC attorneys asked the court to make an effort to increase jury diversity by issuing a summons to those who do not respond to the notices, the court forgot that juries were for the protection of the accused. The court put its own interest first. It denied the request after first offering this rebuke: "Defendants fail to account for the daunting financial and public-relations costs that would accompany their proposed solution of serving a summons to conscript into jury service each prospective juror."[184]

Are Black jurors missing in action or are they missing by practice? Often, intangibles, such as financial insecurity and increased mobility, contribute to the exclusion of Black jurors. Another consideration is the way the labor market affects residential mobility. Fewer Blacks are homeowners with permanent addresses. Those who move about due to migrant work, evictions or the impact of poverty miss jury summonses. Courts often interpret these undelivered summonses as evidence of disinterest. They designate these potential jurors as undeliverable, giving no thought to the fact that people of color are statistically more transient than whites.

When a Black person defies the odds and makes it into a jury pool, many do not serve because they depend on their hourly employment wage or commissions and cannot forgo it to serve on a jury. At one time, state jurors received no compensation. Now, in criminal cases, the state rate of $25.00 daily for those selected (plus mileage at a rate of 16 cents per mile) is often less than wages. The rate is different from state-to-state, with some states paying as little as $5.00 daily and others as much as $50.00 daily to those selected.[185] Federal jurors earn $50.00 daily.[186] A hardship is grounds for one to be excused from jury service. Blacks seek a disproportionately high rate of hardships over income insecurity issues.

They also distrust the legal system and, for this reason, are reluctant or resistant to be involved with any aspect of it. Many Louisiana officials do not deem these things challenges; they deem them faults. There is proof that Louisiana can and should do more to combat the underrepresentation of jurors of color. One can be found in Elizabeth Hilton, a twenty-seven-year veteran public defender in California. Attorney Hilton prepared a robust defense of her houseless Black client who stood accused of killing a houseless white man. The prospect of a lengthy and complicated trial didn't deter her. Her commitment to providing quality defense services to indigent persons rendered this inconvenience insignificant to her.

She learned the hard way that not everyone saw it the same way. Jurors who had income insecurities viewed jury service as a hardship. That tended to disproportionately be jurors of color, leaving primarily white, financially secure jurors to serve. Her client's self-defense claims fell on deaf ears and he was convicted. "Because of this experience, I realized we needed to give jurors with income challenges more money in order to prevent them from leaving long trials due to economic hardship," says Deputy Public Defender Hilton. Hilton planted her idea upon fertile soil. San Francisco Public Defender Mano Raju had been outspoken about the need for jury diversity.

Hilton's vision was conceived in the form of the "Be the Jury" pilot that was implemented in San Francisco in March 2022. The pilot compensates low to moderate income San Franciscans who would otherwise face financial hardship from serving on a jury.[187] In a San Francisco survey by the Administrative Office of the Courts of California prior to the pilot, 35% of jurors reported that jury service imposed a financial hardship. While California law requires employers to provide time off for employees who are summoned to jury duty, employers are not required to compensate employees who serve on a jury.

"Be the Jury" was implemented through legislation that was signed by California Governor Newsome in 2021 and funded through philanthropic dollars raised by the Financial Justice Project of the state's Treasury Office and accomplished through a collaboration between public defenders Hilton, Anisa Sirur, Carolyn Gooslyn, Danica Rodarmel, Niki Solis, the district attorney, the executive and legislative branches and justice partners. "Be the Jury" increased the rate awarded to the juror from $15.00 to $100.00 a day.[188] The program, by any measure, has been a success, with 86% of those enrolled reporting that they would not have been able to serve on a jury without the program. And it achieved the diversity it set out to accomplish.

On average, juries were composed of: 36% whites, 38% Asian, 7% Blacks, 2% Hawaiian or Pacific Islander, 14% Hispanic and 3% mixed race. A second example is found in Pennsylvania. Chief Judge Juan R. Sánchez, of the Eastern District of Pennsylvania and a jury diversity subcommittee, initiated an effort to encourage more people from different communities across the district to respond to jury summonses. To increase the number of names in its juror pool, the court enlarged the size of its master jury wheel to include driver's license lists and voter registration rolls. To improve response rates of qualification questionnaires, the court improved the accuracy of its mailing list by conducting more frequent address checks through the U.S. Postal Service's system of updated addresses.

"To complement these structural changes, the court also created a community outreach and education program, which involves individuals from community and nonprofit organizations, religious institutions, law firms, and the media."[189] In the Eastern District of Michigan, Chief Judge Denise Page Hood and Judge Victoria A. Roberts led the court's grassroot efforts after a recession caused an increase in unemployment, which directly affected the jury summons response rate.[190] They became community educators and recruiters and they also sought insights from the public and they acted on those insights.

"The effort in the Eastern District of Michigan led to greater minority representation."[191] "And the court's non-response and undeliverable rates for jury summonses dropped by about 10% and 3%, respectively, in the Detroit jury division."[192] Recently, the Washington State Jury Commission conducted an inquiry into the state jury system. One of commission's recommendations involved the need to increase jury pool diversity. The proposal suggested: extensive outreach to targeted communities, which would include educational campaigns targeting high school students, new citizens and minority communities; public service campaigns to promote jury service on radio, television, print media, public transit and other outlets; more extensive advertisement of juror appreciation week; and, outreach to business and labor groups.[193]

New legislation followed in 2023. Starting January 1, 2024, persons on the lists of registered voters and driver's license and identicard holders in Washington State can share their email address for the purposes of electronically receiving jury summons and other communication related to jury service. Washington State has also established a workgroup to make recommendations for the creation of a childcare assistance program for individuals reporting for jury service with the intent to eliminate the absence of childcare as a barrier to performing jury service. Others have advocated for the use of racial quotas in the jury box. They ensure proportional representation of various racial groups by mandating the inclusion of individuals from underrepresented groups.

These efforts to achieve an impartial, inclusive and diverse jury are necessary because of the magnitude of the task that a jury performs. When it performs as envisioned, a jury serves as a "guard against the exercise of arbitrary power [by making] available the commonsense judgment of the community as a hedge against the overzealous or mistaken prosecutor....or the biased response of a judge."[194] "This prophylactic vehicle is not provided if the jury pool is made up of only special segments of the populace or if large, distinctive groups are excluded from the pool."[195] "This purpose is attained by the participation of the community in determinations of guilt and by the application of the common sense of laymen who, as jurors, consider the case."[196]

Many accused persons of color in Louisiana have been left vulnerable in Louisiana courtrooms without the intended safeguards against abuses of power. In light of this, jurors of color must understand that, to the accused, absence from jury service is the same as suppression. In both instances, the unique experiences of jurors of color are not interjected into deliberations. This compromises the process and renders outcomes unreliable. As explained by law professor Ranetta Lawson Mack, its not that the jury trial process contributes to mass incarceration; it's the *avoidance* of the jury trial process that does.[197]

During a trial, exclusion harms the accused and infinitely more. Justice Thurgood Marshall explained that exclusion leaves one unable to "perceive himself to be a full participant...."[198] Jurors of color should also recognize that avoidance and exclusion are not the same. Exclusion adorns an excluded person with "a brand...an assertion of their inferiority, and a stimulant to that race prejudice which is an impediment to securing to individuals of the race that equal justice which the law aims to secure to all others...."[199] "Since the end of Reconstruction, the criminal jury box has both reflected and reproduced racial hierarchies in the United States."[200]

Peremptory[201] or for cause[202] strikes are another means used by some Louisiana lawyers to exclude Blacks from juries. By 1965, the matter of Black juror exclusion was before the SCOTUS yet again after an all-white, Alabama jury found Robert Swain guilty of raping a white woman. Peremptory strikes were used to remove Black jurors. The SCOTUS found it persuasive that no Black person, within the memory of persons living at the time, had ever served on any petit jury in any civil or criminal case tried in Talladega County, Alabama.

As a solution, the court set a standard that could be used to prove intentional discrimination. Some Louisiana officials took full advantage of the near-impossible standard set in *Swain v. Alabama*.[203] There were accusations of entire parishes refusing to seat Black jurors in cases where the victim was white and the accused was Black[204] or findings of prosecutors "impermissibly using challenges."[205] There have even been open admissions by lawyers of race impermissibly being used as the sole factor for deciding if a potential juror should be seated on a jury:

> I have found through experience, some twenty-three years in the district attorney's office, that Blacks, where you have a Black defendant, will generally vote not guilty, in spite of the strength of the state's case... particularly young Blacks, they are very resentful of the white establishment.[206]

The response of the Louisiana judge chosen to review the matter is more jolting:

> The trial counsel involved in this proceeding is a sincere, conscientious and professional prosecutor and in this writer's opinion one of the most capable criminal trial tacticians in this state. What he has done wrong in this case is to choose jurors, in his judgment, who will give the State a fair trial...If anything is wrong, it is the system, not the prosecutor.[207]

By 1986, the SCOTUS saw the need for intervention yet again. In *Batson v. Kentucky*, they decided that a prosecutor could not use peremptory strikes[208] to exclude a potential juror solely because of race and they established a new standard of proof.[209] The court decided, where the circumstances at trial support a mere inference of discrimination in the use of peremptory strikes, the prosecutor must explain why he or she removed Black potential jurors.[210] Many Louisiana prosecutors embraced the challenge.[211]

Louisiana prosecutors have provided an assortment of "race-neutral" reasons for striking Black jurors, such as: being a single, Black male with no children;[212] enjoying rap music;[213] being a "smart ass";[214] being Baptist;[215] being the only juror wearing shorts on the first day of voir dire;[216] being employed at a casino;[217] looking like a drug dealer; [218] being "too stupid to live much less be on a jury"; [219] looking nervous;[220] divulging that he had a school obligation to complete a requisite number of student teaching hours in order to secure a college degree;[221] or, wearing gold jewelry and a t-shirt.[222]

A recent study of peremptory strikes in over 1,000 Louisiana jury trials identified massive racial disparities in how Louisiana prosecutors wield peremptory strikes.[223] These race-neutral reasons are often subtle. In *State v. Melvin Cartez Maxie*, a case that became a game changer in the world of non-unanimous juries, it took skill to recognize the way race surfaced during jury selection, courage to confront it and a commitment to equity to address it.[224] LCAC attorney Meghan Shapiro and co-counsel Casey Secor had this trinity and they released it super-sized portions during this trial.

Prosecutor Don M. Burkett allegedly whispered to co-counsel Anna L. Gracie that Black prospective juror Donald Sweet was "too stupid" to serve on the jury. Later, he used one of his strikes against Mr. Sweet. In an 1895 case that charged Black juror exclusion, a Louisiana judge admitted defying the law that made it a crime to prevent Blacks from serving on juries. His justification was that Blacks lacked intelligence and moral standing.[225] The delegates at the 1898 Constitutional Convention where non-unanimous juries were adopted spoke in like terms. They expressed that one of the aims of the convention was to eliminate "corrupt and illiterate" Black voters.[226]

The association of Blackness with mental inferiority stems from slavery era "science." It became rationalization for segregation, and it appears to have found its way into the Sabine Parish courthouse that day. Fortunately, Attorney Shapiro was culturally literate and she broke the code. Prosecutor Burkett stood in open court and insisted his strike was not race-based. He claimed it was due to Sweet's "demeanor" and his way of "answering questions" and "the way he held himself in the jury box."[227]

Ms. Shapiro replied:

> [W]hen Mr. Burkett and Ms. Garcie were filling out their peremptory strike card, I did not intentionally listen, but I'm sitting very close to them, and so, I heard after the name was written, Ms. Gracie say to Mr. Burkett, 'But we don't have a good reason," and Mr. Burkett say... 'Yes we do. He's stupid.' [228]

Burkett responded: "I didn't know we were going to report private conversations between opposing counsel. I don't deny what I said...I've tried in kinder words on the record to say without putting in those terms...yes, I have very serious concerns about the man's IQ."[229] Burkett, who never questioned Sweet about his intelligence or aptitude during voir dire, spent years defending his actions.[230]

How is this possible? When *Batson* concluded that prosecutors could not use race as a criterion for excluding jurors, it charged mostly white judges, many of whom are former prosecutors, with determining if those reasons were race-neutral. It required judges–Black or white–with no mandated training in bias, racism, systemic racism, cultural competency or stereotypes, to make sound decisions on what is race-neutral.[231] The ruling also did not contemplate its application in the confines of a legal system plagued with the social and cultural complexities that infect the system in Louisiana. And it certainly didn't contemplate that offending prosecutors would train other prosecutors on how to circumvent *Batson* and get away with it.[232]

When they suspected racial discrimination during jury selection, Maxie's attorneys refused to waive the surrender flag. LCAC mitigation specialist Kate Robinson worked tirelessly to gather evidence to refute the allegation that Black juror Sweat lacked intelligence as the state claimed as a basis for having him eliminated. Robinson's commitment to jury justice fueled her many visits with the Sweat family and her pursuit of evidence that could be used for a challenge. Without her efforts, LCAC director Richard Bourke remarked that the subsequent challenge would have been impossible.

In post-trial pleadings, LCAC attorneys Richard Bourke, Gabe Newland and Meghan Shapiro provided evidence that the "stupid" juror: was a high school graduate (unlike many of the selected white jurors); had studied welding; had learned to play a musical instrument and performed in a band; served as a deacon who regularly taught Sunday school and assisted the church with its budget; had served on a prior jury in this parish; and, had a thirty-year career as a trim saw operator.[233] After trial, the court agreed that the elimination of Sweet as a juror was in fact discrimination.[234]

As former Louisiana Supreme Court Chief Justice Bernette Johnson tells it, "When the trial judge, as a gatekeeper, enforces a discriminatory peremptory challenge, the court itself becomes a party to racism, and has elected to use its power and prestige to enforce discrimination."[235] Are there options for Louisiana? Absolutely. In 2018, the Washington State Supreme Court took a significant step against this. It adopted General Rule 37 to eliminate the unfair exclusion of potential jurors based on race or ethnicity. It allows judges to raise the issue of bias in the use of peremptory challenges if neither attorney does. Under the new rule, the court need not find purposeful discrimination in order to deny the challenge. It can be denied if an objective observer could view race or ethnicity as a factor in the decision to strike the juror.

The rule gives judges circumstances to consider and a list of presumptively invalid reasons, so they are no longer left to their own devices to evaluate race-neutral reasons if they wish not to be. Some of those reasons that are on the "red flag" list to judges are: provided unintelligent or confused answers, sleeping, body language or problematic attitude. In addition, in 2020, California Governor Gavin Newsom signed AB 3070 into law. It increases transparency in jury selection by requiring an attorney exercising peremptory strikes to show clear and convincing evidence that his or her action is unrelated to that juror's membership in a protected group or class.

Jurors can also be eliminated through challenges for cause. These challenges are used when a juror cannot be impartial, cannot impose a sentence or find guilt, has a conflict of interest, when there is a stake in the outcome of the case or for other causes. They must be justified (unlike peremptory strikes that only require justification if challenged). Predictably, they are "no less than peremptory strikes...an important-- and unrecognized--vehicle of racial exclusion in criminal adjudication."[236] The Advocate's 2018 *Titling the Scales* Series arrived at this same conclusion. Their study showed that the 967 successful challenges for cause by prosecutors removed 58.9% Black prospective jurors and only 34.4% white prospective jurors.

When it comes to challenging discrimination in the jury selection process, people of color rarely get what Allen Snyder received after his capital conviction. In his case, a Louisiana prosecutor eliminated the only five prospective, Black jurors. More than twenty years after his conviction, Snyder obtained a reversal of his conviction from the SCOTUS; a record acknowledging that the prosecutor engaged in discrimination; a finding that the trial judge failed to make specific findings and, instead, just ratified the reasons given by the prosecutor; and, that the Louisiana Supreme Court signed off on all this when it was brought to its attention[237] (with the exception of dissents from Judges Calogero, Kimball and Johnson).[238]

What is more likely is judicial apathy in the wake of the justice-impacted raising challenges to the serious violation of their constitutional rights and the imposition of long and harsh sentences where justice-impacted people are often admonished for displaying non-conforming behavior behind bars or later emerging after the trauma of incarceration to spectators who judge them for being maladjusted. Meanwhile, prosecutors and judges, while acting in their official roles, enjoy immunity from suit, social standing, upward promotion and complete impunity when they destroy or adversely impact people's lives as they perform as villains or automatons instead of as humans with empathy and a commitment to an equitable and credible process.

Multiple Louisiana studies have corroborated the assertion that race plays a role in determining which jurors some prosecutors seek to remove from the jury. A 2003 study found that Jefferson Parish prosecutors struck Black prospective jurors at more than three times the rate they struck white prospective jurors in felony cases.[239] A 2015 study found that "in 332 trials over a ten-year period...prosecutors from the Caddo Parish District Attorney's Office exercised their discretion to peremptorily strike Black jurors 46% of the time" (and they exercised their discretion 15% of the time to strike non-Black jurors), making them more than three times as likely to strike Black than non-Black prospective jurors. [240] These are not random instances at the hands of select prosecutors. This is a documented practice throughout the state as confirmed by the 2018 *Tilting the Scales* study. This study found evidence of race-based strikes by Louisiana prosecutors in eight of nine parishes.

Louisiana's juries remain a site for the continuation of the white man's dominion over Blacks. These juries are living manifestations of systemic or institutionalized racism that are equally harmful to the accused person of color, the prospective juror of color and jurors of color. As noted in the Preface, non-unanimous juries were implemented to create the illusion of Black juror participation. They remained a part of Louisiana's legal landscape for over one hundred and twenty years. As a state, we still have not fully reckoned with them—not because we can't; because we wish not to.

This inquest into the jury box demonstrates how political rights have been used to extend the life span of systemic inequities. This sheds light on why ending non-unanimous juries did not result in jury justice in the state. Blacks remain underrepresented on Louisiana juries, accused people of color still don't experience the full protections of the Sixth Amendment and those with final non-unanimous jury convictions continue to be victims of an injustice as their defective "trials" today amount to no trial at all. To Blacks in Louisiana, the Sixth Amendment's jury trial protections have come close to being a hoax.

Jurors of color have a role to play in this conversation. Are we absent for legitimate reasons, because of judicial mistrust or because we don't understand that our presence matters? These are treatable maladies. The bias, supremacy and racism that has taken occupancy in and around the jury box is an obstacle of a different degree. Because it was not diagnosed in a timely fashion, it wasn't treated. The lack of treatment caused it to spread to the vital organs as detailed in chapter three.

CHAPTER 3

AN ASSESSMENT: A LEGAL ASSEMBLY LINE

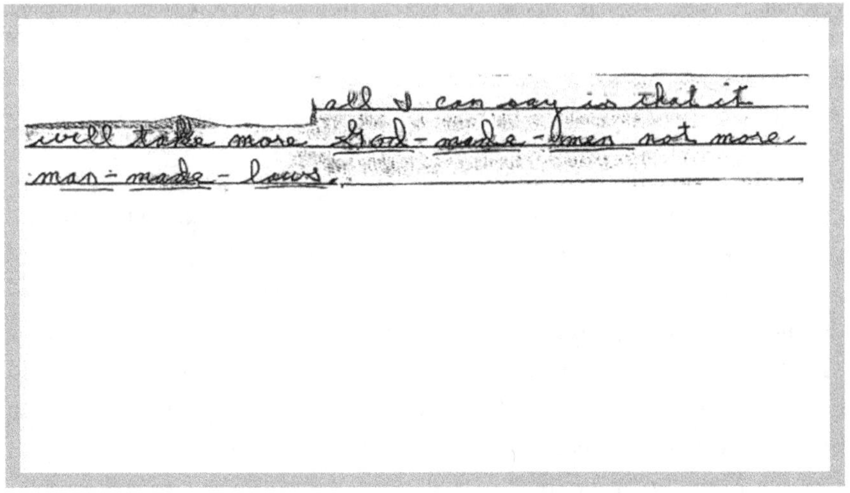

— WORDS OF A LOUISIANA JUSTICE-IMPACTED
MAN

The prior chapters looked back. This one looks at the present. It endeavors to perform an assessment of Louisiana's present legal system. Generally speaking, assessments evaluate how well an entity accomplishes its mission and meets its goals. Entire systems can even be assessed towards the ends of gauging overall performance. Doing so requires a synthesis, analysis and interpretation of outcomes so an action plan for needed improvements can be achieved. Stories, cases, laws and policies will narrate this guided tour of Louisiana's legal system. After, the chapter will synthesize, analyze and interpret findings. The action plan for needed improvements is presented in my second book, *Diversity in the Jury Box and Beyond: A Formula for Transforming Louisiana's Legal System.*

This assessment starts with a look at the pretrial detention process in Louisiana. *Grading Justice* assigns a score and a grade to states based on their pretrial performance. In 2022, Louisiana earned 15 of 100 points and scored an "F." Their study mentions the fact that Louisiana uses a cash bail system, which requires a person who has not been convicted of anything to pay a sum of money if they want to get out of jail, much like a game of *Monopoly* except this is real life. This bears a striking similarity to the chattel slavery era laws that allowed the enslaved to purchase their freedom. If they could, they were allowed to leave the plantation.

If they could not, they had to remain on the plantation. Cash bail is not an impediment to those with means, but, to populations with income insecurities, the lack of funds signals the beginning of the end. Cash bail is used in Louisiana for some misdemeanor charges, as well as for felonies. It causes people to be held in custody for very minor things sometimes. There is a growing movement to eliminate the use of cash bail when the accused is not being held for a crime of violence or being held on serious charges. Louisiana's actions go against the current. Louisiana has shown no interest in ending or limiting the use of cash bail to instances where it is absolutely necessary to ensure the safety of the public and/or the presence of the accused at future court dates.

Grading Justice also observes that Louisiana's Code of Criminal Procedure provides factors for judges to consider as they decide if a person should be detained or allowed to remain free as they await trial. They are critical of those factors, finding them not to be evidence-based. According to *Grading Justice's* state summary, "Louisiana's policies could be improved by implementing evidence-based release policies that ensure detention is only used to protect individuals from a real and present danger, or ensure appearance at trial when no other means can do so."

In its 2022 briefing report, *The Civil Rights Implications of Cash Bail,* the U.S. Commission on Civil Rights indicated that "people of color may also have higher bond amounts imposed and are more likely to be perceived as dangerous during bail hearings." Does Louisiana's legal system improve as a person progresses past the point of pretrial detention? Unfortunately, problems persist and escalate throughout the various stages of the legal process. Sentencing is a great illustration.

Louisiana has an infatuation with long sentences and over sentencing. As of 2022, the Louisiana Department of Corrections (LDC) reported that there were approximately 32,000 people in Louisiana prisons and jails. Of those, about 18,000 were serving sentences of 10 years or more, and more than 8,000 were serving sentences of 20 years or more. Additionally, there are approximately 4,300 people serving life sentences without the possibility of parole. In 2024, The Sentencing Project determined that "Louisiana's share of people serving life without the possibility of parole (LWOP) ranks highest per capita nationally and across the globe."

Long sentences are tantamount to an investment with little return. In fiscal year 2022, the state spent nearly $1 billion on incarceration, with an average annual cost of more than $24,000 per inmate. Research suggests long prison sentences are not always effective in reducing crime or enhancing public safety. In fact, many studies have shown that lengthy sentences can adversely impact the individual and the community. Yet, some Louisiana prosecutors abuse and overuse the state's habitual offender law, causing many sentenced under them to serve grossly disproportionate sentences for nonviolent crimes.

Louisiana's habitual offender law, first enacted in 1928, increases prison time (from a second felony conviction onwards) and significantly removes the discretion of judges. Fate Winslow's life without the possibility of parole for a marijuana conviction is the result of a habitual offender sentence handed down in 2008. At the time, Winslow, a Black man, was destitute and hungry. He was approached by a man looking for $20 worth of marijuana. He got the marijuana from a dealer. In turn, he received a $5 cut. The buyer turned out to be a narcotics officer. The dealer was never charged.

Maurice Lewis, a Black man, spent twenty-three years in custody after being convicted of stealing $20 in cash from a purse snatched from a white woman.[1] It did not matter that the $20 was returned to the victim. To secure this life sentence, prosecutors told the jury he was a "predator" with a history of prior criminal acts.[2] In truth:

> His youth had been punctuated by a series of convictions for minor crimes in which no one was physically hurt and a grand total of $44 was taken and later returned. He was involved in the theft of some stereo equipment aged 19. A purse at the age of 21. And at 27, he took an umbrella from a front porch. It was...raining that day. Lewis was convicted of burgling an inhabited dwelling and sentenced to 80 months in prison. [3]

Clarence Tolbert was sentenced to a life sentence as a habitual offender for possession of $10 worth of crack cocaine. Black defendant Walter Perell Fisher, Jr., received consecutive sentences under the habitual offender law of four years for possession of a minimal amount of methamphetamine and a maximum sentence of ten years for possession of one promethazine pill, a legend drug, after the drugs were discovered in a home he was a guest in, but not on his person or near him.

In a lone dissent, Judge John Michael Guidry protested:

> [W]hen considering the facts of this case, the combined sentence of fourteen years shocks the conscious and is a needless imposition of punishment. This is particularly so in light of the fact that the charge for possession of the promethazine pill would have been a misdemeanor rather than a felony had it occurred fifteen months later, pursuant to the continuation of the Louisiana Justice Reinvestment Reforms...The maximum enhanced sentence of ten years running consecutive to the

four-year sentence violates the prohibition against excessive punishment.[4]

Fair Wayne Bryant, another Black defendant, also had a near fatal encounter with the state's habitual offender law. He was handed a life sentence for the *attempted* theft of a pair of hedge clippers. This did not pose a problem to most members of the two reviewing courts.[5] In her lone dissent from the Supreme Court's denial of review, Justice Bernette Johnson described use of the habitual offender law as a "modern manifestation" of 19th-century Pig Laws, racist statutes implemented shortly after the Civil War for the purpose of criminalizing Black people. Long before, a similar warning bell was rung in Congress shortly after Emancipation *in 1865*:

> The emancipation of the slaves is submitted to only in so far as chattel slavery in the old form could not be kept up. But although the freedman is no longer considered the property of the individual master, *he is considered the slave of society, and all independent State legislation will share the tendency to make him such.* The ordinances abolishing slavery passed by the conventions *under the pressure of circumstances*, will not be looked upon as barring the establishment of a new form of servitude.[6]

Those facing lifetime parole argue they are serving a habitual sentence of another nature. They, in a desperate bid for release from captivity, exchange a literal cell for the bondage that lifetime parole offers. Sometimes parole is for a defined number of years, but lifetime parole has no end date. Parole is granted after a justice-impacted person who has completed a significant portion of their sentence convinces a board that a degree of rehabilitation has happened and there is no obvious threat to the safety of the public if they are released. Once paroled, the justice-impacted person is allowed to leave incarceration before their sentence is completed provided they agree to certain terms and conditions.

Their continued freedom is conditioned on them meeting these conditions for the duration of parole. Some typical conditions are:

visiting the parole officer monthly; forfeiting firearm ownership or possession; performing community service; having travel restrictions or limitations; payment of restitution; not contacting victims or co-defendants; having an employment or education plan; obeying a curfew; and, remittance of a monthly fee. Those on parole also agree to unannounced visits to their place of residence, employment, or anywhere else at any time as may be necessary for the officer to perform their duty. While under parole supervision, one is always subject to random searches of their person or surroundings by the parole officer.

Lifetime parole means this continues until you die, leaving many entrapped in this reality to argue that it is the functional equivalent of chattel slavery because, under both systems, one is perpetually under the authority and supervision of someone else. Opponents contest that characterization, contending that enslavement was involuntary whereas these terms are not. Lloyd Jarrow weighs in. Jarrow says a decision can only be voluntary when there is a choice involved. Jarrow began his hard labor sentence at seventeen-years-old after a prosecutor hid evidence that could have established his innocence. At the time, he was reading on a fourth-grade level. He was poor, the child of an absent father and drug-addicted mother. Without resources, he was left to his own devices to find his way out of what he terms a wrongful conviction.

Jarrow says it took an entire ten years to get the hidden documents and years more of attempts to get a court to listen. After thirty failed filings, the law changed, allowing him to be resentenced before the issue of his innocence could ever be addressed. At the resentencing, this seventeen-year-old was a greying forty-year-old man. He recalls being in court for resentencing and hearing that his life sentence for second degree murder was being corrected to parole eligibility after he served two additional years. He wanted to achieve freedom through a declaration of innocence, but knew that was uncertain whereas parole as a pathway to freedom was certain so he embraced what seemed like an opportunity.

Jarrow remains grateful for the second change at freedom that parole offers, but now comprehends how it can be a barrier to reentry in a way he simply couldn't when he was in custody. Jarrow describes lifetime parole as a potential obstacle to reentry because one is never allowed to separate themselves from the conviction. It hitches them to their past and never allows them to fully rejoin the democracy. It reduces them to a single story and limits opportunities for upward mobility. He, like many others, will spend a lifetime in a cell without bars as did the ancestors. And, like them, dollars will be associated with their bodies.

There are additional concerns, one of which is the process of deciding the suitable candidates for life-time parole. There are cases that might justify lengthy periods of supervision, but my study doesn't show a careful vetting in this regard. What has emerged is an arbitrary selection process that includes people who do not warrant this level of supervision, either at the time of release or in the ensuing years. A further problem involves the view that this is voluntary. The choice between incarceration and parole may be voluntary, but an understanding of the terms of parole is an entirely different matter. Some report *listening* to words and being so traumatized by wrongful incarceration or over sentencing that they couldn't process what was heard.

Others report first understanding what they agreed to when they leave prison and report to the first visit with the parole officer and are then provided verbal and written explanations of the list of conditions. Some say the terms are beyond comprehension as they had lost a societal appreciation of time and revenue while incarcerated. There is no intent to oppose release via parole. It's only a call to consider the way this type of release, as currently used, can prevent one from experiencing the liberty that has been constitutionalized and hailed as an ideal.

On a few occasions, the legislature has contributed to the legal system's failures. In the late 1980s, a series of new "controlled dangerous substances" started appearing on the social scene, especially among young people. Louisiana adopted the philosophy that harsh penalties would deter drug use. In 2001, Sociologist David Garland coined the term "mass incarceration" when he sounded an alarm about the national bent toward mass imprisonment. Many jurisdictions around the country seized this moment to self-assess or change course. This was one of the few times Louisiana acted in accordance with conventional wisdom applicable to legal, justice and penal systems.

In the 2000s, the legislature came to terms with the fact that the drug sentences it imposed in the 1980s and 1990s were too extreme. The legislature drafted a solution that became a problem. The corrective legislation left those already sentenced under the draconian laws uncertain about how to avail themselves to the remedy that the legislature thought it created. The justice-impacted were in an escape room of sorts. The ones that sought relief from courts (through resentencing) were told they were at the wrong door.

Others who sought relief from a newly created risk review panel (that functioned like a parole board) were told they were at the wrong door too. The justice-impacted struggled to decode the legislation. They remained locked inside this escape room for years as legal challenges worked their way through the courts. In a situation like this, state officials should customize legislative solutions out of a spirit of morality and justice and a commitment to the ideals of the state and federal constitution. At times like this, a legislative tweak or a display of legislative concern is often more useful and effective than litigation, but, too often, it's not the response given to justice-impacted populations.

But the legislature did exactly this after Hurricane Katrina. A white medical doctor was criminally charged after patients died in her care, under questionable circumstances, as the region suffered the impacts of the disaster. The charges could be brought because there was no provision in law shielding the medical community from prosecution in instances like this. The legislature didn't need task forces, advisory boards, advocacy campaigns, public testimony, studies or long delays. They swiftly changed laws to ensure that health care providers were protected from civil liability and criminal culpability in the event of future natural disasters.

In the 1960s and 1970s, the "10/6 lifers" accepted plea agreements to life sentences on the promise they would serve ten years and six months then become parole eligible (if they demonstrated good behavior while in custody).[7] The 10/6 sentencing guidelines were established in 1926. As sentencing schemes grew harsher, those who agreed to 10/6 deals were left in prison past their agreements and the state repeatedly raised its parole requirements. In 1979, the legislature abolished parole eligibility altogether.

As of 2022, most of the "10/6 lifers" had been in prison for at least 50 years. Some were wrongfully convicted and others pleaded guilty to crimes they did not commit, opting to spend what they believed would be 10-and-a-half years in prison rather than risk a longer sentence. The overwhelming majority are Black. All are elderly. Lester Pearson would see freedom fifty-seven years later at the age of eighty-four years old only because Jason Williams, the newly elected district attorney of New Orleans saw the injustice and decided to address it.[8]

But the majority of these convictions are not out of Orleans Parish and those with convictions in other parishes did not receive the same prosecutorial concern.[9] The rest remained in cages–excluded–until the next pathway home came in 2022. They weren't released then. The legislature passed a law that made them eligible for parole review, which means yet another obstacle separated them from freedom. No state official will be held accountable. In fact, most won't even lose sleep over the situation.

As of summer 2024, there remains a population of people in custody as a result of non-unanimous jury convictions. Like those medical doctors, they too need a legislative remedy. For those in Oregon that did not get the benefit of their change in law to a unanimous jury system, Oregon's legislature provided the remedy.[10] In 2024, Oregon even agreed to grant a pardon and awarded wrongful conviction compensation to Earl Bain. Bain's 2009 conviction resulted from a non-unanimous jury. Louisiana's legislature has been unwilling to provide a remedy so these men and women languish in Louisiana's prisons still today representing the latest chapter in Louisiana's jury injustice saga.[11]

The stubborn pace of corrective justice is prevalent. In 1997, the state of Louisiana charged Nathaniel Lambert with three aggravated crimes. He was convicted of all three crimes and sentenced to life without parole. In 1999, a state appellate court ordered the resentencing of two of Lambert's crimes. Louisiana did not resentence Lambert until 2018, over eighteen years later. He lost his challenge when the court concluded that he failed to show Louisiana acted with "prejudice" in waiting to resentence him. In addition to that injustice, Lambert's three convictions were by non-unanimous juries.

In 1976, sixty-nine-year-old Kenneth "Zulu" Whitmore was convicted of robbing and murdering a white former mayor of Zachary, Louisiana. For the forty-eight years that he has been in custody, he has consistently maintained his innocence. At Whitmore's trial, the prosecutor told the jury there was "no evidence found, no fingerprints...no nothing." That same prosecutor played what he described as a confession to the jury. Whitmore has always maintained that this statement was not voluntarily given. In a post-conviction effort to prove his innocence, Whitmore sought copies of his taped statement. For years, he was told the tape did not exist. That turned out to be false. It was not the only untruth hovering over the case. The prosecutor's statement to the jury about there being a lack of crime scene evidence was also a lie. Actually, there was physical evidence at the crime scene.

In 2014, Whitmore filed an application for post-conviction relief, asserting actual innocence and accusing the prosecutor of withholding evidence that the defense was entitled to. The state did the predictable. They challenged the timeliness of his efforts, a familiar dilatory tactic in many of these cases. In 2017, the Supreme Court deemed Whitmore's filing timely, but there was no way to fashion a remedy that could restore the time lost as these legal challenges were disposed of. At Whitmore's initiation, demands were made to test the fingerprints found at the crime scene, the ones hidden all these years. State officials fought those attempts, causing more delays. An order from the higher court forced testing of those prints.

During several 2019 proceedings, prosecutors indicated that testing could not be done because of difficulty finding those prints in the crime lab. Eventually, they were located but, according to prosecutors, a ransom-ware attack caused an additional delay in testing. In late 2019, that fingerprint comparison excluded Whitmore as the source of two of the prints and determined that, after forty-eight years, the quality of the remaining four prints were too poor to lead to any conclusive findings. In 2020, a hearing on these matters was set.

As of May 2024, Whitmore was still waiting on that hearing to be held. In many instances, courts don't have enforceable deadlines for action the way parties do. They often don't view time behind bars the way those doing it do. For example, when activist H. Rap Brown complained to a Louisiana court about the harm he suffered by a thirteen month delay between indictment and a trial date, the court was not persuaded that his witnesses might no longer be available. And, as to his wait, the court described thirteen months in custody as an innocent person awaiting trial as "brief."[12]

The same lack of regard for the way encounters with the legal system impact people's lives visits those who are not in custodial settings. Matthew Sims was a government employee and Warren Jordan was a business owner when they had the misfortune of facing criminal charges. When Sims refused the prosecutor's plea bargain offer, the charges were upgraded to felonies. This type of retaliation is routine. Sims represented himself because the lawyers he consulted with all recommended he accept the state's plea offer. This is also routine.

Sims reported to court more than thirty times. The state brought the charges, suggesting they had grounds to prosecute him; yet, they caused repeated delays that prolonged the case. Sims could do nothing but stand on the sidelines and watch his world be reduced to memories. In 2024, Matthew Sims' criminal case ended in dismissal. The news did not result in fanfare because, by that point, he knew what the public didn't: his win had long become a loss. The arrest cost him his job. The pending charges cost him future jobs. The four-year delay between the start and end of the prosecution incrementally destroyed the things it took him a life-time to acquire and accomplish.

Following a billing dispute with a client, Jordan was arrested for residential contractor fraud in 2022 despite him having photos of the work he completed and a contract to document the agreement. Bail was set. He couldn't meet it so he remained in custody for four months on a misdemeanor charge. The prosecutor agreed to freedom on the condition that Jordon enter a plea bargain to a felony. Throughout the duration of this, Jordon claims his public defender never came to see him and did nothing in the way of providing a defense.

With health declining, his worldly possessions slipping away and the challenges of living in a jail, Jordon did what he promised himself he wouldn't. He accepted the plea agreement. After their close encounters with the legal system, Sims and Jordan were left, limp, battered and discarded like debris from the aftermath of one of Louisiana's hurricanes. The public naïvely believes convictions can only happen after the state meets a very high burden at trial.

Pursuant to this thinking, most people are uninterested in the plight of a person who finds themselves behind bars. They believe incarceration has to mean that a criminal law was broken and that a jury carefully made a finding of guilt. As demonstrated in the Sims and Jordon cases, the burden to convict is not as high in practice as it appears on paper.

According to the Plea Bargaining Institute:

> In the U.S., 95% or more of criminal cases are resolved through a plea of guilty. When someone pleads guilty, they waive their right to a trial, something guaranteed by the U.S. Constitution. While a plea bargain may offer advantages, such as a more lenient sentence, plea bargaining often involves coercive incentives that negatively impacts all defendants' right to trial...these incentives can be so coercive that even innocent defendants plead guilty. For example, 21% of the cases entered into the National Registry of Exonerations in 2021 involved false pleas of guilty. These pressures to plead guilty may include pressure from police and prosecutors, the imposition of much higher sentences for those who exercise their right to proceed to trial, and other systemic problems including lack of access to a lawyer, long pre-trial detention periods and high court costs.

The same holds true for Louisiana. More convictions result from plea bargains than from trials.

What was done to the Angola 3–baseless convictions of men already in custody following prior convictions and over one hundred and thirteen years in solitary confinement between the three men–defies human comprehension.[13] After a court reversed Angola 3 member Albert Woodfox's first conviction, it was another six years before this second trial started. Time behind bars is bad for anyone, but Albert's time was done in solitary confinement, so delays took on even greater importance in his case. In the end, his entire forty-one year stay in solitary confinement proved to be one massive time delay because the state reversed his conviction and settled his civil suit over solitary confinement in his favor. No state official has ever been held accountable in any of these instances. The combination of no judicial deadlines and racial hierarchies is lethal for those at the bottom of the hierarchy.

"The American Medical Association, the American Academy of Pediatrics and the United Nations have all condemned the practice of isolating young people as deeply harmful, leading to depression, anxiety and psychosis." That might matter elsewhere. In Louisiana, juveniles have been detained in hidden, round-the-clock solitary confinement chambers and denied education, programming and stimulation. This pales in comparison to what caught the eye of the United Nations (UN) Special Rapporteur on Torture and Other Cruel, Inhuman or Degrading Treatment or Punishment, Juan E. Méndez, who said "Keeping Albert Woodfox in solitary confinement for more than four decades clearly amounts to torture....," said Mendez. "The circumstances of the incarceration of the so-called Angola Three clearly show that the use of solitary confinement in the U.S. penitentiary system goes far beyond what is acceptable under international human rights law," he said

In some of these instances, the justice-impacted person is not in isolation because of any behavioral lapse behind bars. Louisiana prison administrators sometimes place adults in solitary confinement as a matter of discretion. Angola 3 member Robert King had this experience. He was placed in solitary confinement, not because of some action he undertook, but because of a supposed investigation. He recounts, "I was...under investigation for the death of [a guard]...although I had never met the guard, never been in the general population where I could have had the opportunity to meet him, and had not even been in Angola prison at the time of his death."[14] "Without further ado, I was classified to CCR or closed cell restriction..., a classification I would keep for the next twenty-nine years," says King.[15] That twenty-nine-year investigation never ended.

Judges who respond to improprieties with silence are overrepresented in Louisiana. Judges who display zero tolerance for injustices are underrepresented in Louisiana. What Judge John Michael Guidry did in *State v. Burnell* is a gross departure from the norm. In the appeal, Burnell challenged his conviction on the grounds that the state failed to bring him to trial within the time frame allowed by law. In 2005, the *Burnell* panel, knowing the state had the burden of proof on matters such as these, conditionally affirmed the conviction and remanded the matter back to the lower court despite their 2004 attempt to get that same court to supplement the record with all relevant dates in the case so the court could determine whether the state or the accused caused the delay in the case.

The clerk sent the same record in response to that higher court's order that the record be supplemented. In light of this, the appellate panel voted to, again, place the matter in the hands of that same lower court. In his lone dissent, Judge Guidry protested, "I believe it is highly improper to afford the state another opportunity to prove its case once it has been determined that its first attempt was insufficient."[16] Worse happens.

When they perform the powers of their office as intended, prosecutors meet an important public need. Too many don't. Louisiana has a prosecutorial misconduct problem of epic proportions. Silence surrounding this issue has caused it to metastasize. Here, I do not speak of prosecutors who commit unintentional acts of negligence. I speak of prosecutors who, themselves, break the law, engage in intentional acts of wrongdoing or abuse the powers of the office. And I speak of a state judiciary who has, in too many instances, endorsed bad behavior by inaction, dismissiveness or tolerance as is displayed in the following cases.

Prosecutorial misconduct comes in many forms, such as using improper arguments, prosecuting a person without good cause or legal justification for doing so, not disclosing evidence to the defense that the defense is entitled to, introducing false evidence or discriminating during jury selection. It's bad when anyone abuses the power of office, but this is not a case of some random person doing wrong. The prosecutor has more control over life, liberty and reputation than any other person in America. This is so because of the enormity of the discretionary power held by this one person and the virtual lack of oversight that attaches to their decisions.

Prosecutors decide if a charge will proceed to trial, if a plea bargain will be offered or accepted, if bail will be offered and the amount thereof. They even have input over the sentence. By design, they present cases to grand juries with no defense built into the process. The forthcoming examples showcase what many Louisiana prosecutors do with the power we entrust to them.

In David Brown's case, another man provided a statement that he and a third man made the decision to commit the murder of a guard during a prison escape attempt. In that statement, the man never mentioned Brown being a part of the planning or the murder itself. Prosecutors did not share that statement with Brown. He was convicted and sentenced to death. Subsequent challenges brought the issue before the Louisiana Supreme Court to decide if prosecutors had a duty to disclose that statement.

They placed great weight upon the fact that the statement, of who committed the murder, never explained that other people did not commit the murder and did not explicitly say Brown was absent. Upon that reasoning, they concluded the statement was not the kind of evidence that had to be shared with the defense. The response from some SCOTUS justices causes consternation.

This 2023 rebuke from SCOTUS Justices Jackson, Sotomayor and Kagan followed:

> The requirement that the withheld evidence must speak to or rule out the defendant's participation in order for it to be favorable is wholly foreign to our case law...[you] recounted various other reasons why a jury might disregard [the] statement, while completely 'ignoring reasons [it] might not.'...We have repeatedly reversed lower courts—and

> *Louisiana courts, in particular*—for similar refusals to enforce the
> Fourteenth Amendment's mandate that favorable and material
> evidence in the government's possession be disclosed to the defense
> before trial....This Court has decided not to grant Brown's petition for
> certiorari, but that determination should in no way be construed as an
> endorsement of the lower court's legal reasoning...the Louisiana
> Supreme Court misinterpreted and misapplied
> our *Brady* jurisprudence in a manner that contravenes settled law.[17]

The SCOTUS might have had prosecutor Dubelier on their minds
when they wrote that. During a trial, a trial judge, after having his orders
repeatedly ignored by the prosecutor, took custody of the prosecutor's
files for a review. Thereafter, the judge stated:

> Those materials that I reviewed all last night contained what I believe
> to be materials that may possibly be *Brady* material. There is no way...
> you in your competency as an attorney, or any human can review all
> that material taken in context with the testimony thus far given and
> make a determination...positively not *Brady* material.[18]

Later, that same judge wrote in his reasons for decision:

> The Court concludes that Assistant district attorney Dubelier, an
> experienced and technically skilled prosecutor... deliberately and in
> bad faith, suppressed Johnson's earlier statements, first denying the
> statements existed, and then withholding the tape and transcript from
> the Court when ordering to provide each to the Court for in camera
> review.[19]

Astonishingly, the trial court denied the defendant's request for relief
after these scathing revelations were made. The appellate court, seeing
this record, affirmed this. But Judge William Brynes felt compelled to
register a dissent:

> *Brady* material was withheld by the prosecution in direct disobedience
> of the law and the orders of the trial court...where the State's deliberate

disobedience of the orders of the Court created a doubtful situation, I would resolve that doubt in favor of the defendant...it must be noted that the conduct of the district attorney's Office in this case has been deplorable. On at least three occasions the State deliberately disobeyed the orders of the trial court. Such conduct casts a shadow on the integrity of our system of justice. The conduct of the prosecutor should be straightforward, honest, and above reproach. Instead, this case presents the public with a picture of prosecutorial conduct which is unacceptable under any standard of moral or legal ethics.[20]

In another instance, Bruce Mohon served in dual roles as an assistant district attorney (felony prosecutor) and legal counsel for St. James Parish. In the latter capacity, he advised the parish council not to accept payment of a debt from a defendant. As prosecutor, he secured a conviction against that man for not paying that debt. Subsequently, State District Court Judge Jessie LeBlanc of the 23rd Judicial District dismissed all five malfeasance in office counts being prosecuted by Mohon against Blaise Gravois.[21] In so doing, Judge LeBlanc registered her disapproval of the prosecutor's antics: "Mr. Mohon breached his duty to stand as a representative of the people and uphold the integrity of the criminal justice system.... Mr. Mohon's actions thwarted fairness in the search for the truth in the entire proceeding....this Court finds the actions of the state to be so intrusive and over-reaching as to warrant dismissal....[22] A reviewing court agreed with the lower court's finding of misconduct.[23]

In a forth instance, Chris Richard, a prosecutor in the Fifteenth Judicial District, was arrested for felony hit and run, careless operation of a vessel and negligent injury in August 2021 after the boat he was operating struck the inner tube of three children and he allegedly left the scene.[24] His arrest was not immediate. After public pressure, his arrest came days later (long after a sobriety test could be taken). One child sustained a broken pelvis and the other two were injured. Prosecutor Richard was allowed to retain his employment pending trial. After years of unexplained delays, his felonies were downgraded to misdemeanors and he agreed to a comfortable plea that included an apology and talks to students about choices.

On another occasion, former St. Charles Parish district attorney Harry Morel offered female defendants leniency from his office in exchange for sex.[25] In yet another instance, a prosecutor withheld evidence that the law said the accused was entitled to and proceeding to trial, knowing the wrong person is in custody. Louisiana courts viewed this as immaterial.[26] Jason Brown worked in both Caddo and Calcasieu Parishes. His Calcasieu Parish prosecutorial duties ended over alleged dishonesty associated with his handling a continuance motion in the Joey Julian murder trial. One thing he can't be accused of is not helping the state earn its reputation as the forerunner of mass incarceration. He secured a forty-year sentence for James Cass for possessing with intent to distribute 1.5 ounces of marijuana.

During Surcorey Odums' interrogation, an officer presented him with a fake DNA testing report complete with a forged signature, hoping to entice a confession. The fake report wasn't used at trial. Its existence was never disclosed to the defense. Brown prosecuted the case. An appellate court reviewed this and decided it to be harmless because it was never entered into evidence at trial. Brown was also part of a joint police-prosecutor squad called the Zombie Response Team. The squad did "search and arrest operations" and even accompanied law enforcement as they served warrants.

They even had custom-embroidered patches and customized vehicle license plates. They disbanded in July 2012 after a state investigation found two of the squad's ADAs had submitted falsified documents to a military-surplus weapons procurement program. That left Brown more time to do things like testifying at public hearings. In 2016, Brown is said to have attended a meeting of the Caddo Parish Committee where he is reported to have registered objections to the removal of a Confederate soldiers memorial in Caddo Parish. According to minutes, Brown said "our forefathers fought in this country...this City should move forward and focus on growing and making this City better...."

Hugo Holland, also believed to be a part of the Zombie Response Team, was forced to resign his position as an assistant district attorney for Caddo Parish in 2012 after he was allegedly caught falsifying federal forms in order to procure M-16 weapons for personal use through the federal program that gives surplus military gear to police departments. That didn't lower his professional standing. He was hired by parishes across the state as a part-time prosecutor. He was also retained by the district attorneys Association to encourage legislators to oppose criminal justice reform bills. Washington Post Columnist Radley Balko describes Holland as "arguably the most powerful prosecutor in Louisiana, which is odd given that not only has he never run for office, he isn't even officially a full-time state employee."

Holland was part of Bobby L. Hampton's prosecution. Hampton was sentenced to death after "clearly exculpatory" evidence—the grand jury testimony of an eyewitness who identified Mr. Hampton's co-defendant as the shooter–was withheld from the defense. After concluding this happened, the Louisiana Supreme Court ruled that "it does not appear that its suppression denied Defendant a fair trial."[27] Writing in support of a new trial, Justice Bernette Johnson cast the lone dissent at the Louisiana Supreme Court.[28] When asked by a reporter for *The Advocate* about the portrait of Nathan Bedford Forrest, the Confederate general who was an early member and reputed leader of the Ku Klux Klan, that hung in his office at the Caddo Parish DA's Office, Holland is quoted as insisting that "he merely admired Forrest as a cavalry commander."

This type of misconduct was present in the trial of Angola 3 member Herman Wallace. Wallace was charged with murdering a correctional officer inside Angola.[29] On April 17, 1972, Officer Brent Miller was violently attacked in an Angola dorm. Angola retained fingerprints of all inmates, but crime scene blood evidence and fingerprints weren't tested. Wallace was convicted. At his trial, inmate witnesses were incentivized to implicate him. Hezekiah Brown was one. He swore under oath that he was not receiving any incentives for his testimony. That was a lie. Not only did he receive a housing change from the dorm with other inmates to an actual house on the property where a few inmates lived and trained dogs for use in rescues, he also received a weekly carton of cigarettes and early release (from a life sentence).

The defense also learned that he was legally blind, making it impossible for him to see much of what he testified to. Chester Jackson also received a sentence reduction and a housing change. This was hidden during the trial. In absence of forensic evidence, Wallace was convicted and sentenced to life in prison. From a solitary confinement cell, Wallace remained engaged in an over forty-year brawl with the state that took him through a maze of state and federal litigation where he challenged his conviction and raised ancillary issues, like prosecutorial misconduct and grand jury discrimination, before countless judges and magistrates who reviewed these very serious allegations and looked the other way.

In the state court, in over thirty years of filings, only two judges reacted to his pleas for justice. In 1999, Judge John Michael Guidry dissented from the denial of Wallace's application for supervisory review, stating that he "would grant the writ" because Wallace's "attorney should have filed a motion for a mistrial or sought other counsel…and it appears there was a deal not disclosed to the jury." In 2008, Judge Jewel Welch dissented from the denial of the writ, stating: "There was a reasonable likelihood that the verdict would have been different had the jury been aware of the promise and favors to the state's witness, Hezekiah Brown. The state's failure to disclose this information violated relator's constitutional rights, and relator should receive a new trial."

Because he failed at getting relief in state courts, Wallace had to turn to federal courts.[30] As he wrote from the darkness of his solitary cell, dripping in sweat from the lack of air conditioning, an intruder came into his space. As his legal case gained strength in the federal court, his body grew weak from the cancer that had taken occupancy many years earlier. Wallace had no idea his last chapter was being written as he engaged in this fight with the state.

On October 1, 2013, Wallace's forty-one-year incarceration ended when his conviction was overturned due to grand jury discrimination, a claim that he raised in state court over forty years earlier. On October 4, 2013, Wallace succumbed to liver cancer. Had the state courts given him a credible review, Herman would have seen freedom many years earlier and likely would have avoided the cancer diagnosis all together.[31] More importantly, they could have prevented more Herman Wallace's from ever coming to be by reporting and disciplining unethical prosecutors and remedying the injustices they cause.

The next prosecutor of concern is a man who, after work, replaced his business suits with a bedazzled jumpsuit, a cape, a slow moving and shaky leg, super-sized sunshades and a performance closely resembling the workout of a person afflicted with crippling arthritis. Then Attorney General Buddy Caldwell attempted to squeeze all the political juice possible out of the continued prosecution of Angola 3 members Herman Wallace and Albert Woodfox. Their civil suit over their prolonged stay in solitary confinement led to them being placed in specially-created dorms. To fight their suit, the pint-sized Elvis impersonator did what any self-respecting thrift store performer would do, he went bargain hunting for evidence to defeat their suit.

The federal court exposed the shopping spree. State officials searched through Woodfox and Wallace's phone calls for what they could use as sufficient evidence to start a disciplinary proceeding then they wrote the men up. It appears they used the bad behavior (that they manufactured) to place Woodfox and Wallace back in isolation so they could justify, in the civil suit claiming the long-term in solitary confinement as unnecessary and unconstitutional, why the pair needed to be held under these extreme conditions of solitary confinement.[32] The knock-off Elvis seems to have had more tricks up his blinged-out sleeves. When Woodfox was granted habeas relief and a bond was set, the homeowner's association for the property where Woodfox was to be released got an interesting call.

Alternative facts were communicated, leaving the association to believe a violent rapist was headed their way to victimize them all. Woodfox was never convicted of rape. Certainly, his prosecutor knew this. This ended Woodfox's efforts to be released on bond and unnecessarily prolonged his stay in solitary confinement. Elvis had one more act to perform. Years later, in this email excerpt, sent as a reply to Woodfox's supporters, it appears Caldwell improperly commented on pending litigation, and, arguably, engaged in a deliberate misrepresentation:

> Woodfox was…charged with numerous crimes…Among those numerous charges are at least 6 separate, unresolved aggravated rapes and armed robberies. Some of these victims were female patrons or waitresses who were raped during the late night or early morning robberies of bars in the New Orleans area.

> As you know, these convicted murderers filed a civil lawsuit alleging they have been denied due process and have been mistreated. It is important to know that if they win this civil case they could possibly receive money and a change in their housing assignments.

> Let me be clear, Woodfox and Wallace are GUILTY and have NEVER been held in solitary confinement….

> Sincerely,

> James D. "Buddy" Caldwell

> Louisiana Attorney General

One has to wonder—if state officials believed Woodfox committed these rapes, where was their concern for the victims? Why didn't they prosecute Woodfox for rape? Why did they eventually agree to his release and allow him to reenter society if they felt he was a sexual predator? And why did state officials make a secret deal with Hezekiah Brown—not just a convicted rapist, but a serial rapist—if they are so intolerant of those who commit rape? Interestingly, after professing his certainty about the guilt of Wallace and Woodfox, Caldwell offered Wallace freedom in exchange for a plea deal in their criminal case, which Wallace rejected. The state later settled their civil suit involving their prolonged stay in solitary confinement, despite Caldwell suggesting that they were never housed in this way.

Harry Connick, Sr. served as the district attorney of New Orleans (OPDA) from 1973 to 2003. In 1995, SCOTUS Justice David Souter wrote that Connick's office had "descend[ed] to a gladiatorial level unmitigated by any prosecutorial obligation for the sake of the truth." Connick responded to the ruling by saying he had stopped reading legal opinions a long time ago, and saw "no need" to make any changes to any of his office policies. Professor Laurie L. Levenson has served on local and national task forces addressing prosecutorial ethics and she authored an ethics rule relative to *Brady* for the state of California.

Levenson conducted an expert review of convictions obtained while Connick was district attorney. In the report of her findings, she concluded that *Brady* violations, while he was in office, were "systemic and not limited to mistakes by individual prosecutors."[33] Levenson found that "OPDA has been cited in at least 45 cases, affecting 46 defendants, where courts found that OPDA violated *Brady* by failing to disclose favorable information to defendants."[34] She continued, "In addition, OPDA has acknowledged *Brady* violations in at least eight cases, sometimes by offering defendants who alleged credible *Brady* violations plea agreements in exchange for withdrawing their *Brady* claims.[35]

Issac Knapper was sentenced to life in prison after prosecutor David Paddison failed to turnover a police report that contained exculpatory information. Louisiana courts not only permitted this; they later rationalized it. Some of the reviewing judges in a subsequent civil suit for malicious prosecution were of the mind that the hidden evidence "was not sufficient to change the outcome of the proceeding or to create a reasonable doubt that did not otherwise exist."[36] Only Justice Bernette Johnson dissented (in part) from the Louisiana Supreme Court's decision to extend absolute immunity to the prosecutor and deny damages to Mr. Knapper.

Change agents should also consider the legions of unnamed victims convicted in other cases where evidence was withheld.[37] Ellen Yaroshefsky, the Howard Lichtenstein Professor of Legal Ethics at Hofstra University, has written extensively about Louisiana's criminal legal system. According to Yaroshefsky, "Brady violations are a national problem, but Louisiana is an outlier in terms of the number of Brady petitions and Brady errors that have remained unaddressed. It's much more extreme."[38]

The New Yorker's Rachel Aviv reported in 2016 that Louisiana has had 128 death sentences overturned since 1976—25 for prosecutorial misconduct. She said only two were overturned by state judges, who tend to be former prosecutors. Federal courts intervened in all of the others. Recent studies by the Innocence Project and the National Registry of Exonerations both concluded that police and prosecutor misconduct — not faulty witnesses or false confessions — is the primary cause of wrongful convictions in our country.

Does this discussion suggest that Louisiana prosecutors are a group of demon-possessed, conviction-happy beings incapable of managing the power of the office? Absolutely not. I know many prosecutors who are principled and justice-minded people who I proudly call friends. This discussion does suggest there are cultural and systemic explanations for Louisiana's high rate of prosecutorial misconduct.

Attorney A.M. "Marty" Stroud III, of Shreveport, was the lead prosecutor in the December 1984 first-degree murder trial of Glenn Ford, who was sentenced to death for murder. Ford was released from prison March 11, 2014, after the state admitted new evidence proving Ford was not the killer. Stroud issued a rare public apology for his role in the wrongful conviction. In that apology letter, he provided important insights for change agents:

> I was too passive. I did not consider the rumors about the involvement of parties other than Mr. Ford to be credible...my inaction contributed to the miscarriage of justice...My mindset was wrong and blinded me to my purpose of seeking justice, rather than obtaining a conviction...I did not hide evidence, I simply did not seriously consider that sufficient information may have been out there that could have led to a different conclusion...I did not question the unfairness of Mr. Ford having appointed counsel who had never tried a criminal jury case much less a capital one. It never concerned me that the defense had insufficient funds to hire experts or that defense counsel shut down their firms for substantial periods of time to prepare for trial...The jury was all white...

jurors were struck with little thought...because...racial discrimination in the selection of jurors...was a very burdensome requirement that had never been met in the jurisprudence of which I was aware. I also participated in placing before the jury dubious testimony from a forensic pathologist that the shooter had to be left handed, even though there was no eye witness to the murder. And yes, Glenn Ford was left-handed...I was 33 years old. I was arrogant, judgmental, narcissistic and very full of myself. I was not as interested in justice as I was in winning.[39]

Glen Ford & Angela A. Allen-Bell weeks after his release.

State courts ruled against Mr. Ford in 2009 and 2011. As was the case with the enslaved people accused of organizing a 1700's revolt. There was little concern about whether the right Black person was taken into custody. The concern was that a Black person was taken into custody. Those convicted of the Conspiracy of 1731 were hanged or broken alive on a wheel. After, the governor "admitted that it was not clear whether those executed had formed the conspiracy, but a scapegoat was needed to quell the hysteria of the French colonists."[40] Ford served over twenty-nine years before being released in 2015. Within two months, he discovered that he had lung cancer. Then Attorney General Buddy Caldwell opposed his attempts to receive compensation for the time he was incarcerated.

The cost of prosecutorial misconduct is greater than the impact to the individual who is wrongfully convicted. When the suppression of evidence leads to a wrongful conviction, there are certain obvious consequences like expenses involved with proving innocence and unjustified trauma to the accused. There are many more hidden costs, such as the cost to taxpayers. In its *Report on Evidence Suppression in New Orleans* (1973-2002), the IPNO compiled this partial glimpse of the way wrongful convictions create unnecessary tax burdens (illustration based on a select number of cases prosecuted by one D.A.'s office):[41]

COST TO TAXPAYERS: CONVICTION OF INNOCENT MEN				
Name	Years in Prison	Incarceration Cost	Potential Compensation	Total
Earl Truvia	27.5	$516,993	$190,000	$706,993
Greg Bright	27.5	$516,993	$190,000	$706,993
Dwight LaBran	4	$76,591	$100,000	$266,591
Isaac Knapper	12	$229,774	$190,000	$419,774
Dan Bright	8	$153,183	$190,000	$343,183
John Thompson	18	$344,662	$14,190,000	$14,534,662
Curtis Kyles	14	$268,070	$190,000	$458,070
Shareef Cousin	3	$57,443	$85,000	$247,443
Total	113	$2,163,712	$15,325,000	$17,488,712

There are additional costs, including the loss of a contribution to the household by the incarcerated person. This chart helps to begin the process of calculating that: [42]

YEARS OF LIFE LOST IN PRISON: EXONERATED MEN		
Name	Conviction→Discovery of Evidence	Conviction → Release
Earl Truvia	25 Years	27 Years
Greg Bright	25 Years	27 Years
Dwight LaBran	3 Years	4 Years
Isaac Knapper	12 Years	12 Years
Dan Bright	8 Years	8 Years
John Thompson	14 Years	18 Years
Curtis Kyles	4 Years	14 Years
Shareef Cousin	2 Years	3 Years
Average	12 Years	14 Years
Total	93 Years	113 Years

There are also the transportation expenses the family bears in order to see their loved one; the cost of maintaining communication with them; the cost of providing for their unmet needs during incarceration; and, the costs of maintaining them until they can sustain themselves post-release.

Some Louisiana prosecutors approach their work with a "win at all costs" mentality. One of the strategies is interjecting the use of unrelated rap lyrics or social media posts into the trial process for the purpose of othering the person on trial and in an effort to unnecessarily prejudice the jury against that person.[43] In a legitimate prosecution, the facts do that. This is exactly what happened in the criminal cases against Christopher and Jordale Carter and Shelly Davis. In each instance, it worked.

Detective Zac Woodring's testimony was used as part of the prosecution's manslaughter case against cousins Christopher and Jordale Carter, the two Black males being tried before a majority white East Baton Rouge Parish jury.[44] Detective Woodring is a police officer and homicide detective who serves on the federal Alcohol, Tobacco and Firearms (ATF) task force.[45] Besides his experience and training as a member of law enforcement, Detective Woodring completed high school and two years of college.

Attorney Ryan K. Thompson is a SULC graduate living out a life-long dream of providing competent and quality defense services. Unlike the detective in the case against the Carters, he, prior to becoming a lawyer, researched and presented on Ebonics and English as a second language for people of African descent. This perspicacity with linguistics, dialect and culture was evident during his masterful cross examination.

Attorney Thompson cut right to the heart of the matter. He asked the detective if he had been socialized around Black people, and therefore, knowledgeable about their speech patterns, traditions or culture. He asked the "expert" if he had any formal training, certifications, publications or presentations in linguistics, cultural studies, musicology or terminology. Detective Woodring responded in the negative, but he was able to proceed with his testimony. The jury got to hear Detective Woodring testify about a monitored call that he listened to and how he ascribed meanings to words spoken based on his understanding of rap lyrics.

The white detective explained that listening to rap music (as part of his official duties) equipped him with the ability to interpret slang used by non-rappers such as the Carter cousins. Woodring told the jury how rappers "tend to rap about some of the things they do in their songs." After the detective swore under oath, that "75 percent of the rappers that are rapping in Baton Rouge are telling the truth about what they are rapping," Detective Woodring proceeded to interpret the meaning of words spoken during the monitored call made from a jail phone.

During the call, the accused Black man spoke with various Black family members in the vernacular that was native to them. The call involved discussions with his mother, grandfather, brothers and other family members. At a point, verbiage used in a rap song was used by the accused during the conversation. Detective Woodring spoke to the jury about words like "macaroni" (that he described as a mac-10 firearm) or "merc" (that he described as a mercenary) or "upped the rod" (that he described as a pointed a firearm). To him, these words constituted murderous expressions and admissions of criminal acts.

Attorney Thompson countered by asking if those words had a universal meaning or whether they carried a different meaning by state, parish or even neighborhood. Detective Woodring agreed they did, but never reconciled the various meanings with his conclusion. Jurors were also shown social media posts of the accused flashing money. They were told that money was ascertained during the crime at issue. There was no proof of where that money came from. The social media posts weren't even from the day of the crime. Christopher and Jordale Carter were convicted.[46]

In 2015, Shelly Davis, a Black woman, was tried for second-degree murder. The twenty-four-year-old admitted to the murder, but told jurors that she shot as she was under attack and in defense of her life following a feud between her brother and the victim. Prosecutors had a different opinion. Their theory was that it was a case of premeditated murder at the behest of Davis' brother who was in jail upon the accusation that he had previously robbed the victim. To aid the jury in believing their version, prosecutors employed the testimony of a person who testified that he witnessed Davis annihilate the victim.[47]

Additionally, prosecutors used unrelated content from Davis' Instagram account. Posted to her Instagram account were captions, hashtags, explicit rap lyrics and photos of her holding two guns with clip components. Davis told jurors the posts were not associated with the crime or criminal activity. In fact, she explained that posting "selfies" with rap lyrics, captions and hashtags had been a longstanding practice that she shared with millions of other American youth and was, in no way, indicative of criminal activity in this or any other instance.

Shelly Davis Not Long Before Her Conviction

Photo credit to Trellis Davis.

A sentence of life imprisonment without benefit of parole, probation or suspension of sentence was ultimately imposed. Reviewing courts found no merit to her claim that the use of the rap lyrics and social media posts contributed to her not getting a fair trial or to other challenges to the process.[48] With a trial and an appeal concluded, Davis settled into her new abode and the curtains closed. But what's behind those curtains? Years later, the state's main witness, the only person to testify that he actually witnessed an ambush and not a self-defense, sent what the defense describes as a recantation letter expressing "the need to clear" his "conscience."

In the handwritten statement bearing his signature, he says Davis "acted in self-defense" after the victim grabbed her purse. He continued that Davis was "able to grab her gun which was in the purse and that's when she shot." The witness ended by offering an apology "for the lie I told" and by revealing that his conscience had "been eating" him "up ever since." Those curtains also held behind them additional considerations. Davis did not author the lyrics that prosecutors used at her trial. The gun in the social media photos was never connected to the crime. Davis never hid or denied the fact that she was a gun owner, which is a cherished Second Amendment right in this country.

Several of the Davis witnesses were facing criminal charges in the same court, providing a motive for them to cooperate with the State's version of events. The star witness pleaded guilty to attempted manslaughter weeks after Davis' trial (for the shooting of a young man and a toddler). During Davis' trial, he told the jury there were no incentives for his testimony. After Davis' trial, this witness had his criminal charges reduced. For his serious crime, the sentence imposed was forty-four months. The defense interprets this as an undisclosed deal. Attorney Justin Caine Harrell, a graduate of Loyola University New Orleans College of Law with a LL.M. from George Washington University Law School finds himself engaged in a fight again a machine with an extended battery life.

Harrell, through an impassioned 2019 post-conviction application, argues:

> From its opening remarks to its final salvo at closing, the State made every attempt to create an atmosphere of fear, intolerance, xenophobia, and prejudice. The State displayed 'gangsta' rap and hip-hop lyrics outside of their musical or cultural context, hashtags, Instagram post, and other accoutrement of social media in an attempt to alienate the jury and *otherize* Petitioner, transmuting her into a violent, racialized, one-dimensional stereotype. The State admitted photographs of Petitioner...The relevance of these images was clear...folks who listen to violent rap lyrics are violent criminals themselves much in the same way that fans of horror movies are naturally inclined to be axe-wielding homicidal maniacs.[49]

In their response and opposition to Davis' post-conviction application, prosecutors deny a secret deal. They reason the plea bargain to be routine and not evidence of any misconduct. Their filing fails to offer an explanation for the sentencing mercy that the star witness received. In 2020, a court ruled against Davis on all matters. That judgment determined that: (1) the recantation from the witness was not persuasive enough to establish that no reasonable juror would have convicted had they known this information; (2) Davis didn't prove that the star witnesses' testimony was false or that the state colluded to facilitate false testimony; and, (3) Davis didn't prove the admission of the social media and rap lyrics produced a faulty outcome. I remain convinced that Davis, like so many other captives of the carceral state, is a victim of hierarchical, impersonal, empathy-lacking "justice."

One of the most immediate problems with this growing practice is the way it allows social media posts and rap lyrics–many times written long before a crime or removed in time from the crime or not authored by the accused–to be admitted into evidence as relevant to the crime at issue. In instances, there is a potential that the prejudicial effect is simply too great.[50] Evidentiary rules require evidence to be reliable and relevant to the crime at hand before it is shown to a jury. Judges are the interpreters of what is reliable and relevant. In many courts, the scales tip in favor of, not only allowing this content in, but also in allowing it to be presented to the jury as proof of criminal act and not as art. Evidentiary concerns are not the only problem. There are others.

When it disturbed longstanding precedent to end the practice of imposing death sentences on those who committed crimes under the age of eighteen, the SCOTUS did so upon the recognition that there are significant differences between youth and adult decision-making. *Roper v. Simmons* explained:

> [A]s any parent knows and as the scientific and sociological studies... tend to confirm, '[a] lack of maturity and an underdeveloped sense of responsibility are found in youth more often than in adults and are more understandable among the young. These qualities often result in impetuous and ill-considered actions and decisions....' It has been noted

> that 'adolescents are overrepresented statistically in virtually every category of reckless behavior.' The second area of difference is that juveniles are more vulnerable or susceptible to negative influences and outside pressures, including peer pressure.... The third broad difference is that the character of a juvenile is not as well formed as that of an adult. The personality traits of juveniles are more transitory, less fixed... The susceptibility of juveniles to immature and irresponsible behavior means 'their irresponsible conduct is not as morally reprehensible as that of an adult.'

The use of these rap lyrics and social media posts fail to account for lapses in judgment that are synonymous with the age group. It also ignores cultural norms. There is a thirst to be social media famous and many compete for the crown though posts and hashtags that stand out. In fact, this is exactly what social media marketing executives advise if you want to be a social media celebrity. This practice ignores this cultural reality.

An additional problem is how it assumes the, often Black, rapper could not possibly be creative. It assumes that an artist could not possibly be using the songwriting process to communicate or release pain. This furthers the use of racial stereotypes. Additionally, the study of speech is highly specialized. The enslaved brought their culture and language to America. They were prevented from communicating in their native tongue. As a survival tool, those ancestors developed speech patterns. Linguistic experts on pragmatics and discourse analysis have a specialized skill set. Engaging in such scholarly pursuits leads to enlightenment about the way rap, as an artform, specifically calls for the use of wordplay and exaggeration.

It equips one to recognize that, in rap, the speaker is often a narrator (and not one making a confession) and that the artist is, often, the equivalent of a fiction writer. They are also qualified to provide credible testimony on ethnic dialect, speaker meaning and language in the context of out-of-court statements. Allowing a person with no formal credentials, no publications and no grounds for the conclusion they assert to represent to a jury that they are an authority on art forms or speech patterns associated with communities of color delegitimizes certain speech patterns and the study thereof.

The practice also undermines First Amendment protections and injects bias in the trial process. Often, this is done in trials involving people of color. The imagery of Blacks associated with nefarious or criminal activity is rooted in the post-emancipated days when the Black criminal was made by law to sustain the convict leasing system in the state. The imagery survived the era. The use of these images and unrelated rap lyrics is done in an effort to subtly inject race, bias and stereotypes into the deliberation process, a process that, according to the research, is already contaminated with race and bias.

Research shows that this has an influence on jury outcomes. One study concluded that defendants who were associated with negative rap lyrics were seen as more likely to have committed a crime (a murder, in his study) than those defendants who were not presented as having authored any rap lyrics.[51] Prosecutors who do this, simultaneously, promote the continuation of a supremist structure by relegating Blacks to an unequal and inferior position in an unbalanced power dynamic.

In doing so, they successfully inflame racial sensibilities to obtain convictions when convictions should never be the ends sought. Public safety should be. *The Model Rules of Professional Conduct* places upon prosecutors a heightened duty of approaching this work as "ministers of justice."[52] Doing less creates a public safety problem because convicting the wrong person leaves the guilty person amongst the public. This is not to suggest that the mentioned parties wouldn't have been convicted without this "evidence." It is simply to expose the way the unnecessary and reckless infusion of race in a process that always leans in the direction against justice when a person of color is involved and to question how this cocktail might prompt verdicts that are not accurate or reliable.

This assessment must not stop at the offending prosecutors and the judiciary. It must extend to those who are duty-bound to exercise oversight. Conversations with lawyers who have invoked the disciplinary process in cases alleging prosecutorial misconduct capture problems at the onset of the process. Many have encountered difficulty accomplishing a finding of clear and convincing evidence of misconduct at the initial Office of Disciplinary Counsel (ODC) stage. They also reveal that, when cases make their way to the hearing committee, disciplinary board, appeal stage or the Supreme Court–no matter the stage–when considered holistically, the results have been shockingly disappointing. An inspection of some of these complaints are elucidating. Let's first consider a case that went through all stages of the process and, in the end, resulted in discipline.

In 2005, a prosecutor who suppressed information favorable to the accused in a capital case was disciplined. That discipline was not the result of agreement at all stages of the process. The ODC initially dismissed the complaint. An appeal by the complainant forced action and the hearing committee heard the matter only to recommend that formal charges be dismissed. It took an objection from ODC to move the case forward. ODC put up another fight against the disciplinary board who determined that the prosecutor technically violated the rules, but found that no discipline was appropriate. In *In re Jordan*, the Supreme Court concluded that prosecutor Roger Jordan knowingly withheld information. It imposed discipline, but a victory lap is premature. The convicted man Shareef Cousins, the source of the complaint, got what we can all agree was discipline. He was sent to death row at the age of seventeen. Meanwhile the "disciplined" prosecutor received a suspended sentence.

Justice Bernette Johnson concurred (that evidence was withheld intentionally) and dissented (relative to the sentence imposed). She explained, "In determining whether respondent caused an actual injury...our focus should be on the unnecessary and unlawful suffering of the wrongfully convicted...not just the reversal of the wrongfully imposed sentence...loss of a liberty interest is more valuable than financial loss or injury to one's credit, I would impose an actual period of suspension."[53] In 2022, a complaint against this same prosecutor was pending in connection with the role he played in convicting Robert Jones, another entry on Louisiana's growing list of exonerees. A cycle of repeat offenders has become the norm.

The late John Thompson's case illustrates how this repeat offender syndrome works. James "Jim" Williams participated in Thompson's 1985 prosecution. After eighteen years of wrongful incarceration, Thompson was exonerated. Prosecutor Williams was involved in the 1984 trial of Curtis Kyles. Kyles was exonerated from a death sentence after five trials and fourteen years in custody, but only after he got help from the SCOTUS.[54] Louisiana courts permitted this.[55]

In reviewing that case, some SCOTUS justices described the prosecutor's transgressions as "blatant and repeated" and remarked that "cases in which the record reveals so many instances of the state's failure to disclose exculpatory evidence are extremely rare."[56] Williams is featured in a national publication with a model electric chair displayed on his desk. Taped to the seat of the chair are photos of five Black men sent to death row (all of whom were later released after courts found improprieties).

In this next instance, the complaint never made it past go. Attorney Lawrence "L.T." Dupre III filed a complaint against prosecutors Hugo Hollard and Thomas Block in connection with the previously discussed *Louisiana v. David Brown* prosecution. The ODC opened an investigation, but later dismissed the complaint so it never got pass the initial step in the process. Though less than the desired result, then Chief Disciplinary Counsel Charles B. Plattsmier did extend the courtesy of a detailed reply. In his February 29, 2016, reply, Attorney Plattsmier openly acknowledged that the ODC's investigation determined, as alleged, that the two prosecutors did not turn over a recorded statement to the defense.

Plattsmier continued, "there is significant debate across the country…[as to]whether…Rule 3.8(d) [which explains the special responsibilities of a prosecutor] is 'co-extensive' with *Brady* such that showing of 'materiality to outcome' must be shown or whether the 'materiality to outcome' is not a component of the ethical consideration." He then stated that the ODC's position on the matter is "that 3.8(d) does not incorporate the 'materiality to outcome' considerations…."[57] Mr. Plattsmier ended by reserving the right to reopen the matter should a different ruling relevant to the analysis be handed down.

In this next example, the complaint that Attorney Ben Cohen filed against former New Orleans prosecutor Eusi Phillips made it to the end of the process, but discipline was not recommended. The complaint followed a discovery that former New Orleans prosecutor Phillips withheld the fact that incentives were offered in exchange for the testimony of two inmates who testified at trial as prosecution witnesses.[58] The ODC brought charges that the disciplinary board's hearing committee recommended be dismissed. In 2020, the Louisiana Supreme Court dismissed the case, but some judges did not agree with that decision. Justices Weimer and Boddie were of the position that the matter should be remanded to the disciplinary board for further action.

Justice Bernette Johnson also wanted the matter remanded to the disciplinary board. She explained, "We have a duty to use our lawyer disciplinary system to ensure fundamental fairness for defendants and prevent repeated constitutional violations by prosecutors."[59] Johnson continued, "If we have trepidation about disciplining prosecutors whose deliberate misconduct sends people to jail, we have abdicated our responsibility." In the Michael Williams case, the Louisiana Supreme Court had an opportunity to reverse course and send a message to prosecutors that they, too, must play by the rules to ensure justice and fairness.

Williams spent sixteen years in prison before evidence discrediting the state's only witness surfaced from the prosecutor's file. Once the witness' inconsistent statements came to light, the charge against Williams was dismissed and he was freed. Williams' attorney urged the ODC to hold the prosecutor Ken Dohre accountable for his misconduct. The Hearing Committee recognized the grave injustice caused by Dohre and suspended him from practice of law for a year and a day. Dohre appealed to the Attorney Disciplinary Board. The Supreme Court concluded the matter should be dismissed.[60] Only Justice Jefferson Hughes dissented.

Attorney Richard Davis, legal director at the IPNO, earned his Master of Law degree from Loyola University New Orleans. Despite them being very time-consuming endeavors, he has filed disciplinary complaints over a course of years because he sees them as one of the only possible ways of trying to hold prosecutors that misuse their power to account. But he admits his efforts have so far produced dismal results. "In the last five years I have filed nine bar complaints against prosecutors that contributed to wrongful convictions and, while all of them are still pending, none of them have yet led to a prosecutor being charged with misconduct," says Davis. "For several of the complaints, the ODC dismissed the complaints without investigation and it took the Louisiana Supreme Court to reinstate them. The current disciplinary process has utterly failed to hold lawless prosecutors to account," he continued.

Because of immunity protections and obstacles set by prior court rulings, courts are usually not able to resolve these types of cases. That is why a legitimate disciplinary process is so crucial. Reginald Adams is one of the few victims of prosecutorial misconduct to achieve a favorable outcome through litigation. His case underscores the central issues that lie at the heart of this problem. Adams was twice convicted of murder. Ronald Bodenheimer led the prosecution in the first trial. Bodenheimer followed the predictable pedigree. He ascended to a judgeship. After his release, Adams sued. Amongst other things, the suit accused Bodenheimer of withholding evidence helpful to the defense.

During those proceedings, Bodenheimer arrogantly marched into court and said he was immune from suit. He never denied what he was accused of. He wanted the law, the same law that held Adams accountable for something he did not do, to shield him from accountability for what he did do. The suit ultimately settled. The court placed the settlement under seal. The law allowed the world to see Adams cast in the light of a murderer. And it held him very accountable. The same law protected the reputation of Bodenheimer and shielded him from any real level of accountability.

Later, Bodenheimer had the gall to demand reimbursement for the legal fees he incurred defending himself against the allegations Adams made. This sense that judicial spaces are playgrounds or sporting venues is not something most Blacks identify with, whether they are lawyers or lay persons. His character issues that the disciplinary process did not address continued as is often the case. Bodenheimer was eventually sent to prison after being convicted of accepting bribes and other charges.

Adams was left to try to reassemble his life after thirty-four years of wrongful conviction.

A Louisiana prosecutor having Jim Crow era signs signifying segregated restrooms in a building he owned and frequented has been viewed as inconsequential.[61] A Louisiana prosecutor objecting to the removal of Confederate monuments outside of courthouses has been viewed as inconsequential.[62] Elected district attorneys using unauthorized subpoenas to compel witness attendance at pre-trial interviews, complete with the threats of fines and imprisonment have not evoked any consequences.[63] For Renata Singleton, a victim of domestic violence, the threat became real. She was jailed for five days on a $100,000 bond after she ignored two of the fake subpoenas. In the end, her punishment was harsher than the defendant in her case.

In an effort to address abuses associated with material witness warrants, legislation was enacted in 2019. It requires prosecuting agencies to report, on an annual basis, the number of material witness warrants sought and executed.[64] Data provided by Jim Craft, director of the Louisiana Commission on Law Enforcement and Administration of Criminal Justice, in the summer of 2022 shows: (1) for 2020, at least seven parishes disregarded the law and did not submit the data; and, (2) for 2021, at least twenty-four parishes disregarded the law and did not submit the data. The law doesn't include a penalty for noncompliance.

In light of what this book has so far revealed, Jena 6 member turned attorney Theo Shaw challenges change agents to embrace a more expansive definition of "wrongful conviction," which is often associated with being proven innocent of the crime that resulted in a conviction. Shaw contends that "an excessive sentence" is a form of wrongful conviction because an excessive sentence remands a person to custody for the time needed to redress their wrongful acts plus additional time beyond that. When a person remains in custody longer than best practices suggests or longer than needed to protect the public from harm, Shaw feels this is analogous to holding the body of a person who does not owe a debt to society.

The view from the bench is not exactly picturesque. On a sweltering 2023 summer day, defense attorney Ryan K. Thompson entered a Louisiana court dressed in his Sunday best. Thompson was present in court that day to delicately accuse the court that summoned his client in to answer for being a law breaker of breaking the law itself. When called, Thompson cited legislation that allows for a grand jury venire to be set aside when some great wrong that causes irreparable injury to the defendant is committed.[65] The injury, according to Thompson, involved the routine and systematic exclusion of a certain group from East Baton Rouge Parish grand juries. Thompson explained, with great diplomacy, the scientific harms of excluding groups from grand jury service and he delicately cited law indicating that the accused is entitled to a selection process free of systematic exclusion of identifiable groups.

Before Thompson could proceed with a recitation of the witnesses he was prepared to present in order to establish that people with felony convictions were, for months, excluded from grand jury service after the Louisiana legislature changed the law to allow them to participate, the judge told him it wouldn't be necessary to call those witnesses.[66] The judge's response to the charge encapsulates the many shortcomings, failures, defects and dysfunctions that present themselves in Louisiana's legal system.

Judge Eboni Johnson Rose replied: "You didn't even need to call anybody because I know that the rules weren't being followed....."[67] In the next breath, she denied the defense motion, reasoning no law had been broken by a court who did not follow a law because they did not know it existed. Meanwhile, the law prevents citizens from circumventing accountability by asserting ignorance of the law. It seems the court eventually took measures to follow the law once it learned of it, but what about the people harmed by its failures in the interim?

Louisiana does more than exploit Black bodies at the jury stage or in custodial settings. The entire judicial system is infected with this poisonous aim.[68] Louisiana employs a non-unified court system to "fund" its judicial branch.[69] Under such a system, the State provides limited funding for the various arms of the justice system. The lower courts–district, city, parish, and municipal–are funded through multiple sources, including a limited appropriation by the state legislature; funds from local governing bodies; self-generated revenues from fines, fees and court costs; and, federal grants. This funding structure incentivizes players in the carceral state to create revenue streams that their budgets, desires and future political dynasties become dependent on.

It also serves as another pathway for crime, incarceration and profit to remain intertwined. Vendors depend on people in custody to buy music, tablets and commissary items and use the paid phone and email services. Courts depend on fines and fees generated by crime. For-profit prisons depend on bodies to house. Free and low-cost labor from those in custody is also profitable. With this many people profiting from crime and punishment, there is greater opposition to abolishing the carceral state or decarceration.

Another problem created by Louisiana's funding structure is that Louisiana's public defender system has been persistently underfunded. Louisiana's public defender offices are partially funded by local criminal fines and fees combined with a small portion from the state. This revenue structure results in the office's dependance on fluctuating and unreliable funding that is largely generated by traffic tickets and local court costs. Without an adequately funded public defender system, trial delays can occur and convictions and plea bargains can increase, all leading to mass incarceration.

A discussion of Louisiana's underfunded public defense system is enlightening:

> The state relies, in part, on a $45 fee attached to criminal convictions to fund public defense. Convictions—and therefore collection of the $45 conviction fee—have dropped 22 percent from where those collections were before the COVID-19 pandemic hit in 2020...The drop in convictions mean fewer conviction fees for public defenders...*if convictions don't pick up to at least pre-pandemic levels, the public defenders could end up as much as $5 million short of what they need to function*...Approximately three quarters of the public defenders' conviction fees actually come from traffic tickets....A relatively small portion of the revenue from the fee comes from criminal convictions

that are handed down in court—in part because people who are convicted of crimes and sent to prison often can't afford to pay their fees. [70]

The economically-challenged who depend on the state to furnish them with legal representation suffer under this justice algorithm. Since its inception, Louisiana's public defender system has been persistently underfunded due to reliance on an inadequate, unstable, and unreliable funding stream based primarily on traffic tickets and local court costs.

The district attorney of Calcasieu Parish is a perfect illustration of why the state's funding structure is, itself, an injustice. In the first of three revenue-generating schemes, district attorney John DeRosier allowed defendants to donate gift cards in lieu of performing community service. One account attributes a revenue increase "from...$182,000...to $5.9 million in 2017."[71] This same office used traffic citations as a way of generating income. In this instance, overtime was paid to some members of law enforcement as they wrote traffic citations. Instead of those citations being processed through the court where a considerable portion of the fine would have gone into the public defender budget, motorists were given a choice of paying the parish the cost of the ticket or having it dismissed by paying a fine to the district attorney's office. Predictably, payments to the parish decreased while payments to the district attorney's office increased.[72]

Diversion programs have become a part of routine operations. Mr. DeRosier's office also used the pretrial diversion program as a source of revenue. Consistent with most diversion programs, the one in Calcasieu Parish, afforded defendants arrested for minor offenses an opportunity to avoid charges if they satisfied certain conditions, such as completion of a class or counseling. Under Mr. DeRosier, the enrollment fee increased from $50.00 to $600.00.[73] This pretrial diversion program reportedly generated in excess of $300,000 in a single year.[74]

Housing inmates is another part of the fiscal windfall associated with corrections. "Louisiana is relatively unique in the U.S. for using local jails to house approximately 50% of people serving their state sentences."[75] "Jails and private operators receive a per diem per person per day, which cost the state approximately $175 million for fiscal year 2019-2020."[76] In the mid-1970s when the federal court wanted overcrowding addressed, sheriffs argued for a reduction in the size of Louisiana's prison population. At the time, DOC paid a per diem rate of only $4.50/day per prisoner. The greater dependency on local jails to house convicted people resulted in a per diem increase to $18.25 by 1980.

By 2022, the rate was $26.39 per prisoner, per day. Many sheriffs now drink the longer sentences and more incarceration Kool-Aid. Lengthy cooperation endeavors between DOC and sheriffs in various parishes exists. As of 2023, approximately 13,000 people serving state sentences in DOC's custody were housed in 104 local parish jails, at a cost of approximately $350,000 per day.[77] If anyone were in doubt about how attractive this arrangement is, they need only listen to Sheriff Steve Prator's public reaction to news that Louisiana's Justice Reinvestment Package was enacted with the hope of reducing Louisiana's prison population.[78]

Sheriff Prator told reporters: "In addition to the bad ones...they're releasing some good ones that we use every day to wash cars, to change oil in the cars, to cook in the kitchen, to do all that where we save money...they're going to let them out—the ones that we use in work release programs."[79]

Evidence of this fiscal dependence on mass incarceration presented itself again in 2022 when James "Jimmy" LeBlanc, Secretary of Louisiana's Department of Corrections, lent his support to Mister Coffee Bean, a program that would provide a pathway to reentry for low risk, low level, nonviolent inmates near completion of their sentences who had the will and aptitude to complete college coursework. Only justice-impacted persons recommended by the warden could participate in the program.

The program allowed the highly screened and most suitable justice-impacted participants to earn a bachelor's degree while in prison and become elementary school teachers and mentors for at-risk youth once they get out of prison. Once they earned their elementary education degrees, and passed their teacher certification exams, they would be paroled and placed in the most at-risk elementary schools in their states to serve as teachers and role models. After LDOC asked wardens and sheriffs around the state to recommend inmates for the program, it was soon ended because of their opposition.

Sheriff Prator was an outspoken opponent of this program too. The labor and financial dependency built into the criminal legal system prompts resistance to Black bodies leaving state control, much like there was resistance to them escaping the controls of the plantation. What could be more convincing than the words of the Chief Justice of the state's supreme court?

In her 2018 State of the Judiciary address, then Justice Bernette Johnson said candidly:

> Rather than using state funds to fully fund our Judiciary, we push much of that obligation off onto local governmental entities. Those, in turn, pass much of that unfunded mandate onto civil litigants and criminal defendants in the form of court costs, fees, and fines. These user fees help pay for courthouses and salaries of court clerks, as well as district attorneys, sheriffs, and public defenders....*Let us be candid: Innocence, though presumed by our system, is currently bad for our bottom line.*[80]

Four years later, Justice John Weimer assumed the role of Chief Justice. Members of the legislature heard the same tune sung in a different pitch during his 2022 State of the Judiciary Address:

> Louisiana's system of court costs and fees is an immensely significant issue that needs attention....We cannot afford to fund our judicial system strictly on the backs of the impoverished. Additionally, for far too long our state has shifted the costs of our state court system to local government and has done so with fines, fees, and costs to keep the system afloat....This system of funding is antiquated and does not ensure justice or equality statewide.[81]

It would be an exercise in dishonesty to suggest that a single person or group is responsible for all wrongs in the legal system. There is blame to go around. The late forensic pathologist Dr. Paul Anthony McGarry is a good point of illustration. In 2011, ProPublica, PBS "Frontline" and NPR spent a year looking at the nation's 2,300 coroner and medical examiner offices. *Medical Examiners In America: A Dysfunctional System* found that many pathologists working in the busiest morgues in the nation are not board certified in forensic pathology and some are not doctors. The investigation found that "Blunders by doctors in America's morgues have put innocent people in prison cells, allowed the guilty to go free, and left some cases so muddled that prosecutors could do nothing."

The findings about Dr. McGarry were chilling. They said, "a review of medical records, court documents and legal transcripts shows McGarry has made errors and oversights in autopsy after autopsy." A quick search of Louisiana criminal cases shows McGarry to have been a regular in Louisiana courtrooms during his lifetime. Astonishingly, many Louisiana *defense attorneys* routinely consented to his use as an expert and rarely ever questioned his capabilities.[82] McGarry's obituary touts of his three decades of work in multiple states on the Gulf Coast. There's more.

My review of transcripts shows *defense* attorneys physically present during proceedings, but silent while the wrong law was applied at sentencing. It reveals others who did not fully investigate leads or prepare a defense for a person on trial when there were police or medical reports, witnesses or other evidence that could have mitigated or exonerated the accused person. I uncovered a culture of "plea happy" *defense* attorneys who urge clients to enter plea bargains in an attempt to minimize their workloads.

The coup de grâce of my findings was the proud, smiling, white face in a East Baton Rouge Parish Public Defender's 2022 Facebook post that read: "Saturday with our young Confederates...The South will rise again...Port Hutson/Civil War Battle." The post shows several images of him, a female and five small children dressed in red, white and blue and smiling proudly at a Confederate memorial event a few days before he would appear in court as appointed counsel to an indigent defendant in a primarily Black district.

Like other aspects of the carceral state, the custodial conditions in Louisiana have been uncomfortably consistent over the years. In 1975, a federal judge ruled that state corrections officials violated a number of constitutional rights. That judge explained that the conditions at Angola, "shock the conscience of any right-thinking person" and that "the State authorities, who have the power to do so, are either failing or refusing to take the necessary steps to correct these conditions."[83] By 1977, there was a federal ruling validating inmate claims that racial discrimination against the justice-impacted was practiced; that conditions violated the Eight and Fourteenth Amendments; and, that violations of the fire and sanitation codes existed. In *Hayes v. Williams*, the federal court concluded that conditions at Angola violated state law and the U.S. Constitution. The ruling did not inspire change.

More declarations of constitutional violations followed. In the late 1990s, the DOJ sued the state over allegations that ranged from physical abuse to excessive use of handcuffs and solitary confinement. The 2008 allegation of inmates in the Orleans Parish Prison (OPP) were so serious, the DOJ decided it needed to intervene in the litigation. The justice-impacted complained of deficiencies in: prisoner safety from physical and sexual assaults; medical and mental health care; suicide prevention; environmental and life safety; and, limited English proficiency services for Spanish-speaking prisoners. The expert testimony offered during the litigation was jarring.

Manuel Romero, an expert in jail administration, with a particular emphasis on security, staffing, and use of force, concluded that OPP is "totally dysfunctional in terms of overall security," and that it is an "unsafe facility for both staff and inmates."[84] Jeffrey Schwartz, an expert in security and operations of jails and prisons who has worked with more than forty of the fifty state departments of corrections and toured hundreds of prisons and jails, concluded that, in over 35 years of working with and reviewing jails and prisons, "OPP is the worst jail I've ever seen," and "it is likely the worst large city jail in the United States."[85]

Schwartz described an "extraordinary and horrific situation," in which OPP is "plagued" by "suicides and other in-custody deaths, rapes and other sexual assaults, stabbings, and severe beatings."[86] The evidence also supported a finding of severe deficiencies in medical and mental health care, environmental deficiencies and staffing shortages at OPP. In short, it was determined that the conditions at the New Orleans jail were unconstitutional. *Jones v. Gusman* resulted in a consent decree and federal oversight from 2012 until 2022.[87]

A 2013 suit alleging the excessive heat at Angola was exacerbating existing illnesses forced officials to stop violating the constitution.[88] In 2018, justice-impacted people entered the federal court claiming Angola provided constitutionally inadequate healthcare. The undisputed testimony revealed that: Angola's medical staff included five doctors and one nurse practitioner to service a total population of 6400 men; each of the doctors had been disciplined by the Louisiana State Board of Medical Examiners prior to being employed at Angola; each of the doctors had a restricted license or was restricted to practicing in institutional settings at the time they were hired by Angola, but some completed requirements imposed by the Medical Board and were no longer under restriction.[89]

The court concluded that Angola lacked the infrastructure necessary to provide a constitutionally adequate health care system for patients with serious medical needs, including a lack of adequate organizational structure, credentialing and peer review processes, health care policies and procedures, clinic space, and a quality control program.[90] "Under [Burl] Cain's leadership, prisoners reported endless experiences of degradation and cruelty: a man denied access to a specialist for four years while his throat cancer advanced; a man denied medical attention four times during a stroke, which left him blind and paralyzed; a blind man denied even a cane for 16 years."[91]

By 2016, a light shined past the cells and upon the internal culture. Warden Cain, the celebrated plantation Jesus, resigned in disgrace after "The Advocate exposed a series of questionable arrangements involving prison labor and private real estate deals with relatives and friends of favored inmates."[92] By May 2020, the Mississippi Department of

Corrections had employed Cain as a commissioner, describing him as a "transformative and innovative" leader while at Angola, highlighting another shortcoming in many Southern criminal legal systems.[93]

This type of inbreeding (where family is hired, retained and promoted whether qualified or not) and recycling (where misfits are moved like chess pieces and given new assignments instead of terminated) remains a current obstacle inside Louisiana's detention facilities. This creates a culture of corruption that disregards best practices and, often, law. A 2021 review of Angola's internal operations exposed racist hiring and pay practices. In a diverse environment where roughly half of the LDOC employees are Black, Blacks remain deeply underrepresented at the highest levels of leadership.[94]

It seems "most Black employees hold relatively low-ranking jobs, leaving the top spots for their white counterparts."[95] Little has changed with the passage of time, making the fight for jury justice even more pressing. Juries are the barrier between these conditions and freedom. For that to be achieved, race and profits must no longer be proxies for incarceration.

In January 2023, the DOJ determined that the LDOC routinely confines people in its custody past the dates when they are legally entitled to be released from custody, in violation of the Fourteenth Amendment. The DOJ determined that DOC knew of its over detention problem and failed to take adequate measures to ensure timely releases of incarcerated individuals for at least ten years.

Back in 1804, Governor William C.C. Claiborne toured the newly purchased territory. When he made his way to the New Orleans jail, he made a nearly identical allegation.He communicated to the U.S. Secretary of State the high number of prisoners who had been held from "ten to thirteen years on suspicion of crimes which it does not appear they were ever convicted."[96] Dates have passed, names have changed, but little else is different in all these years.

I even uncovered a case of a man who had a stroke many years before he was granted parole. After that stroke, he worked doing physical labor around the prison for years. He was released to a halfway house where he was to remain as a condition of parole. Once the halfway house learned of his prior stroke, they concluded, without consultation of a medical professional, that he could not meet their labor demands. They refused to keep him and they refused to release him so they took him back to prison and dropped him off. No one at the prison attempted to communicate that he was capable of performing physical labor and had for many years after the stroke. No one at the prison was motivated to assist him in finding a new location so, as of the time of this writing, he languishes in purgatory.

One of the trademark's of Louisiana's legal system is the way it manifests a general disregard for human life . This lack of concern for humanity becomes involuntary when equity, inclusion, belonging and human dignity are not priorities and where racial hierarchies exist. This explains the longevity of this type of conduct in, of all places, a professed "pro-life" state.

In 1913, Henry Ford introduced the assembly line to the country. An assembly line is a manufacturing process that constructs a final product more efficiently by adding components sequentially. Each worker or machine on the line performs a specific task then the product progresses along the line for the next task to be performed. Eventually, the process ends with the creation of a product, such as a cell phone, a piece of furniture or an automotive part. Because of the way assembly lines optimize time and labor, they revolutionized production in the U.S.

When quantified, the composite happens to be a legal system that operates much like a legal assembly line where production is swift, ritualistic, void of a personalized quest for truth or justice or sense of fair play and or a respect for sanctity of life. The progression of lapses discussed have given way to a "system" that currently harms–not by color alone. The abridged criminal appellate review process and financial incentives built in, eventually obliterated the racial lines that once penetrated the legal system. Seeing poor whites or poor people of color crushed by the scales of justice is no longer remarkable.

For those who have the misfortune of finding themselves in the grips of the current legal system, they can experience the same systemic failures that have been born of all these years of misdeeds. Louis Schexnayder's case illustrates this very point. Schexnayder is a white man who was tried by a non-unanimous jury. Two jurors voted to acquit him. He was still convicted and he was sentenced to a life sentence without parole. In absence of a post-conviction lawyer, Schexnayder filed his own appeal, which was denied. Had Jerrold Peterson, central staff director at the Fifth Circuit Court of Appeal, not written a suicide letter before he killed himself in his office, Mr. Schexnayder likely would not have known he was getting the automated "justice" that is frequently administered in the state.

That suicide letter detailed a secret practice that resolved cases without a judge ever reviewing them.[97] The cases were covertly reviewed by staff attorneys who did not have the option of granting relief to justice-impacted people seeking appeals without legal representation.[98] They only had a choice of several grounds upon which to deny the appeals. The publicity of the matter did no good. The state's high court's solution was to return all these cases (nearly 300 appeals) to the very judges who concocted the scheme. Schexnayder's appeal was denied again.

Furnell Severin, another justice-impacted victim of the scheme, sued and was denied relief against the judges. The court reminded him that, "judges enjoy absolute judicial immunity from lawsuits that cannot be overcome by allegations of bad faith or malice."[99] Rendell Washington, another justice-impacted victim, asked the court for a declaration that the judges violated his constitutional rights by failing to properly review his writ application. His request was denied also. The court said his request for declaratory relief was "nothing more than a veiled attempt to challenge the validity of his... confinement."[100] The system that failed to follow the proper procedure admonished him for not following the proper procedure. This hypocrisy is reoccurring.

When Jamaal Reine complained to an appellate court that he was sentenced under a law that he was never charged with breaking, the appellate court said it could not help because he did not follow the proper procedure by raising an objection at the time of sentencing or through a subsequent motion.[101] In a lone dissent, Judge John Michael Guidry called that reasoning into question:

> Our review for error in this case is pursuant to La.C.Cr.P. art. 920,
> which provides that the only matters to be considered on appeal are
> errors designated in the assignments of error and 'error that is
> discoverable by a mere inspection of the pleadings and proceedings and
> without inspection of the evidence.'...The sentence imposed on remand
> is illegal...[T]he sentence imposed by the trial court should be vacated,
> and this matter should be remanded to the trial court for resentencing
> on each count. [102]

"Reasoning by hypocrisy" entered the jury box.

While white people are amongst the ranks of Louisiana's incarcerated citizens, they are not overrepresented. They are statistically less likely to be stopped, arrested, convicted of sentenced to extremes.

During the many conversations I had as I worked on this book, the appeal that I heard consistently and most often was: "don't forget about the victims." Stiles P. King's conviction affords me a unique opportunity to honor those requests. Stiles is white. In 2016, he was sentenced to twelve years in prison after being convicted of carnal knowledge of a juvenile and child pornography. This makes him a sex offender under Louisiana law, a designation that won't wash off no matter how hard he scrubs.

By the summer of 2024, Stiles' "victims" were no longer the freshman high school girls they were when the video of two freshman performing oral sex on a high school senior found its way to the high school principal's hands. They are adults with intact memories who give a very different account of the person prosecutors portrayed as a sexual predator. Stiles and "the victims" all agree on the facts that led to Stiles being deemed a sex offender and having to exchange his comfortable middle-class existence for a prison cell.

Stiles was a high school senior at the time of his 2016 arrest. He was dating a freshman at his same high school. His at-the-time-girlfriend decided to record a sexually explicit video and send it to Stiles as a birthday gift. Stiles is experiencing hard labor Louisiana style for doing what many of us do when we get a treasured birthday surprise. He shared his gift. That was not a good choice. Four years after his convictions for carnal knowledge of a juvenile and child pornography, three victims gave sworn statements in support of his release.

In 2021, Victim A.O. swore under oath:

> Our relationship was consensual...I do not think any of us understood the consequences...A lot of 18-and 19-year-old boys had sexual relationships with girls who were freshman and sophomores in high school. We would always hear about underaged girls sending naked pictures and then the older guys sharing them....I think Stiles lacked guidance in dating, but prison is not the answer for someone who may not be a good boyfriend....

In 2021, Victim P.S. swore under oath:

> While we were in school, we always heard about girls at our school taking naked pictures of themselves and sending them out to other guys. The guys would then send the nudes out to all of their friends. We would, also, hear about other girls and guys recording sexual acts with each other. It was something that everyone was doing. It was the cool thing to do....The video [redaction] and I recorded with Stiles was consensual. I was upset when I heard the video was leaked, but I never wanted Stiles to go to jail for something we all played a part in.

In 2021, Victim S.S. swore under oath:

> Stiles and I dated while we were in high school. He was a senior and I was a freshman....freshman girls were always chasing seniors. Many underaged girls sent nudes to upperclassman guys...the guys would gloat about the nudes and leak them to friends...We are meant to do dumb things and make mistakes when we are kids, but prison is not the answer for that. With mine and Stile's relationship, I went after him... the first night we hung out, I had my friend distract my brother so I could sneak out of the house. I left the house with no pants on that night, just an oversized sweatshirt on...I knew what I wanted from him. I made the move on Stiles....With the video me and [redacted] recorded

with Stiles, that was my Valentines Day gift to him. I came up with the idea to have a threesome with Stiles, but [redaction] did not want to hurt our friendship. So, she and I decided to give him a blowjob instead...My thoughts were what boy would turn down a video of two hot girls giving him a blowjob. None of us, including Stiles, knew what could have happened to him had people found out we recoded that....

In 2021, Victim T.C. swore under oath:

> The police made me feel bombarded. They put me on blast in front of
> my family and embarrassed me in front of my mom....I felt forced to talk
> to police when I never wanted this...Stiles never should have gone to
> prison for doing something the majority of teenagers do...Junior and
> senior guys were always dating freshmen girls and having sex with
> them. Naked pictures of underaged girls, mainly freshman, were always
> floating around.... Someone even made an Instagram account where
> freshman and sophomore nudes were posted. No one got in trouble for
> this. The Instagram account got reported and taken down...Stiles is not
> a child predator...He was just doing what we were all doing, and at that
> time, none of us, including Stiles, were mature enough to understand
> the situation.

Stiles' case includes an additional victim whose name has been completely omitted from all official case records. Her name is Juliane E. King. King, a former high school teacher and coach, abandoned her career plans after the state trafficked her baby bother. King entered law school for two reasons: to free her brother and to change the law so this can't happen again. King earned her Juris Doctor as magna cum laude from the SULC in record time then passed the state bar on her first attempt. She is no longer Stiles' sister alone. She is his lawyer too.

Attorney King is adamant that "no high school student who engages in non-violent, consensual sexual activity with other high school students should ever face criminal punishment." King feels Louisiana's law should account for the obvious differences between high school students engaging in sexual activity with each other and an adult taking sexual advantage of a minor. King feels this conviction and Stiles' continued confinement is an indictment upon the entire legal system. I concur.

A credible justice system is not one that is activated for deployment at the smell of a bad decision or at the sight of one being impacted by life's challenges, such as houselessness, substance abuse or mental illness. Instead, a credible legal system should be efficient, consistent, impartial, transparent, accountable, assessable and used in moderation. It should issue customized outcomes that are restorative in nature so it leaves the person it touches better off and not worse. It should not respect racial hierarchies. It should operate with human rights tenants at its core. Profits and finances should be a nonfactor in the justice outcomes. Additionally, it should promote confidence among members of the public and it should display a reverence for the rule of law. Stiles and everyone else mentioned got far less than this when they made contact with Louisiana's legal system.

It's safe to say dismal has turned dire. Following the proposal of the Louisiana Justice Reinvestment Task Force, in 2017, Louisiana Governor John Bel Edwards signed ten bills projected to reduce the prison population by ten percent, and state officials agreed to reinvest 70 percent of the savings into reentry programs for youth and adults. At the time, the state was spending $700 million annually on corrections. As of 2022, the effort was reportedly yielding favorable results and the state's prison population was believed be declining.[103] However, those results did not end Louisiana's reputation as "one of the most notoriously punitive states in the country."[104]

Nor has it removed Louisiana from the top rankings when it comes to highest incarceration rates amongst states.[105] Perhaps that's because immigrant detention, a growing industry that is thriving in rural parishes, is not included in that count. "The state's population is roughly 62% white and 33% Black, but those numbers nearly flip behind bars, where 34% of inmates are white and 64% Black."[106] "The greater the sentence, the higher the disproportionate impact on Black people."[107] "When examining the population serving life sentences (or equivalent), 73.4 % of the population is Black compared to 26% white."[108]

In its 2023 report, *Out of Balance*, the Southern Poverty Law Center's Action Fund observed, "Although people of color are grossly overrepresented at every point of the criminal legal system in Louisiana, white individuals hold the power to influence Black citizens' interactions with racial profiling, criminalization, and incarceration." According to *Out of Balance*, "Of the 64 sheriffs across the state, only four (6%) are Black. Only 12% of the 42 district attorneys are Black. This is in a state where almost a third of the population is Black." The report concluded that the "people being sentenced in Louisiana are 3.8 times as likely to be Black as white – even though 31.2% of the population is Black and 57.9% white."

A synthesis, analysis, and interpretation of the outcomes presented in this chapter suggests that Louisiana's criminal legal system is the closet that stores the baggage of the past eras. Speed, bias, racism, caste, human exploitation[109] and capitalism were–over time, circumstances and through multiple players–hemmed into the fabric of the state's legal system. These inheritances have infected the state's legal system in such critical ways and places that outcomes lack reliability. The result is a people who have been walking on a treadmill for nearly one hundred and sixty years. And a system that now operates as if it were a legal assembly line.

By 2023, when Jeff Landry was elected governor, Louisiana remained a reflection of the country that has the "the highest incarceration rate in the world."[110] In 2023, Consistent with his campaign promises, the February 2024 special session was devoted to addressing crime. In his opening remarks, Governor Landry described Louisiana's sentencing schemes as lenient, the state's "post-conviction programs that feed recidivism by constantly returning un-reformed, un-repentant, and violent criminals to our neighborhoods" as "misguided" and he referred to the legal system as a "revolving door." He denounced good time as a reward that comes with "no effort" and described it as "a participation trophy for jail!"

In 2024, Governor Landry signed into law a tough-on-crime reform package that expands the permissible methods for executions, limits the use of post-conviction relief, reduces pardon, parole and good time release options, lowers the age for trying a person as an adults, increases certain sentences and grants unprecedented access to juvenile court records. 2024 headlines now describe Louisiana as "one of the toughest states in the nation on crime." Landry insists these steps will lead to greater public safety and less recidivism. As is often the case, science or data didn't drive this process. Law enforcement, prosecutors and crime victims seems to have served as the authorities.

Those devoted to the study of recidivism and public safety discourage the state and country's overreliance on incarceration. They lean in the direction of community-based sentences instead. They favor sentences that are not extreme, excessive or void of human rights protections and they advocate for addressing the conditions that create crime instead. They also feel that the only time incarceration can lead to rehabilitation is when meaningful programming and human rights principles are built into the design. Thanks to legislation signed by Governor Landry, Louisiana won't be meeting that need anytime soon.

New 2024 legislation prohibits "Louisiana or any agency, department, board, commission, political subdivision, governmental entity of the state, parish, municipality" from "enforcing or implementing any rule, regulation, policy, or mandate of any kind of the United Nations." Governor Landry's actions do align with the experts when it comes to reentry, however. Landry shares their view that reentry should be an option for those who prove deserving. He explained, "What we need is truth in sentencing that will incentivize inmates to complete certain re-entry programs, earn a GED, learn a job skill, and in doing so earn a reduction in sentence; preparing them to re-join society in a productive, safe, and responsible manner." After saying this, guess who he appointed to the Board of Pardons? None other than former Sheriff Steve Prator. The saga continues.

AFTERWORD

History, despite its wrenching pain, cannot be unlived, and if faced
with courage, need not be lived again.[1]

— MAYA ANGELOU

Non-unanimous juries needed to come to an end. When a system that
harms is destroyed, there is cause for jubilation. Nothing less is
warranted in this instance. But, in the case of race and juries in
Louisiana, there is a danger in not fully appreciating what was
accomplished. What was accomplished was a reform, not a
transformation. Transformation still awaits.

Over time, a lethal combination of deposits were made to Louisiana's
legal system: supremacy and racial hierarchies; Black Codes; convict
leasing; a non-unified court funding system; cash bail, non-unanimous
juries; long or mandatory sentencing schemes; incompetence and
inbreeding where employees are concerned; excessive use of habitual
offender laws; overuse of pretrial incarceration; restricting good time
credits; limiting releases through parole; not holding prosecutors who
engage in misconduct accountable, which allows them to wrongfully

convict more people; excluding crimes of violence from sentencing reform proposals; charging youth as adults; not acting on as many pardon and clemency requests as is in the public's interest; adopting national "tough of crime" and "the drug war propaganda"; not formulating meaningful responses to racism and/or bias on the part of those who hold discretionary power in the criminal justice system; and, the mindset to respond to every human shortcoming and transgression punitively and harshly.

These policies, customs, laws and beliefs interlock and overlap. This has produced a legal system wherein speed is its heart, profits are its soul, caste is its pulse and callousness is its aorta. Juries are not stand-alone institutions. They are components of this structurally unsound legal system. And that local justice system is a component of a Western system that is fundamentally flawed. As a result, Black juror suppression can no longer be viewed in isolation. How it overlaps with other systems to maintain white power and privilege and how it interfaces with systems that respond punitively to human shortcomings and transgressions must now become simultaneous considerations.

There is no intent to suggest that every person of color who interfaces with the carceral state is wronged or convicted. In some rare instances, Blacks have escaped the grips of the legal system. There are even slavery era accounts of this, such as the case of Jacob who was found not guilty of insurrection after the largest slave revolt in the state and nation[2] or the enslaved man Dick who was charged with "rebranding cattle" after he was accused of removing the name of the cattle's owners and replacing it with another name. A St. Landry Parish court acquitted Dick in 1816, at the height of slavery.[3]

Greater odds rest on Blacks being overpoliced, over sentenced, overcharged, over corrected, over fined or looking in the face of a legal system that is too often situationally impotent, such as it was with O'Neal Moore and Creed Rogers. O'Neal Moore and Creed Rogers, the first two Black Washington Parish sheriff's deputies, were shot during a patrol.[4] The bullet to his head killed Office Moore instantly. Officer Rogers was shot in the shoulder. The case against the white suspect, who was an active member of the KKK, was dropped. No one was ever held accountable.

A similar thing happened to some college students on SU's campus back in 1972. Students United wanted to be enriched by the unique possibilities that a HBCU could offer. They wanted agency in their educational experience, which translated into input on matters relative to student life, policy, hiring, retention and curricular. And they wanted the institution to direct resources toward meeting the needs of the Black community. Instead, a false narrative of them engaging in violent unrest and seizing buildings was promoted by officials.[5] It didn't matter that these students were making reasonable demands, particularly in light of the fact that many were veterans returning from service in the Vietnam War who felt, expecting rights at home, was a normal course after fighting for rights on foreign soil.

First, the perceived leaders of Students United were jailed and placed under civil orders that prevented them from returning to campus. Next, On November 16, 1972, law enforcement officials descended upon SU's Baton Rouge campus with a militarized response, killing some and injuring others. Then there's the countless numbers of public lynchings where perpetrators posed for celebratory photos, making apprehension easy. Arrests and prosecutions were rare. There are too many others to name.

For anyone inclined to exit this conversation dismissively, believing this is not your burden to bear because you don't live in Louisiana or have ties to the state, know that the *National* Association of Criminal Defense Lawyers (NACDL) refuses to use the word "justice" to describe criminal systems *in the country*. Instead, their mission statement now refers to "criminal *legal* systems."

NACDL's former Executive Director Norman Reimer explained that a realization about the injustice of the system prompted that shift:

> Society is . . . fallible. It has spawned a criminal legal system that is so flawed that we have stopped calling it a criminal justice system. It is an engine of oppression that denigrates humanity and the dignity of the

individual. It emphasizes harshness and vengeance over compassion. It focuses on revenge instead of redemption.[6]

If you desire better, don't stop here. Complete the series. Read my book, *Diversity in the Jury Box and Beyond: A Formula for Transforming Louisiana's Legal System* next. It unveils a plan for transforming Louisiana's legal system. After, I encourage you to read my book, *The Summons: Advocacy Insights for Systemic and Transformative Change*. It will aid you in doing the system change work that awaits.

When the Bambara people resisted enslavement and an oppressive legal system, resistance was a reflection of their "beliefs about how things should be, how society should work."[7] From their story, we learn that resistance "not only challenges a thing—it champions another thing."[8] Each member of the jury justice society accepted their summons to "champion another thing." Will you?

ACKNOWLEDGMENTS

Here and elsewhere, all acknowledgments are credited to the King and ruler of my life. I have lived a life a dependence on a God who has never failed me. In Jeremiah 1:5, he said, "Before I formed you in the womb I knew you, before you were born, I set you apart; I appointed you as a prophet to the nations." This book is a manifestation of that assignment. And this occasion requires a recognition that every challenge imaginable visited me as I wrote this book. Hurricane Ida left my spouse in the hospital and my home without Internet for months. It caused property damages to our vehicles and home and it forced a temporary relocation.

My teaching load changed every semester, causing already long workdays to be longer. Efforts to censure this book and books like it that discuss race or diversity presented themselves. Of all times, as I wrote this book, my Achilles tendon ruptured, causing a surgery and horrible recovery, which included four-months of limited mobility. During that recovery, a blood clot formed in my leg as I sat for long hours trying to finish this book. Not long after, my husband and I were infected with COVID-19. After months of blows came the knockout punch. Angola 3 member Albert Woodfox contracted COVID-19 also. Within two weeks, my dear friend was pronounced dead. August 4th will never be the same again. I don't know that I will ever recover from that loss.

Celebrating Albert's 71st Birthday in February

2018. Photo credit David Bell.

Angola 3 members Albert Woodfox and Herman Wallace (who died on October 4, 2013, two days after his release) taught me so many sage lessons in life, but, with their deaths, came some of the more profound ones. The first is the importance of completing the task assigned to you at birth (and not ignoring it upon the belief that someone else will do it). Additionally, it is to do it with all deliberate speed (because death comes life a thief in the night). Also, that God maintains power. He, no one else, is the taskmaster. Once your task is complete, there is no negotiating with him. He will have the last say. And, finally, to, in all things, put God front, middle and center (if you dare expect the same from him).

One of my last 2013 visits with Herman Wallace while he was still in custody and dying of cancer that was

ignored for many critical months.

Photo credit to the justice-impacted person who took the photo inside Elayn Hunt Correctional Center

Herman and Albert completed their respective tasks. They owed the world no more. I thank both for the final lessons, and I, with profound sadness, am forced to embrace the vision of both finally achieving something greater than release–freedom. This hindsight view of my last few years hopefully explains the imperative of this initial acknowledgement. My mere presence on this earth to see this book to completion is an act of Grace. I reverently acknowledge God before and above all else.

Agreeing to write a book under the circumstances that I wrote meant simultaneously agreeing to temporarily absent myself from the people and things that matter most. This project consumed the hours I was not teaching or sleeping. Having a support team in life is not something I take for granted. My team includes my two daughters and my husband of thirty-two years. I cherish the three of you and thank you for the sacrificial spirit you have all shown throughout this process. I am also profoundly grateful to each of you for your editorial and technical contributions. My team also includes K-9 companions Drama, Bailey and Justice, my walking and office mates, who bring me immeasurable joy. They took occupancy at the window near my desk and were tortured by the presence of squirrels and birds that they could not chase as I wrote. Let the games begin again!

Beyond the above, there is a village of friends, comrades, allies and family (both through birth and marriage) that sustains and supports me and keeps me grounded. Lisa, Regina, Monica and Kacy, you are the best girlfriends the world has to offer. You never compete, envy or judge. You only love, support and call me out on those very rare instances when it is needed. Angola 3 member Robert King, Malik Rahim, Students United, attorney Ernest Jones, attorney Willie Zanders, Sr., Dr. Clyde Robertson and Calvin Duncan, I'm watching your moves and trying my best to emulate them. I leave every conversation with you improved and wiser. You are deeply cherished. My village understood years of autoreplies, unanswered calls and emails, my unavailability for partnerships and my failure to attend events during this period. It took this for me to finish. I am immensely grateful for the understanding and support. You know I am speaking of you if you have secretly wished I stop sending all those dog photos or social justice emails and text messages.

There are several current and former SULC students and staff members who played a critical role in this project. They provided research support and critical insights and feedback. Chukuma O. Akubeze, Bobbi Davis, Tiffany Rainey, Derrick West, LaCrisha Mcallister, Whitley Triplet, Amari Spraggins, Jeremee Henry and Abeer Farid—your contributions enriched and fortified this work. Research Assistant Brittany Dunn embraced this project with an enthusiasm and excitement that gave me the encouragement to persevere. And when it came to work, Brittany went at it with all she had. She located hard to find sources, scheduled and joined remote sessions, attended meetings and events around the state, tracked leads, provided critiques and conducted interviews. Your devotion to the project shall never be forgotten.

Adrienne Shields and Angela Mason, both SULC library employees, had every reason to avoid me because they knew my research requests were going to be complicated. They never did though. They embraced the opportunity to assist me with acquisitions and research needs and always exceeded my expectations. Colleagues Staci, Donna and Tiffany, I thank you for doing just what sisters should do for each other. You insisted that plant I my feet and stand firm!

The sacrificial work of the Black Panther Party (both national and Louisiana chapter) inspired this work. To each chapter member who has served as teachers and disciples, know you are valuable part of my universe. In this same trailblazing vein, I recognize the work of two Black female authors who are to be credited with starting the modern conversation about racial inequities in the criminal legal system: Angela J. Davis (*Arbitrary Justice: The Power of the American Prosecutor*, first published in 2007) and Michelle Alexander (*The New Jim Crow: Mass Incarceration in the Age of Colorblindness*, first published in 2010).

I lift up the earthshattering work of another yet Black woman whose intellectual gifting is changing the world for the better. I extend that salute to Dr. Gail C. Christopher, the architect of the Truth, Racial Healing & Transformation (TRHT) framework. Your body of work has given definition and direction to my life's work and the cohort training has caused me to make bolder moves.

To the following for the contribution of time, insights and content: Anne Sobol (relative to her late husband Richard Sobol); Okyeame Haley and N. Sundiata Haley, Esq. (relative to their mother the late Oretha Castle Haley); and, the many unnamed justice players (who shared documents and experiences that allowed me to present such a detailed window into the legal system). Throughout the book other contributors are named and recognized. There is no way this book could have been written without their assistance. Each interrupted their schedules to provide materials and/or interviews. To this collective, I am appreciative beyond measure and I remain in awe of your respective fights for justice and equality for all people.

I thank SULC for the award of summer writing stipends used to partially fund my summer research endeavors and the Culture of Health Leadership Institute for Racial Healing for the award of partial summer funds and for enriching content that inspired hope in the ideas advanced in this book. Writing books of this nature and pursuing the scholarship and path of an activist scholar is not something that every law professor is created to do and it is not something they are all free to live. I pay homage to SULC for never devaluing scholarship that contradicts or questions prevailing themes in law.

I also owe a debt that I can never pay to law professors Alfreda Diamond, Raymond Diamond, John Guidry, the late Thomas Jones, Russell Jones, Virgina Listach, Teri A. McMurtry-Chubb, Okechukwu Oko and the late Evelyn Wilson who molded and nurtured me over the course of many years. These "greats" introduced me to the power of scholarship and compelled me to assume my place on those scrolls. They taught me to be uncompromising—not only by words spoken, but also by actions lived. They forced me to grow analytically. They taught me how to clench principles with a firm grip and to never thirst for power or prestige. They taught me that gaining entry to places by connections and not knowledge would ultimately end in disgrace so I learned to earn my way.

I am most appreciative of Sonia Bu for being the best coach on the planet. The suggestions given, the questions posed and the insights shared during ours sessions stretched me and aided me in the visioning work this project required.

A final extension of gratitude is given to all those unnamed teachers and persons who poured into me, counseled me, prayed and encouraged me through this process and over the years leading up to it. Your presence has been felt and has been consequential. You are my sustenance.

POST-SCRIPT

On March 7, 2019, those directly involved with the historic November 6, 2018, election that ended the use of non-unanimous juries, celebrated this victory at the Governor's Mansion with Louisiana's Governor John Bel Edwards, a supporter of the change in law.

Erin Monroe-Wesley, Allen-Bell, Gov. John Bel Edwards, Carlton Miller, Desni Scaife. Photo credit Checo Yancy

Allen-Bell & Representative Edmond
Jordon. Photo credit Checo Yancy

Ed Tarpley, Will Harrell & Allen-Bell
Photo credit Desni Scafe

Sateria Tate-Alexandria & Allen-Bell

Photo credit Desci Scafe

Allen-Bell, Vera Lynn Dampeer.

Photo credit Checo Yancy

Allen-Bell, Mary-Patricia Wray

Photo credit Mary-Patricia Wray

Will Snowden & Angela A. Allen-Bell

Photo credit Checo Yancy

NOTES

Dedication

1. Shannon Frystak, *Oretha Castle Haley (1939-1987)*, in *Louisiana Women Their Lives and Times* 318 (Janet Allured & Judith F. Gentry eds., 2009).

Introduction

1. *See* HR 248, Reg. Sess (La. 2019).
2. The maroons were enslaved people who escaped and established settlements outside of colonial control and lived independently.
3. Virginie Ladisch & Anna Myriam Roccatello, *The Color of Justice Transitional Justice and the Legacy of Slavery and Racism in the United States*, International Center for Transitional Justice (ICTJ), p. 3, April 2021, *available at* ICTJ_Briefing_TJ_US_Race_0.pdf (last visited May 20, 2022) (citations omitted).
4. Carter G. Woodson, *The Mis-Education of the Negro* 22 (1933).
5. Emily Bernard, *Autobiography of an Ex-Black Man*, Harpers Magazine, 84, 85 (Dec. 2019).
6. Andru Okun, *Digging Up the Roots of the Family Tree*, 64 Parishes 56 (fall 2020).
7. *Id.*
8. *Id.*
9. Gail C. Christopher, *Px Racial Healing A Guide to Embracing our Humanity* xiii (2022).
10. The Reconstruction Amendments' Debates (Alfred Avins ed, 2nd ed. 1974) 41 (39th Cong., 1st Sess. 149 (Feb. 26, 1866) (Statement of Senator Lot Morrill).
11. Douglas L. Colbert, *Challenging the Challenge: Thirteenth Amendment as a Prohibition Against the Racial Use of Peremptory Challenges*, 76 Cornell L. Rev. 1, 15 (1990).
12. Allan J. Lichtman, *The Embattled Vote in America From the Founding To The Present* 2 (2018).
13. In this book, "People of Color" includes all non-white individuals who may identify with one or more of the following racial groups (but not limited to): African American/Black, Asian (Central/East/South/Southeast), Hispanic/Latino/a/x, Middle Eastern/North African, Native American/Indigenous, and/or Native Hawaiian/Pacific Islander.

Preface

1. The Reconstruction Amendments' Debates, 655 (Alfred Avins ed, 2nd ed. 1974) (42nd Cong., 2nd Sess., May 21, 1872) (Statement of Senator Charles Sumner).

2. Acts Passed by the General Assembly of the state of Louisiana at the Regular Session Begun and Held in the City of New Orleans on the Twelfth Day of January 1880, 141-2.

3. *Official Journal of the Proceedings of the Constitutional Convention of the State of Louisiana*, pp. 76 (1898); La. Const. art. 116 (1898).

4. *Official Journal of the Proceedings of the Constitutional Convention of the State of Louisiana*, pp. 381 (1898); This was a pattern in all Confederate states. John B. Knox, President of the 1901 Alabama Constitutional Convention explained that the task of the delegates was "establishing white supremacy" in a manner "within the limits imposed by the Federal Constitution." John B. Knox, President, 1901 Alabama Constitutional Convention, Address at the Official Proceedings of the Constitutional Convention of the State of Alabama 8 (May 22, 1901), *available at* http:// www.legislature.state.al.us/misc/history/constitutions/1901/proceedings/ 1901_ proceedings_vol1/day2.html.

5. *U.S. v. La*, 225 F. Supp. 353, 374 (quoting La. Senate J. 1898, 33-35) (emphasis added).

6. *See* Daniel Brantley, *Blacks and Louisiana Constitutional Development, 1890-Present: A Study in Southern Political Thought and Race Relations. Phylon* (1960-), vol. 48, no. 1, 1987, pp. 55.

7. *Id.*

8. Martinet, who lived from 1849-1917, shaped the legal strategy and mobilized the community effort to challenge Louisiana's Separate Car Act. He raised funds to underwrite Homer Plessy's legal fight and he defended Daniel Desdunes in the first separate but equal car law test case. He was a committed public servant who served two terms as state representative (from 1872-1875). He was also an activist lawyer, a journalist and a medical doctor. He refused coveted opportunities to leave the South because of his commitment to the achievement of civil rights in Louisiana. He and the Citizens Committee began their campaign against jury suppression after a local man was removed from a jury in the *Thezan* case after officials discovered they mistook his light complexion for something other than Black.

9. The Comité was again at the forefront of activist efforts in 1897, when all prospective Black jurors were dismissed from a high-profile federal criminal trial in New Orleans. Their protest landed before the U.S. Congress on the eve of the Constitutional Convention in Louisiana. *See* Resolution: Service on Juries in Louisiana, 31 Cong. Rec. 1019 (Jan. 26, 1898).

10. *See* 31 Cong. Rec. 1019 (1898).

11. *See* Daniel Brantley, *Blacks and Louisiana Constitutional Development, 1890-Present: A Study in Southern Political Thought and Race Relations. Phylon* (1960-), vol. 48, no. 1, 1987, pp. 52.

12. In the post-Civil War South, "recognition of freed slaves as full humans appeared to most white southerners not as an extension of liberty but as a violation of it, and as a challenge to the legitimacy of their definition of what it was to be white." Douglas A. Blackmon, *Slavery By Another Name* 41 (2008); "The notion that farms could be operated in some manner other than with groups of Black laborers compelled by a landowner or his overseer to work as many as twenty hours a day was antithetical to most whites." *Id.* at 26.

13. *See* Marjorie R. Esman, *Non-Unanimous Jury Verdicts Steeped in Racist Past*, The Advocate, Jan. 28, 2016, *available at* http://www.theadvocate.com/ba-

ton_rouge/opinion/our_views/article_e9fefca4-c278-57f6-a0fa-24eb1c93d2fd.html (last visited 02/19/18); Angela A. Allen-Bell, *How The Narrative About Louisiana's Non-Unanimous Criminal Jury System Became A Person Of Interest In The Case Against Justice In The Deep South*, 67 Mercer L. Rev. 585 (2016); Thomas Aiello, *Jim Crow's Last Stand: Nonunanimous Criminal Jury Verdicts in Louisiana* (2015).

14. When the matter of jury unanimity was before the SCOTUS in 1972 in the *Johnson v. Louisiana* (arguing a 9-3 verdict violated the Fourteenth Amendment) and *Apodaca* cases, there were no distinctions between grades or degrees of homicide and aggravated kidnapping, aggravated rape and homicide carried a death sentence under Louisiana law. Because there were no grades or degrees of murder, all homicides were deemed capital cases, which required unanimous verdicts. Later changes led to the possibility of some murders, which carried life sentences, being decided by split juries.

15. Article I, Section 3 of the 1974 Louisiana Constitution, states:

   No person shall be denied the equal protection of the laws. No law shall discriminate against a person because of race or religious ideas, beliefs, or affiliations. No law shall arbitrarily, capriciously, or unreasonably discriminate against a person because of birth, age, sex, culture, physical condition, or political ideas or affiliations.

   La. Const. of 1974 art. I, § 3 of the 1974 (amended 1989).

16. Z. Melissa Lawrence, *Constitutional Revision by Amendment—A Louisiana Tradition*, 51 La. Law Rev. 849, 850 (1991).

17. *State v. Eames*, 356 So.2d 1351, 1364 (1978).

18. Joe Massa, *Crisis is Near, Governor Says*, Times-Picayune, Jan. 16, 1970.

19. *See Louisiana State Board of Education v. Anthony*, No. 160, 895 (19th JDC Dec. 10, 1974); The following students were "restrained, enjoined and prohibited from entering on the campus of Southern University in Baton Rouge, harassing other students or members of the faculty or in any manner disrupting or interfering with the operation of said educational institution": Charlene Hardnett (also known as Sister Saikari Siti); Ricky Hill (also known as Malik Kambon); Nathaniel Howard; Herget Harris (also known as Sababu Taibika); Paul Shivers; Louis J. Anthony, Donald Mills Willie T. Henderson and Fred Prejean. Later the injunction was vacated, recalled and set aside as to: Louis J. Anthony, Donald Mills, Willie T. Henderson and Fred Prejean.

   These injunctions ended the future aspirations of some. Others endured the hardship of being educated in other states. Today, those student leaders are engineers, mathematicians, accountants, IT specialists and experts, professors, ministers, authors, government managers, lawyers, community activists, proving in the end who they were and were not. Beyond the 2022 "ban lifting" photo op effort in a jurisdiction with no legal authority over the matter, at an assembly where the 1972 student leaders were never named, acknowledged, mentioned or invited, there has been no legitimate effort undertaken to formally dissolve those injunctions.

20. In 1976, his death sentence was commuted to life after the state's mandatory death penalty was ruled unconstitutional. The *Miller* ruling allowed for a resentencing hearing where Tyler accepted a plea bargain of 21 years for manslaughter, having already served twice that time, he walked out of court, free at last.

21. The Reconstruction Amendments' Debates, 85 (Alfred Avins ed, 2nd ed. 1974) (38th Cong., 2d Sess., Jan. 16, 1865) (Statement of Senator James Kelley), citing to *Is There Any Justice For the Black?*, N. O. Tribune, Dec. 15, 1864.

22. Murder! Murder!, Colored Trib., Mar. 4, 1876, at 2.

23. Cong. Globe, 42d Cong., 2d Sess. 822-23 (1872) (statement of Sen. Sumner).

24. The Crusader was a Black Republican newspaper founded by politician, attorney, and journalist *Louis André Martinet* (1849-1917), and descendants of Free Persons of Color in New Orleans, in 1889. During the 1890s, it was the only Black Daily Newspaper available in the United States.

25. *See Come Forward*, The Daily Crusader, March 13, 1895 (discussing efforts to raise funds in order to litigate challenges to jury discrimination and citing to the case of James Murray as one example).

26. *Not Quite*, The Daily Crusader, March 6, 1895.

27. The meeting records are signed by president Arther Esteves and acting secretary N.E. Mansion. But the members of the Citizens' Committe who met and decided on the action are A. Esteves, R.L. Desdunes, A.J. Gurinovich, Dr. Milanes, L.J. Joubert, L.A. Martinet and N.E. Mansion. See *Citizens' Committee*, DAILY CRUSADER (New Orleans, La.), Feb. 14, 1895 (Tulane University, Amistad Research Center, Charles B. Rousseve Papers, 1842-1994, New Orleans, La.); The Citizens Committee also registered Black voters and encouraged Black civic participation. *See* Mary Gehman, *The Free People of Color of New Orleans* 92 (2014).

28. Booker T. Washington lived from 1856-1915.

29. Booker T. Washington, *An Open Letter to the Louisiana Constitutional Convention*, Feb. 19, 1898, Page 2.

30. *See Lee v. New Orleans Great Railroad Company*, 125 La. 236 (1910).

31. *See Patton v. State of Mississippi*, 332 U.S. 463 (1947).

32. *Edmonson v. Leesville Concrete Co., Inc.*, 500 U.S. 614 (1991).

33. *See* Alejandro De La Fuente & Ariela J. Gross,Â *Becoming Free, Becoming Black Race, Freedom, and Law in Cuba, Virginia, and Louisiana*Â 209 (2020).

34. *Id.* at 217.

35. United States Commission on Civil Rights Report, *Justice*, 103 (book V) (1961) ("The practice of racial exclusion from juries persists today even though it has long stood indicted as a serious violation of the 14th amendment. As a result, the bar of race and color is placed at the only gate through which the average citizen may enter for service in the courts of justice.")

36. Caddo parish supported the amendment at 70 percent, East Baton Rouge at 71 percent and Orleans at 85 percent.

Chapter 1

1. *I Am Not Your Negro* (Velvet Films 2016); *see also* The James Baldwin Estate, *I Am Not Your Negro* 154 (2017).

2. "Free people of color are the "fictional shadows" between Black and white... Numbering in the thousands in New Orleans of the early 1800s, the free people of color had their own identity in a caste that was neither Black nor white, neither slave nor entirely free. French speaking Catholics, well-educated and middle class

for the most par, they were respected members of New Orleans society who attended the French opera and theater, debated the latest politics in their own newspapers, and worshipped in St. Louis Cathedral." Mary Gehman, *The Free People of Color of New Orleans* 1-2 (2014).

3. "[Sieur de] La Salle would have encountered or passed by settlements of several different Native American tribes while sailing down the Mississippi River. In 1700 there were 13,000 American Indians living in Louisiana who can be categorized into six different language groups; the Caddo inhabited the northwest section of Louisiana, the Tunica in the northeast corner, the Natchez in the mideast, the Atakapa in the southwest, the Muskhogee in the southeast and the Chitimacha in the southern part of Louisiana." *Id.*

4. "Within the Muskhogean family are the Choctaw, who lived primarily in Mississippi, but also inhabited the area north of Lake Ponchartrain in Louisiana. The Choctaw were the first of the major tribes to form an alliance with the French in Louisiana and even aided the French against other rival tribes. The Choctaw actively worked with the European settlements and traded European cloth and weapons for goods." Kathy Alcaine & Mary Antee', *Art in Louisiana 1700-1900* 6 (2004).

5. French Colonial Rule (1682-1763); the Spanish were in power (1763-1800); France's second rein was from 1800-1803.

6. Many Louisiana slaves originated from the Senegambian region of West Africa. Others were Bambara who descended from the Mande' or from Angola or the Bight of Benin.

7. The Louisiana 1724 *Code Noir* was based on the 1685 *Code Noir* that was compiled for the French Caribbean colonies. It required the enslaved (both current and former) to be non-violent and respectful to masters at all times and it outlawed slave labor on Sundays and Holy days. It prohibited the enslaved from carrying weapons (without written permission from an owner whose work required the use of said weapon). It barred the enslaved from: engaging in paid transactions involving their products or services, owning property, marrying whites, marrying other enslaved people without permission from a master, serving as a witness at a trial, and gathering with enslaved people belonging to other masters. The 1724 *Code Noir* further required slave owners to provide food and care for their slaves and obligated them to baptize and marry their slaves in the Roman Catholic faith. It provided for the prosecution of owners and overseers who killed or mutilated slaves. The *Code* mandated that children of slaves would be slaves and prohibited slaves from receiving inheritances. It also mandated that slave owners could only free enslaved people after obtaining permission from the colony's Superior Council. By 1751, the idea of slaves buying their own freedom had caught on and was growing in appeal. The 1751 *Code Noir* sought to limit this. One of the functions of the French Superior Council, which comprised of a body of slaveholders, was to make sure the *Code Noir* was upheld.

8. It would be irresponsible for me to use this verbiage without recognizing that race was socially constructed as a way of justifying different treatment in society. Race is a "social identity deeply connected to history and power, privilege and disadvantage." Ian Haney Lopez & Michael A. Olivas, *Jim Crow, Mexican Americans, and the Anti-Subordination Constitution: The Story of Hernendez v.*

Texas, in Race Law Stories 305 (Rachel F. Moran and Devon W. Carbado eds., 2008).

9. "In the early 1680s, King Louis XIV of France instructed two top officials in the Antilles—Jean-Baptiste Patoulet and Comte de Blénac—to draft a legal instrument by incorporating past ordinances and judgments from the islands of Martinique, Guadeloupe, and St. Christophe from the previous 50 years....Louis XIV wrote to Patoulet and de Blénac in 1681, requesting that they draft the "ordinance" regarding "the Blacks . . . in order that His Majesty may lay down the prohibitions, injunctions, and everything touching the conservation, policing, and judging of these people." In 1685, the *Code Noir* was promulgated and applied to the French Antilles....In March 1724, Louis XV issued the *Code Noir* for the Louisiana colony, which was patterned after the original Code, integrating 51 of the original Code's 55 articles." Angi Porter, *Africana Legal Studies: A New Theoretical Approach to Law & Protocol*, 27 MICH. J. RACE & L. 249, 289 (2022) (citations omitted); "Because chattel slavery was uncommon in the 1500s in England..., the existing legal system that colonists brought to the early British colonies in North America did not suffice, so nearly all law related to slavery was forged in the colonies, borrowing from existing practices in Spanish, Portuguese, and English Caribbean plantation colonies...." Roxanne Dunbar-Ortiz, *Loaded A Disarming History of the Second Amendment*, 59-60 (2018).

10. Michael T. Pasquier, *French Colonial Louisiana*, 64 Parishes (Aug. 4, 2011).

11. Spain became owner of the Louisiana territory, but it would be another six years before the Spanish took possession.

12. "The different bodies of law in force in Louisiana under the dominion of Spain were the *Siete Partidas*, the *Neuva Recopilacion* of Castile..., the *Recopilacion* of the Indies..., whatever royal edicts (*Cedulas*) had been directed to the courts of Louisiana...." John H. Wigmore, *Louisiana: The Story of Its Legal System*, Southern Law Quarterly, 1, 5 (1916). The Spanish also created a militia, including a battalion of free men of color. Under the Spanish slave code, Indian slavery was banned. The customs became law when Governor Francisco Carondelet issued a 1795 decree, which legalized them.

13. This practice was stopped following a City Council meeting because of the ongoing was between Spain and England. *See* City Council Meets to Discuss Attorney General's Suggestion that Blacks and whites Not Celebrate Together While Soldiers are in Town, 1781 # wp004012, Jan. 19, 1781, *available at* http://www.louisianadigitallibrary.org/islandora/object/state-law%3A1028 (last visited 11/29/18).

14. Elizabeth Berenguer, Lucy Jewel, and Teri A. McMurtry-Chubb, *Gut Renovations: Using Critical and Comparative Rhetoric to Remodel how the Law Addresses Privilege and Power*,23 Harv. Latinx L. Rev. 205, 231 (2020) ("They were not offended by the notions of owning and controlling their perceived unequals; in fact, ownership and dominion over them was essential to establishing in-group identities and preserving their power and hierarchical superiority.")

15. Charles Chamberlain & Lo Faber, *Spanish Colonial Louisiana*, 64 Parishes (Feb 7, 2014).

16. *See* John T. Hood, Jr., *The History and Development of the Louisiana Civil Code*, 19 La. Law Review 1, 19 (1958).

17. By the Act of 1805, the Territory of Orleans Adopted the forms and procedures of the common law of England in its criminal proceedings, including the methods of trials. *See* Act of 1805 § 33.

18. "The Civil Code...was not based on the Spanish law, as the legislature had directed, but it was based instead on the then newly adopted French Code, the Code Napoleon." Hood, Jr., *supra* note 66, at 26.

19. Grant Lyons, *Louisiana and the Livingston Criminal Codes*, 15 *The Journal of the Louisiana Historical* 243, 249 (1974) (noting that a new penitentiary was approved during this same session in an effort to implement these criminal laws, which were based on rehabilitation and not retribution). Adoption of this *System of Penal Law Prepared for the State of Louisiana* was subject to perpetual delays and ultimately disregarded. He later produced a 1821 *Code of Reform and Prison Discipline*. A criminal code would finally be adopted in 1942. *See Id.* at 270 (1974).

20. *See* Merritt M. Robinson, *A Digest of the Penal Law of the State of Louisiana, Alphabetically Arranged* (New Orleans, 1841).

21. Just Lead Washington, *Washington Pro Bono Equity Training Guide: Race Equity & Cultural Competency Curriculum for Volunteer Lawyers*, p. 11, *available at* Washington Pro Bono Equity Training Guide: Race Equity & Cultural Competency Curriculum for Volunteer Lawyers (justleadwa.org) (last visited March 8, 2022).

22. Gail C. Christopher, *Px Racial Healing A Guide to Embracing our Humanity* 72 (2022).

23. "Ever since the first settlement of Louisiana all persons with any appreciable degree of negro blood have been considered as colored; that is to say, as belonging to the African race." *Lee v. N.O.Great Railroad Company*, 125 La. 236, 239 (1910).

24. Alejandro De La Fuente & Ariela J. Gross, *Becoming Free, Becoming Black Race, Freedom, and Law in Cuba, Virginia, and Louisiana* 35 (2020).

25. *Id.* at 15.

26. *Id.*

27. "All other free persons" included free Black and the Native Americans who lived under US jurisdiction. Other Native Americans were considered "Indians not taxed," a term used in the Constitution to refer to the Native population who lived outside of US jurisdiction. Native Americans would not be fully included in a count until 1900.

28. De La Fuente, *supra* note 76, at 9.

29. *See* W.E. B. Du Bois, *Black Reconstruction in America* 372 (2007).

30. *See Lee v. New Orleans Great Railroad Company*, 125 La. 236 (1910).

31. *See Doe v. State*, 479 So.2d 369, 371 (1985).

32. That litigation produced testimony from Suzy Guillory Phipps; depositions of elderly relatives and neighbors of the Guillory family; testimony of state employees who register and maintain vital statistics; expert testimony of genealogists and a geneticist; genealogical charts supported by official and unofficial records spanning some two hundred years; and, photographs of scores of Guillory family members.

33. *See* Alejandro De La Fuente & Ariela J. Gross, *Becoming Free, Becoming Black Race, Freedom, and Law in Cuba, Virginia, and Louisiana*Â 209 (2020).

34. *Id.* at 217 (2020).

35. *See* Garner, 368 U.S. at 180 (revealing segregation to be a state policy and "the intention... that such a policy be continued"); *see generally* Rachel L. Emanuel &

Alexander P. Tureaud, Jr., *A More Noble Cause: A. P. Tureaud and the Struggle for civil rights in Louisiana* (2011).

36. From 1943 through the 1960s, the state library sponsored the Negro Services Department, a library housed at Southern University for Negro adults. It was segregated and staffed with Blacks who were trained to provide library services to Black patrons.

37. La. Rev. Stat. Ann. § 4:451 (2012) (required segregation at social functions and sporting events).

38. *See Garner, supra* note 85, at 180 n.1 (Douglas, J., concurring) (making reference to: La. Rev. Stat. Ann. § 4:5 (2012) (required that all circuses, shows, and tent exhibitions have segregated entrances); La. Rev. Stat. Ann. § 4:452 (2012) (required separate seating arrangements and separate sanitary drinking water at public functions); La. Rev. Stat. Ann. § 14:79 (2012) (prohibited interracial marriages); La. Rev. Stat. Ann. § 17:10 (2012) (required that the blind be segregated); La. Rev. Stat. Ann. §§ 17:443, 17:462 (2012) (prohibited public school teachers from advocating desegregation); La. Rev. Stat. Ann. § 17:523 (2012) (prohibited state employees from advocating desegregation); La. Rev. Stat. Ann. §§ 45:528-532 (2012) (required segregation on trains); La. Rev. Stat. Ann. § 45:1301 (2012) (required separate waiting rooms on carriers; La. Rev. Stat. Ann. § 45:1303 (2012) (required separate toilets and separate facilities for drinking water on common carriers); La. Rev. Stat. Ann. § 23:971 (2012) (required employers to provide separate sanitary facilities); La. Rev. Stat. Ann. § 23:972 (2012) (required employers to provide separate eating facilities and separate eating and drinking utensils); La. Rev. Stat. Ann. § 33:5066 (2012) (required segregated neighborhood unless integration was approved by the majority of the other race); La. Rev. Stat. Ann. § 13:917 (2012) (required that the race of the parties in a divorce action be made a part of the court docket); and La. Rev. Stat. Ann. § 33:4558.1 (2012) (required that recreational facilities be segregated)).

39. W.E. B. Du Bois, *Black Reconstruction in America* 573-4 (2007).

40. *Id.* at 574.

41. *Id.* at 25.

42. *See* Daniel Brantley, *Blacks and Louisiana Constitutional Development, 1890-Present: A Study in Southern Political Thought and Race Relations. Phylon (1960-),* vol. 48, no. 1, 1987, pp. 52.

43. *Id.*

44. W.E. B. Du Bois, *Black Reconstruction in America* 25 (2007).

45. *See* Daniel Brantley, *Blacks and Louisiana Constitutional Development, 1890-Present: A Study in Southern Political Thought and Race Relations. Phylon (1960-),* vol. 48, no. 1, 1987, pp. 52.

46. Tobias Barrington Wolff, *The Thirteenth Amendment and Slavery in a Global Economy,* Columbia Law Review, 102 CLMLR 973, 1049-1050 (2002); Race & Slavery Petitions Project, *available at* Petition Details (uncg.edu)https://library.uncg.edu/slavery/petitions/details.aspx?pid=16076https://library.uncg.edu/slavery/petitions/details.aspx?pid=6903 (last visited May 7, 2021) (noting that the male slave Frank's heels were exposed to extreme cold and frozen, resulting in a permanent disability).

47. W.E. B. Du Bois, *Black Reconstruction in America* 7 (2007).

48. The Reconstruction Amendments' Debates, 44 (Alfred Avins ed, 2nd ed. 1974) (38th Cong., 1st Sess., Fe. 29, 1864) (Statement of Charles Sumner).

49. Records of the French Superior Council #1747-06-26-02, June 26, 1947, *available at* http://www.louisianadigitallibrary.org/islandora/object/lsm-p15140coll60%3A819 (last visited 11/29/18) (Referencing the case of Bellile, who, in 1747, hanged himself inside his slave quarters).

50. *De Merveilleux v. Gaulaz, French Superior Council* #1727-07-20-01, July 20, 1727, *available at* http://www.lacolonialdocs.org/document/1124 (last visited 11/29/18).

51. Records of the French Superior Council (1714-1769), WPA 1739-07-19-0 , Folder #1739-07-19-03:, *available at http://www.louisianadigitallibrary.org/islandora/object/lsm-p15140coll60%3A905,* (last visited Nov. 28, 2018).

52. *Legal Experts Discuss Relevance of the 13th Amendment 150 Years Later,* American Bar Association News, Dec. 07, 2015.

53. The Reconstruction Amendments' Debates, 66 (Alfred Avins ed, 2nd ed. 1974) (38th Cong., 1st Sess., March 19, 1864) (Statement of Henry Wilson).

54. Michael Tisserand, *A Priest on the Color Line In New Orleans and Breaux Bridge, Father Antoine Borias Navigated Race and Saved Souls,* p. 35, 64 Parishes (Winter 2020), *available at* A Priest on the Color Line | 64 Parishes (last visited May 3, 2021) (Describing Louisiana's Catholic Churches as having a "tolerant—even enthusiastic—attitude toward slavery."); *see also Why Did So Many Christians Support Slavery?,* Christian History Today, *available at* Why Did So Many Christians Support Slavery? | Christian History | Christianity Today (last visited Oct. 31, 2022); John Lee Eighmy, *The Baptists and Slavery: An Examination of the Origins and Benefits of Segregation,* 49 Social Science Quarterly, 427, 666-673 (1968).

55. The Fugitive Slave Act of 1850 was passed by the United States Congress. It obligated white citizens to aid federal agents in recapturing runaways and imposed severe penalties on anyone assisting escaped slaves. Law enforcement was allowed to arrest Blacks suspected of being runaway slaves. Many free people were caught in these dragnets and criminalized because of their skin color. This also created a dynamic where Blacks were subject to twenty-four-hour suspicion by law enforcement. The Fugitive Slave Law also created a devaluing of the testimony of Blacks. It allowed a white slave owner to give a statement as to ownership. When the accused Blacks attempted to defend his freedom with a statement, the law deemed his statement inferior to the white slave owner. He was taken into custody and returned to slavery. He had no trial rights. In the eyes of the law, the word of one white man was worth more than the life or freedom of a Black man. These interactions and this profiling was the manifestation of law criminalizing Blackness. The Fugitive Slave Act of 1850 was part of the package of legislation known as the Compromise of 1850, designed to heal the growing rift between the North and the South. The South got its own Fugitive Slave Law as a result of this compromise.

56. Mary Gorton McBride & Ann Mathison McLaurin, *Randall Lee Gibson of Louisiana Confederate General and New South Reformer* 15 (2007).

57. Allen Pusey, *Abolitionist Beaten Senseless on Senate Floor,* ABA Journal, 72 (May 2018).

58. Andrew Delbanco, *A Den of Braggarts and Brawlers Politics on Capitol Hill Has Never Been Civil,* The Nation, p. 14 (Nov. 19/26, 2018).

59. The January 26, 1861 Ordinance of Secession officially: (1) ended Louisiana's membership in the union of states known as the United States of America; and, (2) declared Louisiana a sovereignty and a free and independent state. There were 113 votes in favor of this action and 17 votes in opposition.

60. On January 18, 1864, by way of Act 2 of the Seventh Legislature of the state of Louisiana, a four-million-dollar appropriation was made towards the support of families of Confederate soldiers. This does not suggest there was no opposition. Unionist James G. Taliaferro, a Delegate to Louisiana's 1861 Secession Convention, requested that his protest resolution against the Ordinance of Secession be entered into the journal of the proceedings of the Louisiana secession convention. Thereafter, he stated his opposition: "[S]ecession may bring anarchy and war, as it will assuredly bring ruinous exactions upon property in the form of direct taxation, a withering blight upon the prosperity of the state, and a fatal prostration of all its great interests." *See* New Orleans During the Civil War (Teacher's Guide), The Historic New Orleans Collection (2016), p. 21, *available at* LessonPlan_CivilWar.pdf (hnoc.org) (last visited 4/27/21) (emphasis added). His protest was dismissed and repudiated overwhelmingly by the vast majority of delegates and was refused inclusion in the official journal.

61. *Who, What, Why: How Many Soldiers Died in the US Civil War?*, BBC News, April 4, 2012, *available at* Who, What, Why: How many soldiers died in the US Civil War? - BBC News (last visited July 13, 2021).

62. Gloria Browne-Marshall, *Race, Law, and American Society* 37 (2013).

63. *Who, What, Why, supra* note 111.

64. "Black people freed themselves. Over 200,000 Black soldiers fought in the war on behalf of the Union." Brown-Marshall, *supra* note 112, at 87; "[S]ome [free men of color] owned slaves and joined the Confederacy in the Civil War." Gehman, *supra* note 52, at 3; The role of Blacks in the confederacy should not go unnoticed:

Black men had formed a large and highly visible portion of the population at every major Confederate army encampment, but not as soldiers. They washed clothes, cooked meals, cared for the personal property of individual owners, groomed horses, drove wagons, unloaded trains, built walls and bridges, and nursed the wounded. One former slave, when interviewed by an employee of the Works Progress Administration, claimed he had done a soldier's work during the war, and this was certainly a valid interpretation. Black men serving the Confederate army did almost all of the tasks that actual Confederate soldiers did on a regular basis—everything except fighting in battle. And while it is possible (perhaps even probable) that a few of the personal body servants or hired slaves working in camp could have picked up a gun and joined a battle at one point or another, there is no credible evidence to suggest that large numbers of them did so. Certainly, their numbers are statistically insignificant when compared with the thousands of Black men who were forced to perform manual labor for the Confederate armies.
*****

The history of the Louisiana Native Guards or the "hospital" company formed in Richmond in March 1865 demonstrates that there were certainly Black men who chose to fight for the Confederacy as a means to obtain personal or familial goals, although it is important to remember that their freedom of choice was often limited by the legal prescriptions of slaveholding societies. Even more important is that these examples of Black Confederates should not undermine two fundamental realities: the Confederate States of America was founded primarily to protect the institution of slavery, and slavery was at its heart an institution based on violence and exploitation.

Black Confederates in Memory and Imagination, Encyclopedia Virginia, *available at* Black Confederates – Encyclopedia Virginia (last visited July 12, 2021).

Black Union soldiers lost their lives in the 1864 Fort Pillow Massacre. Maj. Gen. Nathan Bedford Forrest, a slave owner who later became the first grand wizard in the Ku Klux Klan, led the Confederate forces. Instead of treating the Union soldiers as prisoners of war upon their surrender, they were first robbed then starved, executed, drowned, burned or buried alive. 295 white soldiers and 262 Black soldiers were involved. *See Fort Pillow Massacre Joint Committee Report*, 38th Cong., 1st Sess., H. Rep. No. 65 (May 6, 1864), *available at* Fort Pillow Massacre Joint Committee Report 1864 PDF (1).pdf (last visited 5/7/21); Formed in 1861, the 1st Louisiana Native Guard was the first official Black regiment in the Confederate Army. All of the initial members of the Native Guard were French Speaking Creoles. Among those who joined the militia were successful architects, brick masons, dentists, doctors and carpenters.

65. During the Civil War, in 1863, the Emancipation Proclamation was issued. It ended slavery in Confederate states only.

66. It is the product of a contentious, eight-day debate. The debates began on January 6, 1865 and ended eight days later. The vote on the amendment was postponed to January 28, 1865 . *See* CONG. GLOBE, 38th Cong., 2d Sess. 138 (1865).

67. Political rights were viewed as the right to serve on juries, to hold elected office and the right to cast a vote.

68. The Reconstruction Amendments' Debates (Alfred Avins ed, 2nd ed. 1974) (39th Cong., 1st Sess. 43 (1865).

69. "In some Northern states...intense debates over the expansion of federal power preceded the eventual vote to ratify the amendment...South Carolina tried to find a middle course, reluctantly voting to ratify with a resolution approving section 1 of the amendment but not section 2." George A. Rutherglen, *The Badges and Incidents of Slavery and the Power of Congress to Enforce the Thirteenth Amendment*, in the promises of liberty the history and contemporary relevance of the thirteenth amendment 170 (Alexander Tsesis ed., 2010).

70. *See Id.* at 170.

71. Several drafts of the amendment were considered. Representative James Ashley suggested:

Slavery, being incompatible with a free Government, is forever prohibited in the United States; and involuntary servitude shall be permitted only as a punishment for crime.

The Reconstruction Amendments' Debates, (Alfred Avins ed, 2nd ed. 1974) (38th Cong., 1st Sess., Dec. 14, 1863).

Mr. Sumner later amended his earlier proposal to read:

All persons are equal before the law, so that no person can hold another as a slave; and the Congress may take all laws necessary and proper to carry this article into effect everywhere within the United States and the jurisdiction thereof.

The Reconstruction Amendments' Debates, 67 (Alfred Avins ed, 2nd ed. 1974) (38th Cong., 1st Sess., April 8, 1864).

Representative Howard then proposed: "All persons are free before the law so that no person can hold another as a slave, etc." The Reconstruction Amendments' Debates, 68 (Alfred Avins ed, 2nd ed. 1974) (38th Cong., 1st Sess., April 8, 1864) (Statement of Jacob Howard).

Representative Lazarus Powell responded to the various proposals with an accusation that proponents were not acting in good faith toward the southern states. The Reconstruction Amendments' Debates, 67 (Alfred Avins ed, 2nd ed. 1974) (38th Cong., 1st Sess., April 8, 1864) (Statement of Lazarus Powell).

72. The Northwest Ordinance, authored by Thomas Jefferson, chartered a government for new territory towards the Pacific Ocean, and provided a method for admitting new states. It created a legal structure for the settlement of land in five present-day states: Ohio, Indiana, Illinois, Michigan, and Wisconsin. It also established rules for the admission of its constituent parts as states into the union. Under the ordinance, slavery was forever outlawed from the lands of the Northwest Territory, freedom of religion and other civil liberties were guaranteed, the resident Indians were promised decent treatment, and education was provided for. The ordinance of 1787 for the government of the Northwest Territory declares: 'There shall be neither slavery nor involuntary servitude in the said territory, otherwise than in punishment of crimes, whereof the party shall have been duly convicted." In *Forsyth v. Nash*, 4 Mart. (o.s.) 385, 387-8 (1816), there is reference to this same exception in a 1797 congressional ordinance. Using the language from the Northwest Ordinance of 1787, they sought inspiration from the states within the limits of the Northwest Territory that prohibited involuntary servitude, but required labor upon public roads and who also allowed the sale of convicts to private individuals.

73. The Amendment was passed on January 31,1865, but two-thirds of states had to ratify it as a condition of it being added to the constitution. Northern states did so swiftly. Southern states were not as eager. Federal Reconstruction efforts conditioned readmission to the Union on ratification of the Thirteenth Amendment. Louisiana ratified the Thirteenth Amendment on February 17, 1865. It was not until December 18, 1865 that the requisite number had been obtained and the amendment was officially added to the United States Constitution. Incidentally, Kentucky (ratified in 1976) and Mississippi (ratified in 1995, but the state didn't officially notify the US Archivist until 2012, when the ratification finally became official) have the distinction of being the last states to ratify the amendment.

74. On March 3, 1865, the Bureau of Refugees, Freedmen and Abandoned Lands (also known as the Freedman's Bureau) was established by Congress in the War Department in the closing year of the Civil War. The Freedman's Bureau was created to provide the newly emancipated people with employment, wages, health, housing, legal and educational assistance. *See* 13 Stat. 507-509 (1865). A second Freedmen's Bill was enacted in 1866. *See* 14 Stat. 173-177 (1866); "During the seven years of its existence (1865-1872), this agency helped freed people rejoin with their separated partners, children, parents, and siblings, and it also presided over and documented marriages between freed couples whose relationships had not been legally recognized during slavery." Bob Nowatzki, *Records of the Freedmen's Bureau and the Reconstruction of Black Families*, Rediscovering Black History Blog, Oct. 27, 2021.

75. With the Thirteenth Amendment formally pending, President Lincoln struggled to reunite a divided country. As a solution, he announced the Proclamation of Amnesty and Reconstruction in 1863, which allowed for a full pardon for and restoration of property to all engaged in the rebellion with the exception of the highest Confederate officials and military leaders. In addition, it allowed for a new state government to be formed when 10 percent of the eligible voters had taken an oath of allegiance to the United States. Third, the Southern states admitted in this fashion were encouraged to enact plans to deal with the formerly enslaved people so long as their freedom was not compromised.

    In 1865, President Johnson issued a far more sweeping proclamation of amnesty. In December 1868, President Andrew Johnson pardoned all ex-Confederate soldiers who were ineligible under the general post-Civil War amnesty.

76. The Reconstruction Amendments' Debates, 238 (Alfred Avins ed, 2nd ed. 1974) (39th Cong., 1st Sess., June 13, 1866) (Statement of William Windom).

77. The Reconstruction Amendments' Debates, 154 (Alfred Avins ed, 2nd ed. 1974) (39th Cong., 1st Sess., Feb. 27, 1866) (Statement of Robert S. Hale).

78. The Reconstruction Amendments' Debates, 151 (Alfred Avins ed, 2nd ed. 1974) (39th Cong., 1st Sess., Feb. 26, 1866) (Statement of Andrew J. Rogers).

79. The Reconstruction Amendments' Debates, 237 (Alfred Avins ed, 2nd ed. 1974) (39th Cong., 1st Sess., June 8, 1866) (Statement of Richard Yates); It was adopted in June 1866 and ratified two years later in July 1868.

80. *See* Reconstruction Act of 1867, ch. 153, 14 Stat. 428 (1867). It was enacted by Congress over President Johnson's veto. "In September 1867, over seventy-five thousand Black Louisianans voted for delegates to the upcoming state constitutional convention." Mark Charles Roudande', *United for Justice How Tow Black-Owned Newspapers Launched Louisiana's Civil Rights Struggle*, 64 Parishes, 46, 50 (fall 2020).

81. Official Journal of the Proceedings of the Convention for the State of La. 2 (1867-68).

82. There were forty-nine white delegates. The president of the convention was Black. Oscar James Dunn was a delegate. The provisions of the 1868 Constitution allowed him to become the first Black elected to a state-level position in the United States. He was Lieutenant Governor of Louisiana from 1868–1871. P.B.S. Pinchback, another delegate, achieved his political ascent during this period. He became Lieutenant Governor under Henry Clay Warmoth when Oscar Dunn died. After Warmoth was impeached, Pinchback became Governor. He held office for only 35 days, but ten acts of the Legislature became law during that time. After William Pitt Kellogg took office as a result of the controversial election of 1872, Pinchback continued his career, holding various offices including a seat on the State Board of Education, Internal Revenue agent and as a member of the Board of Trustees of Southern University. P.B.S. Pinchback, before serving as Governor, was elected to the Louisiana legislature, but the Senate refused to seat him because of his race. He was ultimately given $20,000.00 for expenses associated with his challenge. Antoine Dubuclet won the post of state treasurer.

    Between 1868 and 1896, a number of Blacks held high office in the state: two congressmen, six high state officials, thirty-two state senators, ninety-five state representatives, and one United States Senator, who was not seated. Nineteen

Black men held office as sheriffs in Louisiana during Reconstruction. This was partly due to Black men gaining the right to vote in 1868 and partly due to the disfranchisement of many former Confederate soldiers.

"Over 1,400 Blacks held offices during Reconstruction, and more than 600 Blacks served in state assemblies, the majority of whom were former slaves." Eric Foner, *Freedom's Lawmakers: A Directory of Black Officeholders during Reconstruction* xiv (1993). The largest number of Blacks served as local officials in Louisiana, Mississippi, and South Carolina; the fewest number in Alabama, Florida, and Georgia. In 1870, "hundreds of Blacks were serving as city policemen and rural constables; they comprised half the police force in Montgomery [Alabama] and Vicksburg [Mississippi], and more than a quarter in New Orleans [Louisiana], Mobile [Alabama], and Petersburg [Virginia]. In the courts, defendants confronted Black magistrates and justices of the peace, and racially integrated juries." *Id.* at 362-3.

83. *See* Official Journal of the Proceedings of the Convention for the State of La. 48 (1867-68).

84. *Id.* at 216.

85. *Id.*

86. In fact, with the exception of Tennessee, all Southern states rejected the Fourteenth Amendment initially. It took African Americans voting and, in turn, being elected, for the Fourteenth Amendment to be adopted in Louisiana on its second attempt.

87. Official Journal of the Proceedings of the Convention for the State of La., *supra* note 135 at 16; *See also* Act No. 110, 1868 La. Acts 141. Act No. 94, 1873 La. Acts 156-166.

88. Though slavery was still practiced in Confederate-run parts of the state.

89. *See* Official Journal of the Proceedings of the Convention for the state of La., *supra* note 137 at 91; When Louisiana became a state in 1812, appellate courts had no jurisdiction to review criminal cases. There is a belief this was so because there were no transcripts or means of verifying testimony, evidence or objections and no organized system of law to apply. Public outcry led to that being changed in 1843 when that authority was granted to the Court of Errors and Appeals. Later, the 1845 Constitution conferred that authority upon the Louisiana Supreme Court. *See* Scott Crichton and Stuart Kottle, *Appealing Standards: Louisiana's Constitutional Provision Governing Appellate Review of Criminal Facts*, 79 La. L. Rev. 369, 376-7 (2019).

90. *See* Official Journal of the Proceedings of the Convention for the State of La., *supra* note 139 at 25.

91. *Id.* at 116.

92. Andru Okun, *Digging Up the Roots of the Family Tree*, 64 Parishes 56 (fall 2020).

93. The Reconstruction Amendments' Debates, 89 (Alfred Avins ed, 2nd ed. 1974) (39th Cong., 1st Sess., Senate Ex. Doc. No. 2, Dec. 19, 1865, Schurz Report on Condition of the South).

94. The Life and Public Services of Henry Wilson, *available at* https://www. electricscotland.com/history/wilson/chapter18.htm (last visited 09/16/20).

95. *See* Acts Nos. 10, 11, 12, and 16, 1865 La. Acts 14-24.

96. The Reconstruction Amendments' Debates, 95 (Alfred Avins ed, 2nd ed. 1974) (39th Cong., 1st Sess., Senate Ex. Doc. No. 2, Dec. 13, 1865 (Statement of Henry Wilson).

97. The Reconstruction Amendments' Debates, 95 (Alfred Avins ed, 2nd ed. 1974) (39th Cong., 1st Sess., Senate Ex. Doc. No. 2, Dec. 13, 1865 (Statement of Henry Wilson).

98. The Reconstruction Amendments' Debates, 90 (Alfred Avins ed, 2nd ed. 1974) (39th Cong., 1st Sess., Senate Ex. Doc. No. 2, Dec. 19, 1865, Schurz Report on Condition of the South).

99. This should not be interpreted as a suggestion that using convicted persons for free prison labor was a new concept.

100. *Osborn v. Nicholson*, 80 U.S. 654, 662 (1871) (In holding that a contract that sold a slave "for life" could be enforced despite the passage of the Thirteenth Amendment, the court stated that doing otherwise "would, in effect, take away one man's *property* and give it to another.").

101. *United States v. Stanley*, 109 U.S. 3, 22 (1883).

102. By 1876, federal troops were gone. This was not happenstance. This was the bounty paid in the contested presidential election of Republican Rutherford B. Hayes. One hundred and eighty-five electoral college votes were needed to win the election. Neither Mr. Hayes nor his Democratic opponent Samuel J. Tilden had them. An electoral commission was appointed to decide the election. Politics infected the process. The Presidency went to Mr. Hayes (with only 165 electoral votes and 184 electoral votes to Mr. Tilden) in exchange for his agreement to withdraw federal troops and federal sympathies from the South.

103. The 1790 United States Census was the first census in the history of the United States. It was not until around 1820 that the term "colored" entered the census nomenclature.

104. Mark T. Carleton, *Politics and Punishment The History of the Louisiana State Penal System* 44 (1971); During the slavery era, incarceration for Blacks was problematic for a few reasons. It was viewed as an insult to white convicts as it would carry with it a form of equality that defied the human consciousness. Additionally, there was financial losses associated with it. "white politicians considered housing Black prisoners with whites an insult to the white prisoners and bad for morale...whites made up the majority of the inmate populations in the Deep South, where slave laborers were too valuable to imprison." Gloria Browne-Marshall, *Race, Law, and American Society* 44 (2013).

105. The Reconstruction Amendments' Debates (Alfred Avins ed, 2nd ed. 1974) (39th Cong., 1st Sess. 149 (Feb. 26, 1866) (Statement of Lyman Trumbull).

106. *The New York Times*, Oct. 5, 1865, *available* at The Louisiana Democratic Convention. - The New York Times (nytimes.com) (last visited May 20, 2021).

107. Official Journal of the Proceedings of the Convention for the State of La., *supra* note 141 at 12.

108. *See Id.* at 293.

109. The Life and Public Services of Henry Wilson, *available at* https://www. electricscotland.com/history/wilson/chapter18.htm (last visited 09/16/20); In a speech, Representative Wilson observed that "Slavery organized conspiracies in the Cabinet, conspiracies in Congress, conspiracies in the states, conspiracies in the Army, conspiracies in the Navy, conspiracies everywhere for the overthrow of the Government and the disruption of the Republic." Hon. Henry Wilson, "The Death of Slavery is the Life of the Nation," March 28, 1864.

110. C. Vann Woodward, *Origins of the New* South 1877-1913, 155 (1951).

111. *See Id. at* 156.
112. "The violence of this era took a variety of forms--including beatings, castration, and lynchings." James Forman, *Juries and Race in the Nineteenth Century,* 113 Yale L.J. 895, 918 (2004). One author elaborated:

    How many Black men and women were beaten, flogged, mutilated, and murdered in the first years of emancipation will never be known. Nor could any accurate body count or statistical breakdown reveal the barbaric savagery and depravity that so frequently characterized the assaults made on freedmen in the name of restraining their savagery and depravity--the severed ears and entrails, the mutilated sex organs, the burnings at the stake, the forced drownings, the open display of skulls and severed limbs as trophies.

    Leon F. Litwack, *Been in the Storm So Long: The Aftermath of Slavery* 267-77 (1979).
113. E.D. White, Sr. lived from 1795-1847.
114. *See* Hon. Edward D. White, Review of the Reform Legislation of 1877 and 1878 (March 18, 1878).
115. *Id.* at 10.
116. *Id.* at 11-12.
117. *Id.* at 13.
118. Article 230 gave "authority to transform and create the existing University into a great University having all such departments and faculties as the Administrators might see fit to establish." The existing university at the time was the University of Louisiana, a public college and the only college in New Orleans at the time. *See Guillory v. Administrators of Tulane University of La.,* 203 F.Supp. 855, 862 (1962).
119. Mary Gorton McBride & Ann Mathison McLaurin,Â *Randall Lee Gibson of Louisiana Confederate General and New South Reformer*Â 3 (2007).
120. *Id.* at 4.
121. *Id.* at 232.
122. Only seven of the delegates were Black; Segregated higher education institutions were established. *See* La. Const. art.231 (1879) (establishes in the city of New Orleans a university for the education of persons of color...."); While the 1879 Constitution promises free public schools, it reveals plans to maintain them through the collection of a poll tax. *See* La. Const. arts. 224 & 227 (1879).
123. Official Journal of the Proceedings of the Convention for the State of La., *supra* note 158 at 38.
124. Christopher D.E. Willoughby, *Running Away from Drapetomania: Samuel A. Cartwright, Medicine, and Race in the Antebellum South,* LXXXIV Journal of Southern History 3, 585 (Aug. 2018).
125. United Nations General Assembly, No. A/74/321, Report of the Special Rapporteur on Contemporary Forms of Racism, Racial Discrimination, Xenophobia and Racial Intolerance, Aug. 21, 2019, p. 7, *available at* https://undocs.org/A/74/321 (last visited Aug. 31, 2020).
126. Christopher D.E. Willoughby, *Running Away from Drapetomania: Samuel A. Cartwright, Medicine, and Race in the Antebellum South,* LXXXIV Journal of Southern History 3, 583 (Aug. 2018).
127. *See Id.* at 606.
128. *Id.* at 596.

129. *Id.* at 585.
130. *Id.* at 583.
131. *See* Alejandro De La Fuente & Ariela J. Gross, *Becoming Free, Becoming Black Race, Freedom, and Law in Cuba, Virginia, and Louisiana* 146-179 (2020).
132. *Id.* at 178.
133. *Id.* at 179.
134. *See Bank of US v Merle*, 2 Rob. (LA) 117 (1842).
135. *See McDowell v Couch*, April 1851, Supreme Court of Louisiana, Manuscript Case File No. 2093.
136. *Becoming Serious*, Daily Picayune, May 7, 1867, *available at* Against Blacks riding in the section of street cars reserved for whites - Page 1 | Louisiana Digital Library (last visited May 10, 2021).
137. *See Buck v. Thaler*, 565 U.S. 1022 (2011).
138. In 1886 and a few times after, Louisiana considered, but rejected attempts to establish a code of criminal procedure. *See Senate Journal* (1886), 194.
139. Carleton, *supra* note 154 at 6.
140. See, e.g., *State v. Brown*, 201 So. 2d 277, 280 n.3 (La. 1967)(upholding a nine month sentence for vagrancy), overruled by *Argersinger v. Hamlin*, 407 U.S. 25 (1972) (holding that the right to counsel exists where possibility of incarceration).
141. Louisiana law provided no right to appeal unless the fine exceeded $300 or the incarceration exceeded six months. *See State v. Hunter*, 38 So. 686, 686 (La. 1905).
142. Two sections in Article V of the Louisiana Constitution govern the scope of appellate jurisdiction, one for the Supreme Court and the other for the courts of appeal.
143. *See* Scott Crichton and Stuart Kottle, *Appealing Standards: Louisiana's Constitutional Provision Governing Appellate Review of Criminal Facts*, 79 La. L. Rev. 369, 371 (2019).
144. *See Garner v. La.*, 368 U.S. 157 (1961) (involving the arrest of a law student and undergraduate students of Southern University at Baton Rouge following entry into an integrated Baton Rouge store following their request for service at the segregated lunch counter); *see also Lombard v. La*, 373 U.S. 267 (1963).
145. *See Zanders v. La. State Bd. of Ed.*, 281 F.Supp. 747 (1968) (Discussing the Board of Regents agreement with the institution to expel Grambling State University students following days of protests in 1967).
146. *See Cox v La.*, 379 U.S. 536 (1965) (arrest of a minister and students protesting the earlier arrest of fellow demonstrators).
147. *See Brown v. State*, 383 U.S. 131,133 (1966) (where five Black males were arrested for violating the breach of the peace statute after they entered the public library in Clinton, Louisiana, requested a book then, after being told that the book was not available, decided to sit a table in silence.). These convictions were revered by the SCOTUS, who, in its initial remarks, observed: "This is the fourth time in little more than four years that this court has reviewed convictions by the Louisiana courts for alleged violations, in a civil rights context, of that state's breach of the peace statute. In the three preceding cases the convictions were reversed."
148. Thomas D. Morris, *Slaves and the Rules of Evidence in Criminal Trials*, 68 CHIKLR 1209, 1239 (1993).
149. *See* La. Legislature, House Concurrent Resolution No. 27 (1954).

150. The Citizens' Council was formed directly as a reaction to the *Brown v. Board* decision. They were seen as a form of respectable resistance to integration. Their methods involved both nullification (not adhering to any federal legislation that they viewed as unjust) and interposition (interfering with the implementation of federal legislation). Whereas the KKK sought direct confrontation, the Citizens Councils existed to achieve legal encumbrances. "By the 1950s, the Klan had become a secondary force in the South and lost the majority of its members to the White Citizens' Council." Robert A. Goldberg, *Grassroots Resistance: Social Movements in Twentieth Century America*, 89 (1996).

151. *See Louisiana v. United States*, 380 U.S. 145, 149 (1965).

152. Act No. 18, 1960 La. Acts 230-31 (establishing a "State Sovereignty Commission [composed of, among others, the Governor, the Attorney General, the State Senate President, and the Speaker of the House] ... [that] shall meet immediately ... [and] shall be exempted from the provisions of the Public Records Act ....").

153. This included the entire Congressional delegations from Alabama, Arkansas, Georgia, Louisiana, Mississippi, South Carolina, and Virginia, most of the members from Florida and North Carolina, and several members from Tennessee and Texas.

154. In February 2021, Tulane University's Building Naming Task Force recommended removal of his name from the Hebert Hall on its campus, as well as from the Hebert Research Center.

155. W.E. B. Du Bois, *Black Reconstruction in America* 528 (2007).

156. *Id.* at 528.

157. *See Id.* at 392.

158. *See Id.*

159. Brian M. Davis, *In Search of a Rosenwald School*, 64 Parishes, p. 51 (fall 2021), *available at* In Search of a Rosenwald School - 64 Parishes (last visited April 6, 2022) (Discussing a 1916 study by the Department of the Interior, Bureau of Education).

160. *Id.*

161. *Id.*

162. *See* W.E. B. Du Bois, *Black Reconstruction in America* 571 (2007).

163. The state legislature in November 1960 passed an "interposition resolution," in which it sought to assert "the sovereignty of the state of Louisiana" against the usurping authority of the federal courts. The state argued that the Brown decision was illegitimate—it was not a faithful reading of the Equal Protection Clause of the Fourteenth Amendment of the Constitution. Thus, the state argued, it had a duty to resist the efforts of the federal courts to force school desegregation in Louisiana based on an illegitimate constitutional principle. The state found this duty in the theory of "interposition," which held that states have a duty to protect their citizens from unconstitutional behavior by the federal government. *See Bush v. Orleans*, 188 F. Supp. 916, 922-923 (1960).

164. *See Id.* at 930.

165. On September 4, 1952, Black attorney A.P. Tureaud, with the assistance of Thurgood Marshall and Robert Carter from the Legal Defense and Educational Fund of the National Association for the Advancement of Colored People (NAACP), filed a lawsuit on behalf of a group of Black parents in the U.S. District Court for the Eastern District of Louisiana seeking the racial desegregation of the

New Orleans public schools. *Bush v. Orleans Parish School Board* challenged segregation, claiming that Louisiana's state statutes and constitutional provisions mandating school segregation violated the Equal Protection Clause of the Fourteenth Amendment of the U.S. Constitution. At the encouragement of Thurgood Marshall, Tureaud agreed to suspend his newly filed lawsuit until the Supreme Court of the United States issued its ruling on a pending group of cases that called for a decision on the constitutionality of school segregation. On May 17, 1954, the SCOTUS issued its unanimous ruling in *Brown v. Board of Education*, declaring legally protected public school segregation unconstitutional.

166. After a federal court, in *Bush v. Orleans Parish School Board*, ordered the integration of New Orleans schools, the attorney general of Louisiana, Jack Gremillion, filed suit in a state court seeking to restrain the Orleans Parish School Board from desegregating its schools.

167. *See* Matthew Van Meter, *Deep Delta Justice* 138 (2020) (discussing legislative maneuvers successfully taken by Leander Perez that allowed the white children of Plaquemines Parish to attend segregated private schools that were secretly supported by state dollars).

168. Nikole Hannah-Jones, *Segregation Now*, The Atlantic, May 2014, *available at* Segregation Now -- How 'Separate and Equal' is Coming Back - The Atlantic (last visited March 29, 2021).

169. *Moore v Tangipahoa Parish School Board* has been ongoing since 1965. In 2021, U.S. Eastern District Court Judge Ivan Lemelle signed a court document declaring provisional unitary status to the Tangipahoa Parish School System, inspiring hope that the end of the litigation is in sight.

170. Xavier University (XU) and Dillard University (DU) were each founded by whites as was Southern University, but white segregationists and supremacists were not a part of their organizational structure as was the case with SU. Another difference was the vision for these institutions, in the eyes of its white founders. Mother Katharine Drexel, a white woman of means from Pennsylvania, who was devoted to educating African Americans and Native Americans for societal leadership and global society, founded XU in 1915. DU was founded in 1930 after New Orleans University and Straight College consolidated. The new university, named after James Hardy Dillard, the son of a slaveholder who opposed racial inequities, opened in 1935 to foster the creation of ideas and the development of the higher qualities of the individual.

171. In 1881, during the Jim Crow era, Southern University was chartered for Blacks after a group of Black politicians, P.B.S. Pinchback, Theophile T. Allain, and Henry Demas petitioned the State Constitutional Convention in 1879 in order to establish an institution of higher learning for "colored people." The school operated in New Orleans initially.

172. Whatever the original intentions were, SU has proved itself an asset to Blacks and, eventually, whites seeking higher education in this state. I remain forever indebted to Southern University Law Center for training me as a lawyer and allowing me to pursue my course as an activist scholar.

173. Albert G. Brown, *An address on Southern Education*, p.3 (July 18, 1839), *available at* An address on Southern education - Education1859-001_Cover | Louisiana Digital Library (last visited July 1, 2021).

174. Act 118 (1912), p. 3, *available at* 1880-1914 Legislative Acts Establishing Southern University - Southern University and A&M College - HBCU Library Alliance Digital Collection (auctr.edu) (last visited July 2, 2021).

175. *Id.* at 4.

176. *Southern University Ranks High and Gives Broad Type of Service*, State Times, May 16, 1932, *available at* Southern University ranks high and gives broad type of service | Louisiana Digital Library (last visited July 1,2021).

177. *See* Parish of Jefferson Police Jury Min., 60-62, 1858-1870 (declaring, in art. 122, that white male residents between eighteen and forty-five are subject to patrol duty); *see also Laparouse v Rice*, 13 La.Ann. 567, 568 (1858) (discussing the authorized shooting of a slave by two white men who were "hunting for some runaway negros" on the day in question).

178. "To recover the alleged fugitive, the slaveowner had only to produce an affidavit, signed by an officer of a Southern court, that described the alleged fugitive and said he was owned by the claimant. The Black man could not testify on his own behalf, was not provided an attorney, and was not entitled to a public hearing. There was no right to appeal the commissioner's decision. Finally, the commissioner received a five-dollar fee if he decided that the Black man was free, but ten dollars if he found he was a slave." James Forman, *Juries and Race in the Nineteenth Century*, 113 Yale L.J. 895, 906 (2004) (citations omitted).

179. Dennis C. Rousey, *Black Policemen in New Orleans During Reconstruction*, 49:2 The Historian 223, 227 (Feb. 1987).

180. Elizabeth Hinton, Why We Should Reconsider the War on Crime, TIME (Mar. 20, 2015), https://time.com/3746059/war-on-crime-history/.

181. *Id.*

182. *Id.*

183. The Challenge of Crime in a Free Society, PRESIDENT'S COMM'N ON L. ENF'T & THE ADMIN. OF CRIM. JUST. (1967), https://assets.document-cloud.org/document s/3932081/Crimecommishreport.pdf.

184. *See* Timothy Shenk, Booked: The Origins of the Carceral State, DISSENT MAG. (Aug. 30, 2016), https://www.dissentmagazine.org/blog/booked-origins-carceral state-elizabeth-hinton.

185. *See Id.* (discussing President Johnson's views as having been shaped by Daniel Patrick Moynihan, who felt that Black poverty is the product of behavior patterns and not larger socioeconomic issues. As a result, President Johnson initiated job training and equal opportunity programs, and for the symptoms of poverty that manifest through crime he puts more police on the streets).

186. *See Id.* (discussing President Johnson's views as having been shaped by Daniel Patrick Moynihan, who felt that Black poverty is the product of behavior patterns and not larger socioeconomic issues. As a result, President Johnson initiated job training and equal opportunity programs, and for the symptoms of poverty that manifest through crime he puts more police on the streets).

187. *See Id.*

188. *See Id.*

189. *See Id.*

190. Elizabeth Hinton, *Why We Should Reconsider the War on Crime*, TIME (Mar. 20, 2015), https://time.com/3746059/war-on-crime-history/.

191. Dan Baum, *Legalize it All*, Harpers, April 2016, *available at* Legalize It All, by Dan Baum (harpers.org) (last visited Nov. 2022).

192. *Edenfield v. New Orleans Police Department*, 354 So.3d 661 (2023).

193. The example of the unnamed enslaved person shot by a New Iberia, Louisiana slave patrol when he was innocently travelling on horse to visit his wife at a nearby plantation is one of countless examples. *See Duperrier v. Dautrive*, 12 La.Ann. 664 (1856).

194. It is believed that about 549 people were lynched in Louisiana due to irrational fears of interracial sex, casual social transgressions or allegations of a serious violent crime such as, murder and rape; *See* Equal Justice Initiative, *Lynching in America Confronting the Legacy of Racial Terror in America* (3d ed. 2017).

195. There are a few logical explanations for the shift from chattel slavery to wage slavery, the first of which is the immediate end to slave revolts and the potential for mass loss of white lives.

     The longevity of this system is understood by few. Doc James, Jr. speaks to the plight of many. He was born fifty-six years *after* slavery ended (in 1921). Orange Grove Plantation in Port Allen, Louisiana was his employer for over fifty years. He started work as a young boy and worked various jobs on the plantation, such as plowing and cutting sugar cane. He first earned thirty-five cents per day, then eighty cents per day then, finally, one dollar per day, which was sunup to sundown. *See* Oral History of Doc James, Jr., "Remembrances Collection," p.9 (March 2000). In 1982, Popular Grove Plantation, also in Port Allen, Louisiana, closed after almost one hundred years of planting and refining sugarcane. After slavery, its workers lived in the former slave quarters on site. Many of them remained there until as late as 1995. *See* "Remembrances Collection," p.7 (March 2000); *see also State v. Lavalais*, 685 So.2d 1048,1062 (La. 11/25/96) (Discussing the way defendant Albert Lavalais's family was part of plantation country in that this Black family lived on and worked the land of the white owners in 1985).

196. *See L.J. Dupre et al. Executors v. Prescott*, 5 La.Ann 592 (1850).

197. *Eulalie v. Long*, 9 La. Ann.9, 10 (1854).

198. Race & Slavery Petitions Project, *available at* Petition Details (uncg.edu) https://library.uncg.edu/slavery/petitions/details.aspx?pid=6903 (last visited May 3, 2021) (discussing Elizabeth Godinau's petition before the Parish Court for the Parish and City of New Orleans).

199. *Id.*

200. *Hendricks v. Phillips*, 3 La.Ann. 618, 618 (1848).

201. New Orleans During the Civil War (Teacher's Guide), The Historic New Orleans Collection (2016), p. 11-12, *available at* LessonPlan_CivilWar.pdf (hnoc.org) (last visited 4/27/21) (emphasis added); After the Civil War, Reverend Palmer became instrumental in shaping the false narrative of history called the Lost Cause. His commitment to the cause led him to give a stirring eulogy to the Confederate General Robert E. Lee.

202. Nick Weldon, *On Thanksgiving 1860, a New Orleans Pastor's Sermon Defending Slavery Rallied the Secessionist Movement*, The Historic New Orleans Collection (Nov. 22, 2019), *available at* On Thanksgiving 1860, a New Orleans pastor's sermon defending slavery rallied the secessionist movement | The Historic New Orleans Collection (hnoc.org) (last visited 4/27/21).

203. W.E. B. Du Bois, *Black Reconstruction in America* 196 (2007).

204. Kristen Lewis, *A Portrait of Louisiana 2020*, p. 33. New York: Measure of America, Social Science Research Council, 2020, *available at* A Portrait of Louisiana 2020 — Measure of America: A Program of the Social Science Research Council (last visited Feb. 8, 2021).

205. *Franklin v. State of South Carolina*, 218 U.S. 161, 170 (1910).

206. *See* New Orleans During the Civil War (Teacher's Guide), The Historic New Orleans Collection (2016), p. 27, *available at* LessonPlan_CivilWar.pdf (hnoc.org) (last visited 4/27/21) (emphasis added).

207. *Id.*

208. Calvin Schermerhorn, *The Thibodaux Massacre Left 60 African-Americans Dead and Spelled the End of Unionized Farm Labor in the South for Decades*, SMITHSONIANMAG.COM, Nov. 21, 2017, available at The Thibodaux Massacre Left 60 African-Americans Dead and Spelled the End of Unionized Farm Labor in the South for Decades | History | Smithsonian Magazine (last visited May 12, 2021).

209. *Id.*

210. John DeSantis, *The Thibodaux Massacre* 21 (2016).

211. *Id.* at 20 (referencing the local priest, Father Charles Menard's, journal account of the massacre).

212. Ellen Baker Bell, *Thibodaux Massacre*, 64 PARISHES (2011), *available at* Thibodaux Massacre | 64 Parishes (last visited May 12, 2021).

213. In 1938, the Bogalusa Paper Mill was sold to Crown Zellerbach which continued operations until 1986 when the mill was sold to Gaylord Container Corporation. In 2002, Gaylord was acquired by Temple-Inland Corporation and, in 2012, International Paper acquired Temple-Inland. The Bogalusa Paper Mill is still in operation and employees approximately 400 workers.

214. *See Hicks v. Crown Zellerbach Corporation*, 319 F.Supp. 314, 325 (1970).

215. *Id.* at 317-321.

216. *Id.* at 325 court found:

> The system maintained by the defendants, which gives unskilled white employees greater promotional opportunities than unskilled Black employees, for reasons directly traceable to prior segregation and not founded in any objective business considerations violates [Section 703(a) of the Civil Rights Act of 1964].

217. *See* W.E.B. DuBois, *The Negro Since 1900: A Progress Report*, N.Y. Times, Nov. 21, 1948, at SM24.

218. *See* W.E. B. Du Bois, *Black Reconstruction in America* 293 (2007).

219. *Id.* at 293.

220. Olivia Paschal, *The PRO Act Would Undo Decades of Southern Anti-Union Laws Rooted in Racism*, Facing South (March 11, 2021), *available at* The PRO Act would undo decades of Southern anti-union laws rooted in racism | Facing South (last visited 3/31/21).

221. Du Bois, *supra* note 269 at 285.

222. Three-year-old John Joseph is a good example of the term safekeeping. He was held in custody until he was old enough to work. John Joseph, *The Life and Sufferings of John Joseph, a Native of Ashantee, in Western Africa: Who Was Stolen from His Parents at the Age of 3 Years, and Sold to Mr Johnstone, a Cotton Planter, in New Orleans, South America.* (Wellington: Printed for John Joseph by J. Greedy, 1848).

223. Grant Lyons, *Louisiana and the Livingston Criminal Codes*, 15 *The Journal of the Louisiana Historical* 243, 254 (1974).
224. *See Id.*
225. *See Id.*
226. *See Id.*
227. Mr. Livingston favored the Philadelphia plan with adaptions. He wanted no work and solitary confinement, initially. After good behavior, he offered work as a form of relief from the isolation and as a means to have them reconstitute their social constitutions. He also wanted moral and charter lessons integrated into corrections. His criminal code envisioned a penitentiary modelled as such. *See Id. at* 255-265.
228. *See See Id. at* 252-3.
229. Governor's Message, January 10, 1831, 2.
230. *See* Lyons, supra note 278 at 265 (this followed official complaints about poor conditions in prisons).
231. 'Advertisement: Creole Shoes', BRG, April 18, 1840, 2.
232. *Johnson v Municipality No. One*, 5 LaAnn. 100, p.1 (1850).
233. *Id. at* 2. (There was no culpability for the prison officials who were responsible for the conditions. The white slave owner was awarded $600.00 for the loss of his slave that was caused by the jail. The subliminal message that Blacks got was that their life was of no worth or value.)
234. Convict leasing, which prevailed in Louisiana from 1844 to 1901, was underway, making it a both a pre and post-Civil War enterprise.
235. W.E. B. Du Bois, *Black Reconstruction in America* 173 (2007) (Observing that âoeRailways in the United States increased from three miles in 1828 to 23, 476 miles in 1860, 30, 283 miles in 1870, and over 50,000 miles in 1880.").
236. *See* Mark T. Carleton, *Politics and Punishment The History of the Louisiana State Penal System* 46 (1971).
237. *Id.*
238. *Id.*
239. Angela Y. Davis, *Racialized Punishment and Prison Abolition, in* A Companion to African American Philosophy 363 (Blackwell Publishing 1988) (citations omitted); The United States Supreme Court has acknowledged this. *See United States v. Rhodes*, 1 Abb. U.S. 28, 794 (1866) (noting that "[a]lmost simultaneously with the adoption of the amendment this course of legislative oppression was begun."); Scholars have affirmed this. Woodward, *supra* note 161; Carleton, *supra* note 288 ; Douglas A. Blackmon, *Slavery by Another Name* (2008); Michelle Alexander, *The New Jim Crow* (2010); Dennis Childs, *Slaves of the State Black Incarceration from the Chain Gang to the Penitentiary* (2015). Some members of Congress were troubled by this:

> The emancipation of the slaves is submitted to only in so far as chattel slavery in the old form could not be kept up. But although the freedman is no longer considered the property of the individual master, *he is considered the slave of society, and all independent state legislation will share the tendency to make him such.* The ordinances abolishing slavery passed by the conventions *under the pressure of circumstances*, will not be looked upon as barring the establishment of a new form of servitude.

> The Reconstruction Amendments' Debates, 93 (Alfred Avins ed, 2nd ed. 1974)

(39th Cong., 1st Sess., Senate Ex. Doc. No. 2, Dec. 19, 1865, Schurz Report on Condition of the South).

240. Dennis Childs, *Slaves of the State* 9 (2015).

241. OFFICIAL JOURNAL OF THE PROCEEDINGS OF THE CONSTITUTIONAL CONVENTION OF THE STATE OF LOUISIANA 180 (1879).

242. Upon its creation, it was to assume the leases of convicts and it was purposed with overseeing convicts on State farms, levees, factories roads, and other public works, jobs reserved for the Black convicts. By this juncture, over 80 percent of Louisiana's convicts were Black.; *See also* Carleton, *supra* note 289 at 88 (mentioning a steady increase in the number of Black inmates from 1869, when Major James took charge of the penitentiary, until his leases ended).

243. *See Convict System Changed in the South: Negro Prisoners No Longer Leased Out to Work for Levee Contractors*, Chicago Daily Tribune, August 3, 1901, 13.

244. This was done in 1897 at a meeting held in in Nashville, Tennessee. She grew up in Thomasville, Georgia and witnessed the prisoners working on the roads there.

245. This was published in 1893.

246. In 1907, Terrell published her essay in the magazine *The Nineteenth Century*.

247. *Black Women Reformers*, Colored Conventions Project, *available at* Black Women Reformers - The Colored Conventions and the Carceral States (last visited Aug. 17, 2022).

248. *Id.*

249. *See* Mark T. Carleton, *Politics and Punishment The History of the Louisiana State Penal System* 46 (1971).

250. *Id.* at 90.

251. *See* Shane Bauer, *5 Ways Prisoners Were Used for Profit Throughout U.S. History*, PBS New Hour, Feb, 26, 2020.

252. *Id.*

253. *Id.*

254. *Id.*

255. Louisiana State Penitentiary Museum Foundation, The Angola Story 8-9 (2011).

256. Plantation owner Isaac Franklin purchased property later consolidated as "Angola" in the 1830s. *See* Marianne Fisher-Giorlando and Chris Turner-Neal, *Angola: Fact and Fiction*, 64 Parishes (2020).

257. *See* David M. Oshinsky, *Worse Than Slavery: Parchman Farm and the Ordeal of Jim Crow Justice* (1996).

258. The inmate guard system that was used harkens back to slavery-era practices:

   [A] work gang is given a designated area to hoe, cultivate or cut. Said area is usually rectangular in shape. The inmates are instructed to remain inside the imaginary lines of the rectangle. A guard, armed with a high powered rifle or shot gun, is stationed at each point of the rectangle. If an inmate crosses the guard lines he is considered as trying to escape and can be shot. If an inmate gets too close to the line he might get a warning shot fired over his head or at his feet...This technique is known as working under the gun.

   George v. Sowers, 268 So.2d 65, 66-67 (1972).

259. Prison Enterprises, *available at* http://www.prisonenterprises.org/crops/ (last visited July 24, 2020).

260. Louisiana State Penitentiary Museum Foundation, The Angola Story 9 (2011).

261. Prison Enterprises, *available at* http://www.prisonenterprises.org/crops/ (last visited July 24, 2020).

262. Louisiana State Penitentiary Museum Foundation, The Angola Story 9 (2011); This is consistent with national practices:

    [T]he companies that purchase prison labor or the products developed in whole or in part from the prison system include elite brands and Fortune 500 companies:

    Whole Foods, McDonalds, Wal-Mart,Â Victoria's Secret (no longer purchasing), AT&T, BP, Bank of America, Bayer, Cargill, Caterpillar, Chevron, Chrysler, Costco, John Deere, Eli Lilly and Company, Exxon Mobil, GlaxoSmithKline, Johnson and Johnson, K-Mart, Koch Industries, Merck, Motorola, Nintendo, Pfizer, Procter & Gamble, Pepsi, ConAgra Foods, Shell, Starbucks, UPS, Verizon, Wendy's,Â IBM, Boeing, Motorola, Microsoft, AT&T, Wireless, Texas Instrument, Dell, Compaq, Honeywell, Hewlett-Packard, Nortel, Lucent Technologies, 3Com, Intel, Northern Telecom, TWA, Nordstrom's, Revlon, Macy's, Pierre Cardin, and Target Stores.

    Michele Goodwin, *The Thirteenth Amendment: Modern Slavery, Capitalism, and Mass Incarceration,* 104 CNLLR 899, 962 (2019) (citations omitted).

263. *See* La. Admin. Code 22§331 (2022).

264. Louisiana Commission on Law Enforcement and Administration of Criminal Justice, 2019 Status of State and Local Corrections Facilities and Program Report (April 1, 2020).

265. *Id.*

266. Thomas A. Foster, *Rethinking Rufus Sexual Violations of Enslaved Men* 103 (2019).

267. *Id.*

268. *Id.*

269. *Bobby Jindal's Personal Butler, Also an Inmate, Wants Life Sentence Reduced,* Firstpost, May 20, 2015, *available at* Bobby Jindal's personal butler, also an inmate, wants life sentence reduced-World News , Firstpost (last visited Jan. 20, 2022) (Mansion coordinator Irene Shepherd explaining that inmate Henry Cage handles any duties she asks of him for the household of then-governor Bobby Jindal); Forest C.Hammond-Martin, a former butler, tells of his experience delivering food and beverages to employees in the governors mansion; preparing and serving meals to mansion guests; pulling chairs for female guests as they took seats; responding to the governor's personal requests during meals, such as retrieving items in his office or bringing more food; and, rising at the presence of the governor. *See* Forest C. Hammond-Martin, *With Edwards in the Governor's Mansion: From Angola to Free Man,* 225-238 (2012).

270. *See* Kerry Myers, *Sugarcane Makes a Comeback,* The Angolite 8 (Nov.-Dec. 2012).

271. C.M. Hargroder, *A Look at Angola -- Prison Conditions Better, But Changes Are Still Needed,* Times Picayune, Apr. 15, 1967.

272. Louisiana Advisory Committee to the United States Commission on Civil Rights, *A Study of Adult Corrections in Louisiana,* at 90 (1976) Public-A-Study-of-Adult-Corrections-in-Louisiana.pdf (incarcerationtransparency.org) (last visited Jan. 18. 2022).

273. "Sugar production at the prison was big business for at least 50 years. In addition to the planted acreage, a sugar refinery produced more than 3.5 million pounds of raw

sugar a year from the Angola crop alone." Kerry Myers, *Sugarcane Makes a Comeback*, The Angolite 8-9 (Nov.-Dec. 2012).

274. The Reconstruction Amendments' Debates, 614 (Alfred Avins ed, 2nd ed. 1974) (42nd Cong., 2nd Sess., Feb. 5, 1872) (Statement of Senator Matthew H. Carpenter); The respected political philosopher Alexis de Tocqueville referred to the jury as a political institution. See Tocqueville , Alexis de. (1831), Chapter XVI: Causes Mitigating Tyranny in the United States Part II in *Democracy In America* (Vol. 1).

275. Derrick Bell, *The Law of Racial Standing*, 2 Yale J.L. & Liberation 117, 120 (1991).

276. Just Lead Washington, *Washington Pro Bono Equity Training Guide: Race Equity & Cultural Competency Curriculum for Volunteer Lawyers*, p. 11, *available at* Washington Pro Bono Equity Training Guide: Race Equity & Cultural Competency Curriculum for Volunteer Lawyers (justleadwa.org) (last visited March 8, 2022).

277. *See Strategic Action Plan Report of the Secretary-General's Task Force on Addressing Racism and Promoting Dignity for All in the United Nations Secretariat*, at 7 (2021) (citing foreword by Catherine Pollard Under-Secretary-General for Management Strategy, Policy and Compliance).

278. *See* Just Lead Washington, *supra* note 326 at 11.

279. *See Who Dat Say (We) "Too Depraved to Be Saved"?: Re-membering Katrina/ Haiti (and Beyond): Critical Studyin'for Human Freedom*, 81 Harv. Ed. Rev. 343, 348 (2011); Historian Ibram X. Kendi reminds us that racism describes one's action at a time; it does not anchor one to that action for all of posterity nor does it define who one is for the remainder of their existence on earth. *See* Ibram X. Kendi, *How to be an Antiracist* (Dec. 2, 2020). Albion W. Tourgèe, a Union veteran and former North Carolina judge during Reconstruction, is an example to consider. Tourgèe litigated Homer Plessy's case before the SCOTUS. Prior to his involvement in Plessy, Tourgèe opposed Senator Charles Sumner's efforts to pass the Civil Rights Act in 1874. "Tourgée underwent his conversion to the ideal of racial equality during the Civil War, when he fought in an 'abolition regiment' and came into contact with fugitive slaves and Black soldiers in Union army camps." Carolyn L. Karcher, *The National Citizen's Rights Association: Precursor of the NAACP*, 5 Elon L. Rev. 107, 108 (2013). In 1891, he founded the interracial organization that became the precursor to the NAACP: The National Citizens' Rights Association (NCRA). He used novels, newspaper stories and multi-racial coalitions to change public opinion on matters of race.

280. In Stokely Carmichael & Charles V. Hamilton, *Black Power: The Politics of Liberation in America* 4 (1967), they explained:

When white terrorists bomb a Black church and kill five Black children, that is an act of individual racism, widely deplored by most segments of society. But when in that same city–Birmingham, Alabama–five hundred Black babies die each year because of the lack of proper food, shelter and medical facilities...that is a function of institutional racism.

281. *See Strategic Action Plan Report of the Secretary-General's Task Force on Addressing Racism and Promoting Dignity for All in the United Nations Secretariat*, at 8 (2021) (citing foreword by Catherine Pollard Under-Secretary-General for Management Strategy, Policy and Compliance).

282. *See* Sovereignty Commission Online, Mississippi Department of Archives & History, *available at* Digital Archives | Mississippi Department of Archives &... (ms.gov) (last visited April 5, 2022).

283. COINTELPRO, which is short for Counterintelligence Program, was a series of covert, and often illegal projects conduct by the United States FBI and aimed at surveilling, infiltrating, discrediting and disrupting American political organizations and other voices of dissent; See Anthony Summers, Official and Confidential The Secret Life of J. Edgar Hoover (1993); *See also* Angela A. Allen-Bell, *The Incongruous Intersection of the Black Panther Party and the Ku Klux Klan*, 39 Seattle U. L. Rev. 1157 (2016); Angela A. Allen-Bell, *A Prescription for Healing a National Wound: Two Doses of Executive Direct Action Equals a Portion of Justice and a Serving of Redress for America & The Black Panther Party*, 5 Univ. Miami Race & Soc. Justice L.Rev. 1 (2015); Angela A. Allen-Bell, *Activism Unshackled & Justice Unchained: A Call to Make a Human Right Out of One of the Most Calamitous Human Wrongs to Have Taken Place on American Soil*, 7 J. of Law & Social Deviance 125 (2014).

284. The United States Senate Select Committee to Study Governmental Operations With Respect to Intelligence Activities (Church Committee Report). *See* Senate Select Comm. to Study Governmental Operations with Respect to Intelligence Activities, Final Report, S.Rep.No.755, 94th Cong., 2d Sess., Book III at 185-223 (1976); See also ward churchill & jim vander wall, the cointelpro papers 91-92 (South End Press 1990).

285. See Betty Medsger, *The Burglary: The Discovery of J. Edgar Hoover's Secret FBI* 7 (2014); Angela A. Allen-Bell, *A Prescription for Healing a National Wound: Two Doses of Executive Direct Action Equals a Portion of Justice and a Serving of Redress for America & The Black Panther Party*, 5 Univ. Miami Race & Soc. Justice L.Rev. 69-70 (Spring 2015) (Lead Article) (citations omitted).

286. *See* Curt Gentry, *J. Edgar Hoover: The Man and the Secrets* 34 (1991) (quoting Gus Hall, General Secretary of the Communist Party of the United States).

287. For many years, Black farmers had complained that they were not receiving fair treatment when they applied to local county committees (which make the decisions) for farm loans or assistance. These farmers alleged that they were being denied USDA farm loans or forced to wait longer for loan approval than were non-minority farmers. Many black farmers contended that they were facing foreclosure and financial ruin because the USDA denied them timely loans and debt restructuring. In 1997 and 1998, two class-action lawsuits entitled *Pigford v. Glickman* ("*Pigford*") and *Brewington v. Glickman* ("*Brewington*"), respectively, were filed on behalf of groups of Black farmers. After the *Pigford and Brewington* cases were consolidated, they were settled by the parties in 1999 and became the largest civil rights settlement in history.

288. *See Strategic Action Plan Report of the Secretary-General's Task Force on Addressing Racism and Promoting Dignity for All in the United Nations Secretariat*, at 8 (2021) (citing foreword by Catherine Pollard Under-Secretary-General for Management Strategy, Policy and Compliance).

289. *See* Khiara M. Bridges, *Critical Race Theory A Primer* 148 (2019).

290. Ruby Tapia, *What Is the Carceral State?*, STORYMAPS (Oct. 3, 2018), https://storymaps.arcgis.com/stories/7ab5f5c3fbca46c38f0b2496bcaa5ab0.

291. Ruby Tapia, *What Is the Carceral State?*, STORYMAPS (Oct. 3, 2018), https://storymaps.arcgis.com/stories/7ab5f5c3fbca46c38f0b2496bcaa5ab0.

292. NAT'L ACADS. OF SCIS., ENG'G AND MED., REDUCING RACIAL INEQUALITY IN CRIME AND JUSTICE: SCIENCE, PRACTICE, AND POLICY VIII (2022).

293. *Id.*

Chapter 2

1. The Reconstruction Amendments' Debates, 81 (Alfred Avins ed, 2nd ed. 1974). (38th Cong., 2d Sess., June 21, 1864) (Statement of Representative James Ashley).

2. In 1909, the NAACP (National Association for the Advancement of Colored People) was formed in New York for the purposes of ending lynching, advancing political rights and achieving criminal justice improvements.

3. To do business in Louisiana, "non-trading" organizations were required to submit an affidavit stating that they were not affiliated with any out-of-state associations having links to communist or subversive organizations or communists on their board. Also, non-trading organizations affiliated with any out-of-state association was required to submit its membership list to the state of Louisiana. For failure to comply with these laws, Louisiana sued the NAACP (National Association for the Advancement of Colored People) in state court to stop it from operating in Louisiana. *See State v. N.A.A.C.P.*, 90 So.2d 884 (1956); *see also Gremillion v. N.A.A.C.P.*, 81 S.Ct. 1333 (1961); During its formative years, the NAACP's purpose was to make American Blacks "free from peonage, politically free from disenfranchisement, and socially free from insult." W.E.B. DuBois, *The Negro Since 1900: A Progress Report*, N.Y. Times, Nov. 21, 1948, at SM24; *State ex rel. Gremillion v. National Ass'n for Advancement of Colored People*, 90 So.2d 884 (1956).

4. W.E. B. Du Bois, *Black Reconstruction in America* 237 (2007).

5. The Reconstruction Amendments' Debates, 216 (Alfred Avins ed, 2nd ed. 1974) (39th Cong., 1st Sess., May 9, 1866) (Statement of Representative Andrew Rogers).

6. The Reconstruction Amendments' Debates, 400 (Alfred Avins ed, 2nd ed. 1974) (40th Cong., 3rd Sess., Feb. 17, 1869) (Statement of Representative James W. Nye).

7. The Reconstruction Amendments' Debates, 143 (Alfred Avins ed, 2nd ed. 1974) (39th Cong., 3rd Sess., Feb. 7, 1866) (Statement of Representative Samuel McKee) (A "voter is an officer...as the man who enters the jury box, as any one who holds office. It is a trust imposed upon him by law....")

8. The Reconstruction Amendments' Debates, 327 (Alfred Avins ed, 2nd ed. 1974) (40th Cong., 2d Sess., June 6, 1868) (Statement of Representative James W. Patterson).

9. James Retallack, *Get Out the Vote! Electioneering without Democracy*, in *Germany's Second Reich* (University of Toronto Press, 2015) (referencing "The ballot is stronger than the bullet." Abraham Lincoln, speech of 19 May 1856).

10. Gloria J. Brown-Marshall, *She Took Justice the Black Woman, Law and Power 1619 to 1969* 169 (2021).

11. The Reconstruction Amendments' Debates, 7 (Alfred Avins ed, 2nd ed. 1974) (31st Cong., 1st Sess. (Sept. 12,1850) (Statement of Senator Stephen Douglas).

12. The Reconstruction Amendments' Debates, 85 (Alfred Avins ed, 2nd ed. 1974) (38th Cong., 2d Sess., Jan. 31, 1865) (Statement of Representative John D. Stiles).

13. The Reconstruction Amendments' Debates, 191(Alfred Avins ed, 2nd ed. 1974) (39th Cong., 1st Sess., March 13, 1866) (Statement of Representative James F. Wilson).

14. The Reconstruction Amendments' Debates, 735 (Alfred Avins ed, 2nd ed. 1974) (43rd Cong., 2d Sess., Feb. 26, 1875) (Statement of Senator Augustus S. Merrimon).

15. The Civil Rights Act of 1866 declared that all persons born in the United States are citizens of the United States and, as such, are entitled to enjoy the same basic rights as white citizens. This legislation was a direct response to the Black Codes. Section One of the 1866 Act listed as civil rights the following private law rights: (1) to make and enforce contracts; (2) to sue, and be sued; (3) to give evidence; (4) to inherit, purchase, sell, lease, hold and convey real and personal property; and (5) to enjoy equal protection of the laws. Act of Apr. 9, 1866, ch. 31, s 1, 14 Stat. 27. It also invalidated the Black Codes. The Act as finally adopted did not include a general ban on discrimination in civil rights or immunities, in "an abundance of caution" for those who feared "it might be held by courts that the right of suffrage was included." Cong. Globe , 39th Cong., 1st Sess. 1366-7 (1866) (remarks of Rep. Wilson); Fears that the Civil Rights Act of 1866 might be unconstitutional led to the swift passage of the 1868 Fourteenth Amendment, which, with constitutional backing, conferred citizenship on the emancipated population.

16. Cong. Globe , 39th Cong., 1st Sess. 1366 (1866) (remarks of Rep. Thayer).

17. The Reconstruction Amendments' Debates, 1117 (Alfred Avins ed, 2nd ed. 1974) (39th Cong., 1st Sess., Feb. 28, 1866) (Statement of Representative James F. Wilson).

18. The Reconstruction Amendments' Debates, 205 (Alfred Avins ed, 2nd ed. 1974) (39th Cong., 1st Sess., April 7, 1866) (Statement of Representative William Lawrence).

19. Cong. Globe , 39th Cong., 1st Sess. 2542 (1866) (remarks of Rep. Bingham).

20. Cong. Globe , 39th Cong., 1st Sess. 2766 (1866) (remarks of Sen. Howard).

21. The Reconstruction Amendments' Debates, 613 (Alfred Avins ed, 2nd ed. 1974) (39th Cong., 1st Sess., Feb. 5, 1872) (Statement of Senator Matthew Carpenter).

22. The Reconstruction Amendments' Debates, 141 (Alfred Avins ed, 2nd ed. 1974) (39th Cong., 1st Sess., Feb. 5, 1866) (Statement of Representative Samuel Moulton) (Civil rights "are the great fundamental rights that are secured by the Constitution of the United States, and that are defined in the Declaration of Independence, the right to personal liberty, the right to hold and enjoy property, to transmit property, and to make contracts...I understand that a civil right is a right that a party is entitled to and that he can enforce by operation of law."); The Reconstruction Amendments' Debates, 1117 (Alfred Avins ed, 2nd ed. 1974) (39th Cong., 1st Sess., Feb. 28, 1866) (Statement of Representative James F. Wilson) ("Civil rights are those which have no relation to the establishment, support, or management of government. Civil rights are the natural rights of man....")

23. The Reconstruction Amendments' Debates, 394 (Alfred Avins ed, 2nd ed. 1974) (40th Cong., 3rd Sess., Feb. 17, 1869) (Statement of Representative Henry Wilson).

24. The Reconstruction Amendments' Debates, 407 (Alfred Avins ed, 2nd ed. 1974) (40th Cong., 1st Sess. (Feb. 20, 1869)(Statement of Senator John Logan).

25. The Reconstruction Amendments' Debates, 92 (Alfred Avins ed, 2nd ed. 1974) (39th Cong., 1st Sess., Dec. 19, 1865) (Report of Maj. Gen. Carl Schurz on Condition of the South): *see also* W.E. B. Du Bois, *Black Reconstruction in America* 166 (2007).

26. The Reconstruction Amendments' Debates, 735 (Alfred Avins ed, 2nd ed. 1974) (43rd Cong., 2d Sess., Feb. 26, 1875) (Statement of Senator Augustus S. Merrimon).

27. The privileges and immunities clause, appearing in article IV of the constitution, is an ideal starting point. Voting is not included amongst the "privileges or immunities of citizenship, which means that, as citizens move about the various states, certain individual rights follow, but not political rights.; In *Minor v. Happersett*, 88 U.S. 162 (1874), the Court considered the claim that "a woman, born or naturalized in the United States and subject to the jurisdiction thereof, is a citizen of the state in which she resides, [and thus] has the right of suffrage as one of the privileges and immunities of her citizenship, which the state cannot by its laws or Constitution abridge." The Court agreed that women may be citizens of the United States so as to be entitled to the protection of the Privileges and Immunities Clause,but the court disagreed with the thought that there was an entitlement to vote. The court held that the Privileges and Immunities Clause did not add to the privileges and immunities that existed before it was enacted and they shared that suffrage was not coextensive with citizenship at the time the Fourteenth Amendment was adopted. Therefore, the court concluded that voting was not among the privileges and immunities guaranteed by the Fourteenth Amendment so a provision in a State Constitution that confined the right to vote to "male citizens of the United States" did not run afoul of the privileges and immunities clause.

28. The Louisiana Constitutions of 1812, 1845, 1852, 1861 and 1864 all limit the right to vote to white males. The 1845 constitution, extended voting rights to all foreign-born white men after just two years of residency. This induced many migrants who entered the state through the port of New Orleans to stay.

29. There were overlapping local and national efforts. "Even before the end of the Civil War, African Americans organized to campaign for the right to vote. In 1864, free Blacks gathered in Syracuse, New York, to form the National Equal Rights League (NERL). One of those in attendance was Abraham Galloway, a fugitive slave, abolitionist, and Union spy. He and a delegation of Blacks met with President Lincoln to endorse the suffrage for all African Americans. The president did not commit himself and was assassinated in April 1865 before the issue came to a resolution." Susan Cianci Salvatore, National Park Service, *Civil Rights in America: Racial Voting Rights*, p. 4 (2009).

In *Fogg v. Hobbs*, 6 Watts 553 (1837), a free Black citizen of Pennsylvania sued after being denied the right to vote. He claimed that election officials had violated the state's color-blind constitution—"all men are born equally free and independent." He further contended that he qualified as a legal voter under Article III, Section I of the Pennsylvania Constitution of 1790, which granted voting rights irrespective of race to "every freeman of the age of twenty-one years, having resided in the state two years next before the election, and within that time paid a state or county tax." The Pennsylvania Supreme Court reversed the lower court's ruling in his favor, noting that "no coloured race was party to our social compact," and that there was no basis on which "to raise this depressed race to the level of the white one." The court also concluded that federal constitution was an obstacle to "political freedom of the negro." Hobbs, 6 Watts 553, 560 (1837); This distinction was drawn repeatedly during consideration of the Civil Rights Act of 1866 carried over to, and informed interpretation of, the Privileges and Immunities Clause of the Fourteenth Amendment, which was intended to preserve this barrier between the two.

30. *Yick Wo v. Hopkins*, 118 U.S. 356, 370 (1886).

31. *See* Judith N. Shklar, *American Citizenship: The Quest for Inclusion* 25-62 (1991).

32. Libby Neidenbach, *In 1860s New Orleans, Black Activists Fought—and Died— for the Right to Vote, The Historic New Orleans Collection.*

33. There were simultaneous efforts. In 1864, free Blacks gathered in Syracuse, New York, to form the National Equal Rights League (NERL). In Wilmington, the NERL chapter demanded "all the social and political rights of . . . white citizens" and insisted "that Blacks be consulted in the selection of policemen, justices of the peace, and county commissioners." David Cecelski and Timothy Tyson, eds., *Democracy Betrayed: The Wilmington Race Riot of 1898 and Its Legacy* 111 (1998); Throughout the South in 1865 and 1866, ex-slaves and free Blacks convened statewide conventions to agitate for their political rights.

34. *See* State Convention for the Colored People of Louisiana, Jan. 1865 at 242-249.

35. *The Late President Lincoln on Negro Suffrage; A Letter from Him to Gov. Hahn of Louisiana,*" New York Times June 23, 1865; "Last Public Address," Abraham Lincoln Online, available at http://www.abrahamlincolnonline.org/lincoln/speeches/last.htm (last visited Jan. 9, 2020).

36. W.E. B. Du Bois, *Black Reconstruction in America* 32 (2007).

37. Granting the right to vote to mixed race persons was proposed at the legislature that year. The "Quadroom Bill," proposed by Charles Smith, failed.

38. Emily H. Reed, *Life of A. P. Dostie; Of the Conflict of New Orleans,* 292-3 (2015).

39. *See* Mary Gehman, *The Free People of Color of New Orleans* 90 (2014).

40. *Id.* at 91.

41. As noted in chapter one, the 1868 constitution formalized this right.

42. Official Journal of the Proceedings of the Convention for the State of La. 151 (1867-68); The Louisiana Constitution of 1868 for the first-time permitted Negroes to vote. La.Const.1868, Art. 98.

43. "In 1866, a mere 39,000 hogsheads of sugar were produced in Louisiana...But by 1868, 84, 256 hogsheads were produced at an average market price of $137.80. After that prices and yields were mostly on the upswing ...." John DeSantis, *The Thibodaux Massacre* 60 (2016).

44. A white man named Gibson stopped to make a purchase at a plantation in Bossier Parish. Gibson saw a Black man sitting nearby and yelled, "You was all damned radicals." After concluding that the Black men would vote Republican in the presidential election, he opened fire, but missed. Black men captured and bound him but left him unharmed. News spread, as well as unsubstantiated rumors that two white men had been killed. By the next morning, Whites sought vengeance. Approximately one hundred Blacks were killed.

45. This massacre occurred before the 1868 presidential election, which pitted conservative Democrat Horatio Seymour against Republican war hero Ulysses S. Grant. Republicans used their newspapers to advocate expanding Black people's rights and privileges. Democratic papers aligned with the slogan of their party's presidential nominee Seymour: "This is a white man's Government." In September

1868, a dispute over a column published in an Opelousas, Louisiana partisan newspaper provoked this racial violence. The attackers sought to reverse dramatic political gains made by Black citizens after the Civil War, intimidate them from exercising their newly found rights and restore the racial hierarchy of the slavery era.

46. The massacre preceded the approaching general election. Black men had been granted the right to vote. Whites were afraid the black vote would cause the Democratic Candidate Horatio Seymour not to win the election against Ulysses S. Grant, his rival, so the white Democrats sought to kill the black voters.

47. The massacre started when an official attempted to move the voting site from the court to a plantation. Black protest led to this confrontation. *See* James D. Wilson, Jr., *The Donaldsonville Incident of 1870: A Study of Local Party Dissension and Republican Infighting in Reconstruction Louisiana*, 38 The Journal of the Louisiana Historical Association 329-345 (1997).

48. During the last week of August 1874, some members of the White League murdered ten Republicans: four blacks and six whites. The killings all had the same end: the destruction of Republican government in northwestern Louisiana.

49. The Reconstruction Amendments' Debates, 359 (Alfred Avins ed, 2nd ed. 1974) (40th Cong., 1st Sess., Feb. 5, 1869) (Statement of Representative George Vickers) (Commenting that the purpose of the Fifteenth Amendment "is to give the right of suffrage to the negro, to make him equal in office, equal in all political rights with others."); Some of the shortcomings discussed were realized and verbalized when the Fifteenth Amendment was debated by the United States Congress. Senator Jabob M. Howard indicated that the Fifteenth Amendment would offer no protection to Blacks when state officials wished to use legal schemes to disenfranchise them. The Reconstruction Amendments' Debates, 422 (Alfred Avins ed, 2nd ed. 1974) (41st Cong., 1st Sess., Jan. 21, 1870) (Statement of Senator Jabob M. Howard).

One should not overlook that the desire to prevent the vote was also about preventing office holding. A proposed version of the Fifteenth Amendment included both office holding and voting upon the belief that there should be a "right to select in a republican government the agent who is to execute your will and the right to be selected by your fellow citizens as that agent." That version failed because putting federal might behind the right of a Black person to hold office would be costly.

50. Republican William Pitt Kellogg and Fusion Party candidate John McEnery were candidates for governor. The Fusion Party was an alliance between Democrats and liberal Republicans, Republicans who advocated for the rule of former slave owners and rebels.

51. Knowing the history of resistance on the part of Southern whites, President Ulysses S. Grant sent federal troops to support the Republican candidate. The Fusion Party refused to accept the results. Blacks were unwilling to surrender even a modicum of their newfound freedom. Fearing the consequences of inaction, Blacks took control of the local courthouse (where Republic officeholders were also).

52. The Enforcement Acts of 1870 and 1871, also known as the Klu Klux Klan Acts, intended to guarantee the rights of the formerly enslaved under the 14th and 15th Amendments.

53. *United States v. Cruikshank*, 1 Woods 308 (1874). The defendants are believed to be Ku Klux Klan members.
54. *Id.*
55. *Id*; 25 F.Cas. 707, 712 (1874).
56. In 1951, a monument at the site of the Colfax Massacre was erected. It described the massacre as the "riot that marked the end of carpetbag misrule in the South" and it commemorated the three White men who lost their lives. Because the marker offensively and inaccurately depicted the slaughter of innocent Black men asserting their constitutional rights, the two descents joined forces to do the overdue and necessary work of narrative change. Reverend Avery Hamilton worked for years to have the marker removed. He, along with several other concerned citizens, petitioned the Grant Parish Police Jury to take it down, to no avail. After Dean Woods sent a letter to the Louisiana Economic Department, things began to change. The marker was finally removed on May 15, 2021. Rather than simply replace the historical marker with one containing the correct story, Avery and Dean felt more was needed. As founders of the Colfax Memorial Organization, these two unexpected friends desired to create a new monument and an accompanying reflective space that will properly honor and commemorate those who died fighting for their right to experience full citizenship through the exercise of the vote and participation in governing. Efforts to raise funds for the replacement marker are underway. The unveiling ceremony took place on April 13, 2023.
57. The Reconstruction Amendments' Debates (Alfred Avins ed, 2nd ed. 1974) (39th Cong., 1st Sess. 149 (Feb. 26, 1866) (Statement of Lyman Trumbull).
58. In 1873, the Thirteenth Amendment was interpreted in the *Slaughter-House Cases*, 83 U.S. 36 (1873) where Louisiana granted a monopoly to a corporation for the purposes of butchering in New Orleans. Butchers left out of that monopoly were deprived of a chance to earn a living and they sued in federal court, arguing that the monopoly violated their right to pursue a livelihood. Amongst the several constitutional challenges asserted was the contention that exclusion from the monopoly amounted to involuntary servitude, which the Thirteenth Amendment prohibited. The stakes were high because this was the first time the court was asked to interpret the Reconstruction Amendments. If the rights conferred through those amendments could not be secured, no civil rights law could be and citizenship couldn't be realized for the emancipated population. The Court expressed the feeling that the Reconstruction Amendments were not intended to apply beyond those impacted by chattel slavery. It also rejected the argument that the monopoly violated the privileges and immunities clause of the Fourteenth Amendment. The Court refused to interpret the privileges and immunities clause as protecting economic or labor rights. The Court interpreted it to protect rights of national citizenship only. The Court deemed the law constitutional and granted no relief to the butchers.

    In *Blyew v. United States*, 80 U.S. 581 (1871), a Black couple and a family member was violently murdered inside their cabin. During this attack, their teenage son was struck in the head with an ax and the couple's six-year-old child was also attacked. The son later died of his injuries. Another daughter survived and was able to identify the defendants and the murderers. There was also physical evidence linking the defendants and a dying declaration from the sixteen-year-old. The white defendants were convicted in federal court. These convictions, brought pursuant to the 1866 Civil Rights Act, were later overturned when it was decided the state court was the proper forum for the matter to be heard (despite the fact that Blacks could not testify against a white defendant in state court).

The Tennessee court, in *Charge to Grand Jury --Civil Rights Act*, 30 F. Cas. 1005 (W.D.Tenn. 1875), was asked if a person could be indicted for denying a newly freed person access to accommodations. The Court ruled that it had no authority to involve itself with a state matter and it remarked that Congress had exceeded its powers in so its attempt to grant such authority to the federal court.

In *Le Grand v. United States*, federal charges were brought against two white men who conspired by shooting the Black victim over providing evidence in a proceeding. After being convicted, the white defendants sought to have their convictions reversed. They argued that Congress lacked authority to enact the legislation used to convict them. This law was enacted pursuant to Section II of the Thirteenth Amendment. The court agreed and reversed the convictions, explaining that:

It was never supposed that...congress could pass a law which would punish any private citizen for an invasion of the rights of his fellow-citizen conferred by the state of which both were residents.

*****

The utmost effect of this amendment is to declare the colored as free as the white race, and to give them nothing more than freedom... The second section of this amendment authorizes congress to pass such laws as are appropriate, but not to annul state laws or control their operations....this amendment does not authorize congress to pass laws for the punishment of offences against persons of the colored race— that belongs to the state government.

Le Grand v. United States, 12 F. 577, 582-3 (1882).

The *Civil Rights* Cases were decided eighteen years *after* passage of the Thirteenth Amendment. The *Civil Rights* Cases, 109 U.S. 3 (1883), also involved a challenge pursuant to the Fourteenth Amendment. It involved restrictions placed upon Blacks who sought use and access to establishments and properties owned by whites, such as hotels, theaters, opera houses, railroads. The Supreme Court struck down the public accommodations provisions of the Civil Rights Act of 1875, ruling that it couldn't be sustained under Congress's Thirteenth Amendment powers because the Thirteenth Amendment authorized Congress to regulate private conduct and limited action to instances where slavery or involuntary servitude was at issue. The Court found that the act couldn't be applied to private actors under Congress's Fourteenth Amendment powers because no state action was involved. This Court did note that, when Congress is properly exercising its authority pursuant to section two of the Amendment, Congress is cloaked with authority to pass all laws necessary and proper for abolishing all badges and incidents of slavery in the United States. Then, the Court reasoned that:

Congress did not assume, under the authority given by the Thirteenth Amendment, to adjust what may be called the social rights of men and races in the community; but only to declare and vindicate those fundamental rights which appertain to the essence of citizenship, and the enjoyment or deprivation of which constitutes the essential distinction between freedom and slavery.

The *Civil Rights* Cases, 109 U.S. 3, 23 (1883).

Denying someone access to public accommodations on the basis of race, the Court ruled, didn't rise to the level of slavery. As such, the court concluded that a "badge of slavery" did not exist. Accordingly, the Court held that Congress exceeded its authority by regulating in the domain of states. Though the task at hand had been completed, the Court revealed its thoughts on future attempts at using the Thirteen Amendment as a tool for finishing the work of achieving full emancipation:

It would be running the slavery argument into the ground to make it apply to every act of discrimination which a person may see fit .
*****

When a man has emerged from slavery, and by the aid of beneficent legislation has shaken off the inseparable concomitants of that state, there must be some stage in the progress of his elevation when he takes the rank of a mere citizen, and ceases to be the special favorite of the laws, and when his rights as a citizen, or a man, are to be protected in the ordinary modes by which other men's rights are protected.

The *Civil Rights* Cases, 109 U.S. 3, 24-5 (1883).

In response to an attempt to use the Thirteenth Amendment to challenge segregated rail cars, the SCOTUS explained, in *Plessy v. Ferguson*, 163 U.S. 537, 543-544 (1896), why segregated railcars was not a badge or incident of slavery:

A statute which implies merely a legal distinction between the white and colored races—a distinction which is founded in the color of the two races, and which must always exist so long as white men are distinguished from the other race by color—has no tendency to destroy the legal equality of the two races, or re-establish a state of involuntary servitude. Indeed, we do not understand that the thirteenth amendment is strenuously relied upon by the plaintiff in error in this connection.
*****

[The Amendment was not] intended to abolish distinctions based upon color, or to enforce social, as distinguished from political, equality....

This remained the law until this decision was overruled by *Brown v. Board of Ed.* of Topeka, Shawnee County, Kan., 347 U.S. 483 (1954).

By 1945, matters had not improved. In *Screws v. United States*, 325 U.S. 91 (1945), a Georgia sheriff wanted to teach Robert Hall a lesson about being the type of Black man who dared assert his rights. A suspect arrest warrant was used to arrest Mr. Hall for theft of a tire. He was handcuffed then placed in the patrol car where he was driven to the town square, in front of the courthouse, where the sheriff was waiting. The three members of law enforcement, in the town center in the view of citizens, beat Mr. Hall with their fists and a two-pound blackjack. They beat him until he lay motionless on the ground then the sheriff ordered the two officers to drag him to the jail. Mr. Hall's skull was crushed. He died from his injuries. Georgia officials opted not to prosecute so federal charges were brought. In 1945, the SCOTUS reversed the convictions of these officers, reasoning that manslaughter was a State offense that the federal government lacked authority to prosecute. They declared the federal law that they used unconstitutional, suggesting that it was vague and did not clearly explain what due process rights it was designed to protect. This decision left victims of Southern constitutional violations at the mercy of Southern law enforcement, prosecutors and juries.

59. Gloria J. Brown-Marshall, *She Took Justice the Black Woman, Law and Power 1619 to 1969* 169 (2021).

60. The 1874 Battle of Liberty Place is but one example. Two decades later, this was publicly endorsed with a monument. That monument came down in 2017.

61. *See Williams v. State of Mississippi,* 170 U.S. 213 (1898).

62. Stanley Nelson, *"Equal Rights to All Men" Divergent coverage of Jim Crow– and civil rights–era Violence in Louisiana,* p. 47, 64 Parishes (Winter 2020), *available at* "Equal Rights to All Men" | 64 Parishes (last visited May 3, 2021).

63. *See United States Senate Committee to Inquire into Alleged Frauds and Violence in the Elections of 1878,* S. Rep., 45th Cong. (1979), *available at* Louisiana [and South Carolina] in 1878. Report of the United States Senate Committee to inquire into alleged frauds and violence in the elections of 1878, with the testimony and documentary evidence (loc.gov).

64. *United States v. Louisiana,* 225 F. Supp. 353, 367-70 (E.D. La. 1963).

65. Daniel Brantley, *Blacks and Louisiana Constitutional Development, 1890-Present: A Study in Southern Political Thought and Race Relations. Phylon* (1960-), vol. 48, no. 1, 1987, pp. 55.

66. *Id.*

67. At the height of lynching in 1903, Jackson Giles, a Black man who had voted in Montgomery, Alabama for thirty years, sued over a new Alabama constitution, adopted by the all-white legislature, that denied him the opportunity to vote for a congressperson (due to the use of the grandfather clause). Mr. Giles did not challenge the scheme; he simply asked that he be added to the voting roles. The matter ended up before the SCOTUS. The case was ultimately dismissed because the suit did not seek enough in damages to bring it within the jurisdiction of the federal courts.This disposition left the system that excluded Black voters intact for many more years despite the fact that the court got a firsthand glimpse into how it was undermining both federal legislation and the United States Constitution. *See Giles v. Harris,* 189 U.S. 475 (1903); Many years later, this was corrected through and Equal Protection challenge and with the help of the Voting Rights Act of 1965 (VRA). Incidentally, as we refine our understanding of activist and activism, Booker T. Washington, who is best known for his efforts surrounding educational opportunities for Blacks, secretly arranged for funding and representation for Jackson W. Giles.

68. *Louisiana v United States,* 380 U.S. 145, 147-48 (1965).

69. *See Id.* at 148.

70. Voter registration was first introduced in Massachusetts in the 1800s, but it did not gain popularity around 1890, after the Civil War. In Louisiana, the Constitution of 1852 required residents in New Orleans to register, starting in 1854. The 1864 and 1868 Louisiana Constitutions established statewide registration requirements.

71. Criminal disenfranchisements dates back to Colonial American when these laws were written to exclude "undesirables" from the political process. *See* Jeff Manza & Christopher Uggen, *Locked Out: Felon Disenfranchisement and American Democracy* 53-54 (2006); In 1901, Alabama changed its law to disenfranchise persons convicted of "any crime involving moral turpitude." See *Hunter v Underwood,* 471 U.S. 222, 229 (1985).

    In Mississippi, for example, where voters elected two Black U.S. senators and a plethora of Black state officials during Reconstruction, about 47,000 people — a disproportionate number of whom are Black — were convicted of crimes that disenfranchised them for life just between 1994 and 2017. Although convicted felons can regain their right to vote in the state if they receive permission from the governor and two-thirds of the legislature, only 14 people did so between 2013 and 2017. Currently, there are two federal lawsuits challenging this discriminatory system.

Today, Florida still has the strictest felony disenfranchisement law in the country, and nearly a quarter of its Black population is denied the freedom to vote. The governor and his cabinet have unfettered discretion to grant or deny the restoration of voting rights, and the current governor requires potential voters to wait five years after completing their sentences to even petition the state for the restoration of their voting rights. So many people are now disenfranchised in Florida that some voting rights advocates suspect that their votes could have changed the outcome of the 2000 presidential election. But this November, in the wake of a federal judge's ruling that Florida's system of disenfranchising felons is unconstitutional, voters will get to weigh in on Amendment 4, a ballot initiative that would repeal their state's harsh and discriminatory disenfranchisement law. Andrew Gillum, the Democratic mayor of Tallahassee and now Florida's first Black nominee for governor, has voiced his support for Amendment 4. "Floridians who have paid their debts deserve a second chance," he said. He continued, "Our current system for rights restoration is a relic of Jim Crow that we should end for good."

The Sentencing Project, a criminal-justice nonprofit, estimates that 5.2 million Americans remain disenfranchised because of felony convictions, a disproportionate number of them Black. According to a report the group released in 2019, over 6.2% of the adult African American population is disenfranchised, compared with 1.7% of the non-African American population.

72. Before the Civil War, white men—the only eligible voters—were barred from voting if they committed one of four felonies, all of which related to the integrity of elections. When the U.S. Constitution extended the right to vote to Black men after the war, Louisiana expanded its practice of felony disenfranchisement. In 1868, three years after slavery, persons convicted of treason, perjury, forgery, bribery or other crimes punishable by imprisonment at hard labor were prohibited from voting. *See* Official Journal of the Proceedings of the Convention for the State of La. 179 & 182 (1867-68). At the 1898 Constitutional Convention, the same convention to formally change from a unanimous jury system to a split jury system in felony cases, a change was made to disenfranchise anyone who committed *any* felony. The practice of permanently depriving persons convicted of felonies from voting started under Louisiana's 1921 Constitution.

73. "Under an order of imprisonment" refers to a sentence of confinement, whether or not suspended, whether or not the subject of the order has been placed on probation, with or without supervision, and whether or not the subject of the order has been paroled.

74. *See VOICE OF the EX-OFFENDER v. State*, 249 So.3d 857 (2018); Louisiana's supreme court wouldn't consider the matter. The only concern from that court would be Justice Johnson's dissent acknowledging the inherent injustice of the matter:

In 1969, there were 6,740 people on probation or parole across the state. Today, that number has increased to approximately 71,000 people who are on probation or parole, twice the number of people actually incarcerated in the state. Citizens on probation or parole in Louisiana contribute to our state in various ways. These citizens work, pay taxes, raise families, and volunteer in their communities...This representative group include a Vietnam War veteran, a construction worker, a law school graduate, a college graduate, two deacons, a hospice volunteer, and a minister. Yet these tax-paying citizens have no voice in the political life of their communities and are excluded from our democratic process because they are denied the right to choose their elected officials...Notably, people of color are disproportionately impacted by these voting restrictions. One of every thirteen African-Americans has lost their right to vote due to criminal disenfranchisement laws....

    VOICE OF the EX-OFFENDER v. State, 255 So.3d 575, 576-577 (2018) (Johnson, J., dissenting).

75. In 2018, the Louisiana Legislature amended La. R.S. 18:102(A)(1) to specifically provide an exception to voter registration ineligibility for certain probationers and parolees. The amendment provides, in relevant part:

    A. No person shall be permitted to register or vote who is:

    (1)(a) Under an order of imprisonment, as defined in R.S. 18:2(8), for conviction of a felony; or, except as provided in Subparagraph (b) of this Paragraph.

    (b) Except as provided in Subparagraph (c) of this Paragraph, a person who is under an order of imprisonment for conviction of a felony and who has not been incarcerated pursuant to the order within the last five years shall not be ineligible to register or vote based on the order if the person submits documentation to the registrar of voters from the appropriate correction official showing that the person has not been incarcerated pursuant to the order within the last five years.

    (Emphasis added)

    2018 La. Sess. Law Serv. Act 636 (H.B. 265).

76. In 2021, Louisiana passed another law allowing people who were convicted of felonies would be able to serve on juries after they have been off probation or parole and out of prison for five years. Act 121, 2021 Reg. Session.

77. *See Guinn v. United States*, 238 U.S. 347 (1915), which outlawed grandfather clauses.

78. *Smith v. Alllwright*, 321 U.S. 649 (1944); the State's white primary law kept Blacks from voting in the Democratic Party primary election, the only election that mattered in the political climate of that State.

79. Act No. 613, 1960 La. Acts 1166.

80. Louisiana amended its Constitution in 1921 to adopt the "interpretation test" or "understanding clause." It required every voter who applied to register to be able to understand, as well as give a reasonable interpretation of any section of the State or Federal Constitution "when read to him by the register." By 1940, a total of 897 Blacks were registered in Louisiana. The practice was declared illegal in *Louisiana v. United States* where the court found that "Louisiana's interpretation test, as written and as applied, was part of a successful plan to deprive Louisiana Negroes of their right to vote." *Louisiana v. U.S.*, 380 U.S. 145, 151 (1965).

81. Police juries, the governing authority for a jurisdiction, are cloaked with legislative and executive authority. They have a unique racial history in Louisiana. "The original law that established police juries was passed at the Second Session of the Third Legislature of the Territory of Orleans 1811 [and it stated that it's] duty...

shall be specially to go after runaway negroes and to maintain good order among the slaves." Kelby Ouchley, *Police Juries*, 64 Parishes, Nov. 10, 2020, *available at* Police Juries - 64 Parishes (last visited Jan. 11, 2022). They later became instrumental in voter suppression efforts because they set the eligibility requirements for voters in their jurisdiction and they exercised authority over registrars.

82. In 1890, Mississippi began using the Mississippi plan to disenfranchise voters. This included poll taxes, literacy tests, understanding clauses, malicious voter registration rules, all designed to prevent Blacks from voting.

83. Carol Anderson, *One Person, No Vote How Voter Suppression Is Destroying Our Democracy* 22 (2018).

84. *Id.*

85. *Id.* at 27.

86. The Rev. James E. Orange, an aide to the Rev. Dr. Martin Luther King Jr. was organizing a voter registration drive in southwest Alabama in early 1965 when he was arrested on charges of disorderly conduct and contributing to the delinquency of minors.

87. *See Hunter v Underwood*, 471 U.S. 222, 229-232 (1985).

88. *North Carolina State Conference of NAACP v. McCrory*, 831 F.3d 204, 214 (2016).

89. *Louisiana v. United States*, 380 U.S. 156 (1965).

90. *See In re* Judge Timothy C. Ellender, 889 So.2d 225 (2004).

91. *In re Murchison*, 349 U.S. 133, 136 (1955).

92. The first Black judge elected in the parish in 2014 was a Republican whose campaign, according to the litigation, "was partially funded by interests opposed to Black progress." Oddly and conveniently, no whites ran against him.

93. *See In re* Judge Timothy C. Ellender, 16 So.3d 351 (2009).

94. In *Chisom v. Edwards*, 690 F.Supp. 1524 (1988), the plaintiffs successfully argued that the method for electing supreme court justices diluted the Black vote; *Chisom v. Roemer*, 501 U.S. 380 (1991), was brought by New Orleans residents who successfully challenged the process of electing supreme court justices from multimember districts.

95. The Reconstruction Amendments' Debates (Alfred Avins ed, 2nd ed. 1974) (39th Cong., 1st Sess. 383 (1866)(remarks of Representative Thaddaeus Stevens).

96. W. E. B. Du Bois, *Black Reconstruction in America: Toward a History of the Part Which Black Folk Played in the Attempt to Reconstruct Democracy in America, 1860-1880* 427 (1935)

97. Henry Warmoth, a Republican was the Louisiana governor. He and Oscar Dunn are elected on the same ticket in 1868. The relationship disintegrates when Governor Warmoth betrays Lieutenant Governor Dunn by not supporting a civil rights bill. The party also became divided over this. Some followed Dunn camp and some followed Warmoth. They have separate police forces, separate conventions and they become competitors.

98. A mix-race crowd of over 50,000 people attended his funeral in New Orleans.

99. Act 57 of 1873 created the O. J. Dunn Monumental Association and endowed it with $10,000 to create a monument in memory of their fallen leader. In March 1873, Gov. William Pitt Kellogg approved the bill, but, for unknown reasons, the monument never got made. In 2022, a bill seeking to fulfill that promise unanimously passed the Louisiana legislature and was signed by the governor. House Bill 739 creates the Oscar James Dunn Memorial Commission (to exist from

2022-2027) for the purpose of seeing to the erection of the Oscar James Dunn statute within Memorial Hall within the State Capital. Additionally, the New Orleans City Council recently decided to rename Washington Artillery Park, which overlooks Jackson Square, after Dunn.

100. In the 1960s, school board contenders challenged a law that required the race of each candidate to be printed opposite his name on all ballots, a system that disadvantaged Blacks in majority white districts in *Anderson v. Martin*, 375 U.S. 399, 401-402 (1964) ("[B]y placing a racial label on a candidate at the most crucial stage in the electoral process—the instant before the vote is cast—the State furnishes a vehicle by which racial prejudice may be so aroused as to operate against one group because of race and for another." The court held that the compulsory designation of the race of the candidate on the ballot operates as a discrimination and is therefore violative of the Fourteenth Amendment's Equal Protection Clause.); *Brown v. Post*, 279 F. Supp. 60 (W.D. La. 1968) (wherein the schoolboard election of Madison Parish was found to be in violation of the Voting Rights Act when it was discovered that local officials allowed whites to vote absentee by making absentee ballots available to them in their private residences without extending same opportunity to Blacks, and by making absentee ballots available to white plantation employees without doing so for Black employees similarly situated, and by making absentee voting available to white residents of certain section without a corresponding opportunity being given to similarly situated Blacks.

101. *See, e.g., East Jefferson Coalition for Leadership and Development v. Jefferson Parish,* 691 F.Supp. 991 (1988).

102. *See, e.g., Wyche v. Post,* 297 F. Supp. 46 (W.D. La. 1969).

103. *See Westwego Citizens for Better Government v. City of Westwego,* 946 F.2d 1109 (1991); *Citizens for a Better Gretna v. City of Gretna,* 834 F.2d 496 (1987).

104. In 1971, Dorothy Mae Taylor, after a fight led by Oretha Castle Haley to have New Orleans election districts redrawn, became the first Black woman in the Louisiana legislature.

105. U.S. *v. Post,* 279 F. Supp. 46 (W.D. La. 1969) (where the procedure, which violated the Voting Rights Act, caused Black voters not to cast effective votes for Village Marshall of Tallulah, Louisiana).

106. As a result of *Clark vs. Edwards,* also brought under the Voting Rights Act of 1965, numerous other majority-Black districts were created throughout the state to provide Black voters with the equal opportunity to elect their preferred candidates to Louisiana's trial and appellate courts. This work remains unfinished. First Circuit Court of Appeal Judge John Michael Guidry will begin his term as Chief Judge of the Louisiana First Circuit Court of Appeal on January 1, 2023. He is the second Black American to be elected to the First Circuit Court of Appeal and will be the first Black judge in the 100-plus-year history of the court to serve as Chief Judge.

107. The plaintiffs were Chisom and four other Black plaintiffs and the Louisiana Voter Registration Education Crusade. *Chisom v. Edwards* started in 1987 with Ron Chisom, Marie Bookman, and Marc Morial suing Governor Charles Roemer and the state of Louisiana over the lack of Black representation on the state Supreme Court. Attorneys William P. Quigley, Roy Rodney, New Orleans, La., Pamela S. Karlan, Charles Stephen Ralston, Univ. of Virginia, Law School, Charlottesville, Va., Ron Wilson, New Orleans, La Ron Wilson, Bill Quigley, and Roy Rodney represented the plaintiffs. The *Chisom* plaintiffs, alleging a violation of the

constitution and the VRA, brought suit against the governor and other state officials seeking a remedy that would have divided the first supreme court district into two districts, one for Orleans Parish and the second for the other three parishes.

108. *See Chisom v. Edwards*, 839 F.2d 1056 (1988); The settlement was challenged in *Perschall v. State*, 697 So.2d 240 (1997). Mr. Perschall argued that the seat was unconstitutional. The Supreme Court ruled in July 1997 that the Chisom settlement had, in fact, violated the state's constitution. However, because the seat had been created by the legislature, the court felt it couldn't undo it. In 1992, pursuant to Act 512 of 1992, Justice Revius Ortique, Jr. was elected to the Fourth Circuit Court of Appeal for the purpose of serving on the Louisiana Supreme Court, becoming the first Black to serve on the state's highest court, and served until his retirement in 1994. *See also Chisom v. Roemer, Chisom v. Jindal* and a 2022 version captioned *Chisom v. Edwards*.

109. This litigation began as *Clark v. Edwards* in 1988, later became *Clark v. Roemer* then ended as *Clark v. Edwards* (1992) with the addition of plaintiffs over time. The plaintiffs claimed that the use by Louisiana of multimember election districts to elect these judicial officers operated to dilute Black voting strength in violation of Section 2 of the VRA of 1965. "The parties...stipulated that Louisiana has almost routinely enforced statutes relating to judicial elections without complying with the provisions of Section 5 of the Voting Rights Act." *Clark v Edwards*, 725 F.Supp. 285, 295 (1988). They were represented by: Ernest L. Johnson; T. Richardson Bobb; Robert McDuff, Lawyer's Committee for Civ. Rights Under Law, Washington, D.C.; and, Ulysses Thibodeaux.

110. *Clark v Edwards*, 725 F.Supp. 285, 292-5 (1988).

111. *See Clark v Edwards*, 725 F.Supp. 285, 295 (1988).

112. *See Clark v Roemer*, 777 F.Supp. 445 (1990); *Clark v. Roemer*, 777 F.Supp. 471 (1991) decided that the appropriate remedy for voter dilution on state Court of Appeals, in a district that had no elections planned for immediate future, was to create temporary judgeship.

113. *See Wes Muller, GOP Lawmakers Reluctant to Add Majority-Minority Districts in Louisiana*, Louisiana Illuminator, Jan. 21, 2022, available at GOP lawmakers reluctant to add majority-minority districts in Louisiana - Louisiana Illuminator (lailluminator.com) (last visited Jan. 26, 2022).

114. *Id.*

115. *Id.*

116. "The new maps are likely to have a significant impact on virtually every political election in Louisiana over the next decade...." Wes Muller, *GOP Lawmakers Reluctant to Add Majority-Minority Districts in Louisiana*, Louisiana Illuminator, Jan. 21, 2022, available at GOP lawmakers reluctant to add majority-minority districts in Louisiana - Louisiana Illuminator (lailluminator.com) (last visited Jan. 26, 2022).

117. *See Wes Muller, GOP Lawmakers Reluctant to Add Majority-Minority Districts in Louisiana,*Â Louisiana Illuminator, Jan. 21, 2022, available at GOP lawmakers reluctant to add majority-minority districts in Louisiana - Louisiana Illuminator (lailluminator.com) (last visited Jan. 26, 2022).

118. *Id.*

119. Letter from Louisiana Governor John Bel Edwards to Speaker of the Louisiana House of Representatives Clay J. Schexnayder (March 9, 2022), *available at*

SchexnayderLtr20220309VetoHB1.pdf (louisiana.gov) (last visited March 14, 2022); By operation of law, those maps became law without the governor's signature.

120. The House voted 72-31, with all Republicans and three Independents in favor. The Senate voted 27-11 in favor. This is the Louisiana's first redistricting cycle since the *Shelby County v. Holder decision.*

121. Reginald Turner, *ABA Survey of Civic Literacy Shows People are in Favor of Protecting the Right to Vote,* ABA Journal, 6 (June-July 2022).

122. *Id.*

123. *Id.*

124. This work exclusively focuses on the petit jury, the individuals who decide one's fate during trial. The avoidance of grand jury discussions is the result of project limitations and should not be interpreted as a suggestion that the grand jury process is void of the shortcomings that plague the jury system because that is far from the case.

125. *Taylor v. Louisiana,* 419 U.S. 522, 530-1 (1975).

126. Reid Hastie, Steven D. Penrod & Nancy Pennington, *Inside the Jury* 1 (1983); Other than voting, serving on a jury is the most substantial opportunity that most citizens have to participate in the democratic process. See *Powers v. Ohio,* 499 U.S. 400, 407 (1991).

127. *Pena-Rodriguez v. Colorado,* 137 S. Ct. 855, 860 (2017).

128. United States Commission on Civil Rights Report, *Justice,* 89 (book V) (1961).

129. *Id.*

130. Jeffrey Abramson, *We, The Jury* 1 (1994).

131. *See Taylor v. La.,* 419 U.S. 522 (1975).

132. Renee Lettow Lerner, *The Surprising Views of Montesquieu and Tocqueville about Juries: Juries Empower Judges,* 81 Louisiana Law Review 1, 40 (2020); *see also* Alexis De Tocqueville, Democracy in America, Vol. 1, Part II, Chapter XVI:

> The jury contributes most powerfully to form the judgement and to increase the natural intelligence of a people....It may be regarded as a free public school ever open, in which every juror learns to exercise his rights, enters into daily communication with the most learned and enlightened members of the upper classes, and becomes practically acquainted with the laws of his country, which are brought within the reach of his capacity by the efforts of the bar, the advice of the judge, and even by the passions of the parties. I think that the practical intelligence and political good sense of the Americans are mainly attributable to the long use which they have made of the jury in civil causes. I do not know whether the jury is useful to those who are in litigation; but I am certain it is highly beneficial to those who decide the litigation; and I look upon it as one of the most efficacious means for the education of the people which society can employ.

133. Dale W. Broeder, *The Negro in Court,* 1965 Duke L.J. 19, 26 (1965).

134. Renee Lettow Lerner, *The Surprising Views of Montesquieu and Tocqueville about Juries: Juries Empower Judges,* 81 Louisiana Law Review 1, 44 (2020).

135. *Id.*

136. Raneta Lawson Mack, *Unpacking Race in the American Jury System Cases, Readings, and Perspectives* 3 (2023).

137. The Reconstruction Amendments' Debates, 143 (Alfred Avins ed, 2nd ed. 1974) (39th Cong., 3rd Sess., Feb. 7, 1866) (Statement of Representative Samuel McKee)

(A "voter is an officer...as the man who enters the jury box, as any one who holds office. It is a trust imposed upon him by law....")

138. On April 30, 1803, the United States and France entered into "A Treaty between the United States of America and the French republic" for the purchase of a vast tract of land known as "the colony or province of Louisiana." *See* Treaty Between the United States of America and the French Republic, Fr.-U.S., art. I, Apr. 30, 1803. It provided:

Art.3. The inhabitants of the ceded territory shall be incorporated in the Union of the United States, and admitted as soon as possible, according to the principles of the federal constitution, to the enjoyment of All the rights, advantages, and immunities of citizens of the United States; and in the meantime, they shall be maintained and protected in the free enjoyment of their liberty, property, and the religion which they profess.

The Treaty was ratified by the U.S. Senate on October 20, 1803, and the United States took possession of the territory on October 31, 1803. *See* Journal of the Executive Proceedings of the Senate of the United States of America, Vol.1, at 450 (1803); *see also* Journal of the Senate of the United States of America, Vol.3, at 302 (1803).

After much debate, in 1804, the President signed into law an act that divided Louisiana into two territories, each having a judicial system. *See* An Act erecting Louisiana into two Territories and providing for the Temporary Government thereof, 2 Stat. 283, 8 Cong. Chap. 36 (1804). A subsequent 1805 act conditioned statehood on compliance with the above-referenced Treaty of Paris. *See* An Act further providing for the government of the territory of Orleans, 2 Stat. 322, 8 Cong. Chap. 23, Sec. 7 (1805).

139. According to the political philosopher Alexis de Tocqueville, "[T]he jury is above all a political institution." Alexis de Tocqueville, Chapter XVI. *Causes Mitigating Tyranny In The United States – Part II*, in Democracy In America; Debate on the Federal Jury Selection and Service Act of 1968, 114 Cong.Rec. 3992 (1968) (remarks of Mr. Rogers); *See also* 118 Cong.Rec. 6939 (1972) (remarks of Mr. Poff) (In 1968, when congress established its protocol for selection of federal juries, it "recognized that the jury plays a *political* function...."); "The right to serve in the jury-box strikes me as a political right like that of serving on the bench. It is not inherent in a citizen....the political right to serve as a juror, seems tome tofall into the same class and belong to those political rights as to which the States always have determined and may still discriminate...."). The Reconstruction Amendments' Debates, 609 (Alfred Avins ed, 2nd ed. 1974) (42nd Cong., 2nd Sess., Feb. 5, 1872) (Statement of Senator Matthew H. Carpenter).

140. Derrick A. Bell, Jr, *Race, Racism and American Law* 950 (1973).

141. Douglas L. Colbert, *Challenging the Challenge: Thirteenth Amendment as a Prohibition Against the Racial Use of Peremptory Challenges*, 76 Cornell L. Rev. 1, 16-17 (1990).

142. Glorida J. Brown-Marshall, *She Took Justice the Black Woman, Law and Power 1619 to 1969* 68 (2021).

143. *Id.*

144. The 1845 state constitution enabled the supreme court to hear criminal appeals, but the Black Codes prohibited proceedings from being "annulled or impeded by any error of form."

145. Douglas L. Colbert, *Challenging the Challenge: Thirteenth Amendment as a Prohibition Against the Racial Use of Peremptory Challenges*, 76 Cornell L. Rev. 1, 13 (1990).

146. *Id.*

147. The Reconstruction Amendments' Debates, 635 (Alfred Avins ed, 2nd ed. 1974) (42nd Cong., 2nd Sess., April 13, 1872) (Statement of Representative Henry D. McHenry).

148. Douglas L. Colbert, *Challenging the Challenge: Thirteenth Amendment as a Prohibition Against the Racial Use of Peremptory Challenges*, 76 Cornell L. Rev. 1, 13 (1990).

149. In *Powers v. Ohio*, 499 U.S. 400 (1991), the United States Supreme Court held that jurors have a right not to be excluded based on their race.

150. Glen Jeansonne, *Leander Perez*, 64 Parishes, *available at* Leander Perez | 64 Parishes (last visited Feb. 8, 2021).

151. "By 1966 Plaquemines Parish was one of the few parishes...in which a school desegregation case had not been filed. The reason, presumptively, was that no Black parent was prepared to take on the potential consequences of Perez's wrath. Recognizing this, the U.S. Justice Department instituted a school desegregation suit in its own name." Richard Sobol, *Arrested by Leander Perez Sr. in Voices of Civil Rights Lawyers Reflections From the Deep South*, 1964-1980 189 (Kent Spriggs ed. 2017).

152. Glen Jeansonne, *Leander Perez*, 64 Parishes, *available at* Leander Perez | 64 Parishes (last visited Feb. 8, 2021).

153. Matthew Van Meter, *Deep Delta Justice A Black Teen, His Lawyer, and Their Groundbreaking Battle for Civil Rights in the South* 19 (2020).

154. *Id.* at 68.

155. In *Duncan,* they suggested his sixty-day sentence was too insignificant to justify the relief he sought. Louisiana officials also urged the court to aid them in concealing their misdeeds for fear of a ruling in Mr. Duncan's favor "would cast doubt on the integrity of every trial conducted without a jury" (an argument that they would shameless present again in 2020 before the court in *Ramos v. Louisiana* (2020).

156. The aftermath holds precious insights. In 1977, Leander H. Perez, who, in addition to all this, created the interpretation tests that would be used to disenfranchise Black voters in Plaquemines Parish, was memorialized with a statute and a $1 million, 12-acre park just below Belle Chasse. Instead of grandeur, Gary Duncan would enter the next phase of his life realizing he was little more than an obscure character in historical labyrinth of people trying to break free of Sixth Amendment bondage.

157. "Although the 1866 [Civil Right] Act did not specifically address the issue of the all-white jury, its guarantee that a person receive "the full and equal benefit of all laws . . . for the security of person and property" significantly changed the southern trial jury's composition. Following a 1866 federal circuit court decision that upheld the constitutionality of the Civil Rights Act and the passage of the 1867 Military Reconstruction Act, Black jurors began to appear in several southern states....By 1870, the integrated jury was a common sight in those states." Colbert, *supra* note 491 at 49 (and noting that Louisiana swore in its first Black grand juror in 1867). Additional protection for Black jurors came via Section 4 of the Civil Rights Act of 1875, which provided:

[N]o citizen possessing all other qualifications which are or may be prescribed by law shall be disqualified for service as grand or petit juror in any court of the United States, or of any State, on account of race, color or previous condition of servitude; and any officer or other person charged with any duty in the selection or summoning of jurors who shall exclude or fail to summon any citizen for the cause aforesaid shall, on conviction thereof, be deemed guilty of a misdemeanor, and be fined not more than five thousand dollars.

Civil Rights Act of 1875, ch. 114, §4, 18 Stat. 335, 336-37. The Act was struck down by the Supreme Court in the *Civil Rights Cases*, 109 U.S. 3 (1883); *see also* 18 U.S.C. § 243, which prohibits racial discrimination in jury selection.

Before this, in 1870, Charles Sumner introduced a bill to supplement the Civil Rights Act of 1866. It included a provision prohibiting discrimination in the selection of jurors and providing penalties for officials who disobeyed. After strong opposition, it died. *See* Cong. Globe, 41st Cong., 2d Sess. 3434 (1870).

In *Strauder v. West Virginia*, 100 U.S. 303 (1879), decided twelve years after the Fourteenth Amendment was enacted, the court struck down a state statute that excluded all Blacks (and only qualified whites) from the jury venire and held that, under the Equal Protection Clause, a State could not systemically exclude persons from juries solely because of their race or color; *Ex Parte Virginia* upheld a provision of civil rights law prohibiting the exclusion of Blacks from juries.

In the trial of one of the Scottsboro Boys, the SCOTUS agreed with the accused' assertion that there was a longstanding pattern of excluding qualified Black jurors in Jackson County, Alabama. The testimony estimated that no Black person had ever served on a grand or petit jury despite qualified Blacks being available. See *Norris v. Alabama*, 294 U.S. 587 (1935).

Starting in 1940 with *Smith v. Texas*, 311 U.S. 128 (1940), the Supreme Court began providing substantive protections for minority representation in jury pools and venires instead of simply holding that minorities could not be excluded by statute (as was the case in *Strauder*).

In *Hernandez v. Texas*, 347 U.S. 475 (1954), the SCOTUS barred the exclusion of Latinos from jury participation. The court concluded this to be a violation of the Equal Protection Clause of the Fourteenth Amendment.

In *Carter v. Jury Commission of Greene County*, 396 U.S. 320 (1970), potential Black Alabama jurors sued in an effort to invalidate a law that required jury commissioners to select persons who are honest, intelligent and esteemed in the community for their integrity, good character and sound judgment. They complained that this system facilitated their exclusion from the pool of potential jurors. Despite statistics establishing an under inclusion on juries and only white being appointed to the commission, the SCOTUS would not invalidate the law or practice.

On the same day that the SCOTUS decided *Plessy v. Ferguson* (1896) and branded segregation as legal, it decided *Murray v. Louisiana*, 163 U.S. 101 (1896), upholding the murder conviction of James Murray that followed an indictment by an all-white grand jury.

158. *See State v. Jacko*, 444 So.2d 1185, 1187 (1984).
159. *Id.*
160. See *State v. Cage*, 337 So. 2d 1123 (1976) (finding systemic exclusion of a geographical group).

161. *Pierre v. La*, 306 U.S. 354 (1939).

162. *State v. Montgomery*, 48-489 Motion to Set Aside the Petit Jury Venire Tr, p.103, Dec. 17, 1963; *see also Peters v. Kiff*, 407 U.S. 493, 513 n. 3 (1972) (Discussing how jury lists were made from tax digests that were segregated by race).

163. Dennis Childs, *Slaves of the State* 6 (2015).

164. He was initially sentenced to death but the state's Supreme Court threw out his conviction in 1966, saying he didn't get a fair trial. The case was retried, Montgomery convicted again but this time sentenced to life in prison without the possibility of parole.

165. *Miller v. Alabama*, 567 U.S. 460 (2012).

166. During the 2016 legislative session, legislation was proposed to address those cases in which persons that committed murder as juveniles and were sentenced to life imprisonment without parole eligibility before *Miller* was decided. However, the Legislature ultimately failed to take further action in the last few moments of the legislative session regarding sentences of life without parole for juvenile homicide offenders. *See* HB 264 of the 2016 Regular Session.

167. *See Montgomery v. Louisiana*, 575 U.S. 911 (2015).

168. *See Montgomery v. Louisiana*, 577 U.S. 190 (2016); *State v. Montgomery*, 194 So.3d 606 (La. 6/28/16).

169. Because of his life sentence, he was not able to avail himself to classes for the first thirty years. Though he had no need to attend, he participated in Alcoholics Anonymous because it was the only class available to him for some time. For twenty years, he worked at the prison's silk screen shop and he was named "Employee of the Month" several times. He also founded Angola's Amateur Boxing Association, was a mentor and active in religious organizations.

170. *Eubanks v. State*, 78 S.Ct. 970 (1958).

171. *Wesberry v. Sanders*, 376 U.S. 1, 17 (1964).

172. Thomas Ward Frampton, *The Jim Crow Jury*, 71 VNLR 1593, 1595 (2018).

173. La. Code Cr. P. art. 408.1(A) provides:

   In developing a list of all persons who may be called for grand or petit jury duty:

   (1) It shall be determined by each judicial district whether the names of prospective jurors shall be drawn exclusively from voter registration lists or also drawn from other sources or lists.

   (2) If the district judges of the judicial district, in their discretion, authorize the use of sources other than voter registration lists in developing grand and petit jury lists, a jury commission shall not draw the names of prospective jurors exclusively from voter registration lists, but shall use other sources or lists of prospective jurors as may be legally available.

   La. Code Cr. P. art. 408.1 has been revised a few times. Acts 1997, No. 886 rewrote this article, which had read:

   In developing a list of all persons who may be called for grand or petit jury duty;

   It shall be determined by each judicial district whether or not the names of prospective jurors shall be drawn exclusively from voter registration lists or from other sources, which other sources may include motor vehicle license and registration records.

   (2) A jury commission shall not draw the names of prospective jurors exclusively from voter registration lists or lists of actual voters, but shall use other sources, which may include motor vehicle license and registration records and lists

of individual utility customers, if the district judges of the judicial district, in their discretion, authorize the use of sources other than voter registration or actual voter lists in developing grand and petit jury lists."

Acts 1998, 1st Ex.Sess., No. 124, § 1 rewrote the article, which formerly read:

In developing a list of all persons who may be called for grand or petit jury duty, a jury commission shall draw names from a master list derived from voter registration lists, lists of actual voters, motor vehicle license and registration records, lists of individual utility customers, if made available by the utility company, and such other sources as may be approved by a majority of the district judges of the judicial district for which the master list is compiled.

174. For example, *See State v. George*, 371 So.2d 762 (1979); *State v. Jacko*, 444 So.2d 1185 (1984).

175. *See* Gordon Russell and John Simerman, In Louisiana, *Is It Truly a Jury of One's Peers' When Race Matters?: Tilting the scales*, The Advocate, April 1. 2018, *available at* Tilting the scales: In Louisiana, is it truly a 'jury of one's peers' when race matters? | Courts | nola.com (last visited Jan.17. 2022)("Almost every parish in the state pulls prospective jurors at random from voter rolls, with some also using the list of licensed drivers.").

176. Hong Tran, *Jury Diversity*, Defense, p. 8 (2013), *available at* Jury Diversity Policy Legislative and Legal Arguments.pdf (wa.gov) (last visited March 16, 2022) (Mentioning that the use of church parishioner lists led to increased minority representation the jury pool).

177. *See* Def's Omnibus Motion for New Trial, in Arrest of Judgment and for Post Verdict Judgment of Acquittal, 53 (Jan. 3, 2018) (Delegates "had before them the 'Statement of Registered Voters 1897 and 1898.' Which indicated that African-Americans represented 14.7% of all citizens registered to vote in Louisiana at the beginning of 1898. Thus, the proportionate representation would have resulted in an average of two Black jurors per trial. The effect of the 9-3 non-unanimous verdict scheme was white control over jury verdicts—Black votes could be ignored.").

178. In 1968, the Federal Jury Selection and Service Act was enacted. In that Act, Congress announced a public policy of random selection from a fair cross section of the community for federal jurors (both grand and petit juries). Congress also established the machinery by which the stated policy was to be implemented. 28 U.S.C. ss 1862—1866.

The Sixth Amendment entitles every defendant to object to a venire that is not designed to represent a fair cross section of the community, whether or not the systematically excluded groups are groups to which he himself belongs. The Sixth Amendment requirement of a fair cross section on the venire is a means of assuring, not a *representative* jury (which the Constitution does not demand), but an *impartial* one (which it does). The fair-cross-section requirement serves three important purposes: (1) a guard against the exercise of arbitrary power' and ensuring that the 'commonsense judgment of the community' will act as 'a hedge against the overzealous or mistaken prosecutor; (2) preserving 'public confidence in the fairness of the criminal justice system; and, (3) implementing our belief that 'sharing in the administration of justice is a phase of civic responsibility.

In *Taylor v. Louisiana*, 419 U.S. 522 (1975), the SCOTUS extended the cross-sectional requirement to state juries in 1975.

179. *U.S. v. Goff*, 509 F.2d 825 (1975) (The court found that the underrepresentation was not substantial enough, as defined by the JSSA, to require supplementation of the voter registration list.); *United States v. McDaniels*, 379 F. Supp. 298 (1973) (the court determined that approximately 20% underrepresentation of Blacks on voter registration list was not a substantial deviation from a full cross section of the community requirement of the JSSA.).

180. "A statistical discrepancy alone does not prove a JSSA violation when voter rolls constitute the source list for jury selection." *U.S. v. Age*, 2021 WL 2227244, *16 (2021). The Court denied the defendants' motion, holding that neither the district's jury plan, nor its implementation in constructing the jury wheels from which the grand jury that indicted the Defendants was selected, violated the fair-cross-section guarantee of the Sixth Amendment or the JSSA.

181. *U.S. v. Age*, 2021 WL 2227244, *3-*4 (2021) (mentioning the jury plan that was in effect when the 2017 indictment was obtained was drawn from a master wheel that was filled in 2016).

182. *Id.* at *7: During this litigation, the court said that there "is simply no problem of representativeness with respect to the source list used by the district under the jury plan." After the litigation, the court revised its jury plan for the first time in seven years. The 2020 jury plan supplements the voter rolls with drivers' license lists. The 2021 jury plan supplements the voter rolls with drivers' license and personal identification lists.

183. "The practical result is that in order to be considered for jury service a citizen 'must be sufficiently concerned with the operation of his [or her] government either to register to vote or actually to vote,'…, and to return a completed juror qualification form." *United States v. Age*, 2021 U.S. Dist. LEXIS 103258, at *32 n.100 (E.D. La. June 2, 2021)(citations omitted).

184. *U.S. v. Age*, 2021 WL 2227244, *15 (2021).

185. *See Jury Duty Pay Rates by State*, JuryDuty101/com, *available at* Jury Duty Pay By State - JuryDuty101 (last visited March 16, 2022).

186. *Juror Pay*, UsCourt.Gov, *available at* Juror Pay | United States Courts (uscourts.gov) (last visited March 16, 2022) ("While the majority of jury trials last less than a week, jurors can receive up to $60 a day after serving 10 days on a trial."); The amount is less for those who "attend," which means they respond to the jury summons, but have not yet been selected to serve on jury; Act 237, which became effective on January 1, 2021, increased juror compensation in civil trials from $25.00 to $50.00.

187. Jurors are eligible if their household income is less than 80% Area Median Income ($71,700 for a single person; $102,500 for a household of four) and if they meet one of the following criteria: (1) their employer does not compensate for jury service; (2) their employer does not compensate for the estimated duration of jury service; (3) they are self-employed; or, (4) they are unemployed. Stakeholders will conduct an evaluation of the pilot program once it is completed.

188. *New CA Bill Pilots Higher Compensation for Low-Income Jurors in San Francisco*, sftreasurer.org, June 20, 2021, available at New CA Bill Pilots Higher Compensation for Low-Income Jurors in San Francisco | Treasurer & Tax Collector (sftreasurer.org) (last visited March 16, 2022).

189. *Courts Seek to Increase Jury Diversity*, UScourts.gov, May 2019, *available at* Courts

Seek to Increase Jury Diversity | United States Courts (uscourts.gov) (last visited March 16, 2022).

190. *Id.*

191. *Id.*

192. *Id.*

193. *See* Hong Tran, *Jury Diversity*, Defense, p. 8 (2013), *available at* Jury Diversity Policy Legislative and Legal Arguments.pdf (wa.gov) (last visited March 16, 2022) (Mentioning that the use of church parishioner lists led to increased minority representation the jury pool).

194. *Duncan v. Louisiana*, 391 U.S. 145, 155-6 (1968); "Those who wrote our constitutions knew from history and experience that it was necessary to protect against unfounded criminal charges brought to eliminate enemies and against judges too responsive to the voice of higher authority." *Duncan v. Louisiana*, 391 U.S. 145, 157 (1968); "The framers of the constitutions strove to create an independent judiciary but insisted upon further protection against arbitrary action." *Duncan v. Louisiana*, 391 U.S. 145, 157 (1968); "Providing an accused with the right to be tried by a jury of his peers gave him an inestimable safeguard against the corrupt or overzealous prosecutor and against the compliant, biased, or eccentric judge." *Duncan v. Louisiana*, 391 U.S. 145, 157 (1968).

195. *See Taylor v. La.*, 419 U.S. 522, 530 (1975).

196. *Duncan v. Louisiana*, 391 U.S. 156 (1968).

197. Raneta Lawson Mack, *Unpacking Race in the American Jury System Cases, Readings, and Perspectives* xiii (2023).

198. *Holland v. Illinois*, 493 U.S. 474, 497 (1990)(Marshall, J. dissenting).

199. *Strauder v. West Virginia*, 100 U.S. 303, 308 (1880).

200. Thomas Ward Frampton, *The Jim Crow Jury*, 71 VNLR 1593, 1593 (2018).

201. A party's right to remove a potential juror without giving a reason.

202. Strike for cause is a method of eliminating potential members from a jury panel. During the jury selection process, after voir dire, opposing attorneys may request removal of any juror who does not appear capable of rendering a fair and impartial verdict.;"Recently-gathered statistical data suggests that the primary means through which African Americans are disproportionately excluded from jury service in criminal trials in Louisiana is through the State challenging prospective jurors for cause. The dataset on which the district court relied in *State v. Melvin Cartez Maxie*...demonstrated not only that the State disproportionately uses peremptory strikes against Black prospective jurors, but also that the State disproportionately uses challenges for cause against Black prospective jurors. *State v. Henson*, 20-00785, 304 So.3d 422 (La. 11/18/20) (Johnson, J., concurring); "Misuse of the peremptory challenge to exclude Black jurors has become both common and flagrant." *Batson v. Kentucky*, 476 U.S. 79, 103 (1986) (Marshall, J., dissenting).

203. *Swain v. Alabama*, 380 U.S. 202 (1965).

204. *See State v. Gray*, 285 So.2d 199 (1973) (Barham, J., dissenting).

205. *United States v. McDaniels*, 379 F. Supp. 1243, 1247 (1974).

206. *State v. Washington*, 375 So.2d 1162 (1979); Tragically, this was not the rambling of a lone bad actor. *State v. Eames*, 356 So.2d 1351, 1364 (1978) (wherein the prosecuting attorney admitted to using the State's peremptory challenges to remove Blacks from the petit jury); *State v. Jack*, 285 So.2d 204 (1973) (Barham, J., dissenting) (The State "readily admitted that it had challenged each and every

Black called for possible empaneling for the sole purpose of excluding all Blacks from this jury and forcing the defendant to trial before an all-white jury.")

207. *State v. Washington*, 375 So.2d 1162 (1979) (Blanche, J., dissenting).

208. Attorneys are allotted a limited number of options to remove jurors without stating a reason for the removal.

209. *Batson v. Kentucky*, 476 U.S. 79 (1986).

210. If the prosecutor fails to give a legitimate, race-neutral reason for each strike, the trial court can conclude that the prosecutor acted on the basis of race and put the struck jurors back on the jury venire.

211. This should not be interpreted as a suggestion that other prosecutors aren't using race as the sole basis to strike jurors. It's a national problem that is inflamed by the specific racial challenges of the South. It would be irresponsible to engage in this conversation without considering the Mississippi case of Curtis Flowers who was sent to death row for the murder of four people in Winona, Mississippi, in 1997. Over the next 23 years, Mr. Flowers was tried six times, with three of the cases overturned for prosecutorial misconduct or *Batson* violations. Two more of Flowers' trials ended in hung juries, and the sixth was reversed by the U.S. Supreme Court, which criticized Winona County District Attorney Doug Evans for striking 41 of 42 prospective Black jurors during the trials. In a 45% Black county, none of the juries that convicted Flowers had more than one Black. After this national public exposure, the public reelected Mr. Evans in 2019.

212. *State v. Harris*, 820 So.2d 471 (2002).

213. *State v. Miller*, 83 So.3d 178 (2011).

214. *State v. Collier*, 553 So.2d 815, 823 (1989)("The record in this case strongly suggests that the prosecutor, already frustrated in defendant's first trial by a hung jury which included three Blacks, pursued a strategy in the second trial of limiting the number of Blacks on the jury to two, thus making a conviction possible even if all of the Blacks on the jury voted according to racial bias.").

215. *State v. Collier*, 553 So.2d 815, 823 (1989)("The record in this case strongly suggests that the prosecutor, already frustrated in defendant's first trial by a hung jury which included three Blacks, pursued a strategy in the second trial of limiting the number of Blacks on the jury to two, thus making a conviction possible even if all of the Blacks on the jury voted according to racial bias.").

216. *State v. Jacobs*, 32 So.3d 227, 234 (2010) (In her dissent, Justice B. Johnson cited to statistical evidence that the prosecutor used peremptory strikes to exclude 100% of the minorities from the jury. She concluded this to be a case of discriminatory intent that was evident from the record.).

217. *State v. Jacobs*, 32 So.3d 227, 234 (2010) (In her dissent, Justice B. Johnson cited to statistical evidence that the prosecutor used peremptory strikes to exclude 100% of the minorities from the jury. She concluded this to be a case of discriminatory intent that was evident from the record.).

218. *State v. Crawford*, 873 So.2d 768, 776 (2004).

219. *Id.* at 781.

220. *Snyder v. La.*, 552 U.S. 472 (2008).

221. *Id.* at 472.

222. *State v. Banks*, 694 So.2d 401, 408 (1997).

223. *See* Thomas Ward Frampton, *The Jim Crow Jury*, 71 Vand. L. Rev. 1593, 1624-35 (2018); The national findings are comparable. "A study found that most peremptory

challenges were based on group stereotypes, and judges almost always accept neutral explanations for these." See JEFFREY ABRAMSON, WE, THE JURY: THE JURY SYSTEM AND THE IDEAL OF DEMOCRACY xxiv, xxvi (2000).

224. *State v. Melvin Cartez Maxie*, No. 13-CR-72522, (11th JDC Oct. 11, 2018).

225. *Come Forward*, The Daily Crusader, March 13, 1895 (discussing Judge Moise saying that Blacks were excluded on the account "of their lack of intelligence and of moral standing."); In *State v. Broussard*, 201 So.3d 400, 404 (2016), a Black, female was struck after the prosecutor explained that "she does not appear to be as intelligent as I would like to see." There too, nothing had been asked concerning her intelligence and nothing was done in the presence of the court to call it into question. The conviction was revered after the court deemed this a case of discrimination.

226. OFFICIAL JOURNAL OF THE PROCEEDINGS OF THE CONSTITUTIONAL CONVENTION OF THE STATE OF LOUISIANA 9-10 (1898).

227. ALL PROCEEDINGS Hr'g Tr. 36, March 20, 2017.

228. ALL PROCEEDINGS Hr'g Tr. 37, March 20, 2017.

229. ALL PROCEEDINGS Hr'g Tr. 37-8, March 20, 2017.

230. Over defense objection, the prosecution used peremptory challenges against three Black jurors/Mercedes Hale, Victoria Reed and Donald Sweet.

231. Louisiana judges can voluntarily train in these areas, but this type of training is not required.

232. Then-assistant Philadelphia district attorney Jack McMahon trained fellow prosecutors to strike Black jurors. The tape advised that Blacks from low-income areas are less likely to convict, that "young Black women are very bad... because they're downtrodden on [sic] two respects," that prosecutors do not want "the real educated ones," and that if they are "going to take Blacks, you want older Blacks." See *Today: Philadelphia Attorney Jack McMahon and Defense Attorney Roy Black Discuss Videotape Made by McMahon 11 Years Ago in Which He Appears to Advocate Using Race as a Basis for Selecting Jury Members* (NBC television broadcast, Apr. 4, 1997); "In the nineteen-nineties, the North Carolina prosecutors' association held training sessions where prosecutors got one-page handouts such as 'Batson Justifications: Articulating Juror Negatives,' which listed reasons for striking jurors based on traits like age and body language. A similar list distributed in 2004 to Texas prosecutors included justifications like 'Agreed with O. J. Simpson verdict' and 'Watched gospel TV programs.' *See also* Gilad Edelman, *Why Is It So Easy for Prosecutors to Strike Black Jurors?*, The New Yorker, June 5, 2015 (last visited Jan. 26, 2022).

233. Def's Omnibus Motion for New Trial, in Arrest of Judgment and for Post Verdict Judgment of Acquittal, 25-6 (Jan. 3, 2018).

234. ALL PROCEEDINGS Hr'g Tr. 8, March 20, 2017 (On March 20, 2017, the court initially ruled that the state's reasons were not pretextual. In its October 11, 2018 ruling on Defendant's Motion for New Trial, the trial court found that the peremptory challenges against the three Black jurors wanted a new trial.)

235. *Alex v. Rayne Concrete Serv.*, 951 So.2d 138, 158 (La. 2007) (Johnson, J., concurring in part and dissenting in part).

236. Thomas Ward Frampton, *For Cause: Rethinking Racial Exclusion and the American Jury*, 118 Mich. L. Rev. 785 (2020).

237. *State v. Snyder*, 942 So.2d 484 (2006).
238. *Snyder v. La.*, 552 U.S. 472 (2008).
239. Richard Bourke, Joe Hingston, & Joel Devine, Louisiana Crisis Assistance Center, *Black Strikes: A Study of the Racially Disparate Use of Peremptory Challenges by the Jefferson Parish District Attorney's Office* 2 (2003).
240. Ursula Noye, Repreive Australia, *Black Strikes: A Study of the Racially Disparate Use of Peremptory Challenges By the Caddo Parish District Attorney's Office* 11 (2015), *available at* Blackstrikes_Caddo_Parish_August_2015.pdf (prisonpolicy.org) (last visited Jan. 17. 2022).

Chapter 3

1. *See* Oliver Laughland, *Life in Prison for Stealing $20: How the Division is Taking Apart Brutal Criminal Sentences*, The Guardian, May 7, 2022, *available at* https://www.theguardian.com/us-news/2022/may/06/prosecutors-new-orleans-mass-incarceration Life in prison for stealing $20: how The Division is taking apart brutal criminal sentences | New Orleans | The Guardian (last visited June 9, 2022).
2. *Id.*
3. *See Id.*; Because of a new civil rights division in the Orleans parish district attorney's office that was created to address past harms, Mr. Lewis was released from custody in 2021.
4. *State v. Fisher*, 19-0669, (La. 1 Cir App. 05/13/21), 2019 WL 6045310 (Guidry, J., dissenting); The Supreme Court later overturned the entire conviction. *See State v. Fisher*, 19-01899 (La. 05/13/21); 320 So.3d 400.
5. After serving twenty-three years in prison for attempting to steal a pair of hedge clippers, Fair Wayne Bryant was granted parole and released in 2020. The Committee on Parole voted 3-0 to release the 63-year-old.
6. The Reconstruction Amendments' Debates, 93 (Alfred Avins ed, 2nd ed. 1974) (39th Cong., 1st Sess., Senate Ex. Doc. No. 2, Dec. 19, 1865, Schurz Report on Condition of the South).
7. In 1973, when legislators established different classes for murder–such as first degree and second degree)–they also raised the minimum sentence for people serving life to 20 years. Three years later, they changed it to 40 years and eliminated any chance of parole for people with life sentences in 1979. In 1979, eligibility for parole was stripped away altogether. Those who went to prison before 1973, believing they'd be released after 10 1/2 years, found themselves stuck behind bars and at the mercy of new laws. The majority of said inmates (who are still alive) are Black.
8. Lester Pearson was released on October 19, 2021.
9. In 2022, Sen. Regina Barrow (D) and Sen. Franklin Foil (R) introduced two bills that would provide parole eligibility to 10/6 lifers. Sen. Barrow's bill would have made inmates eligible if they committed the crime before July 2, 1973, but it did not get enacted into law. Sen. Franklin's bill did. It provides parole eligibility to 10/6 lifers who pleaded guilty, excluding those who went to trial and were convicted. This helps, but did not solve the problem because those who did not plead guilty remain behind bars.

10. A December 2022 ruling by the Oregon Supreme Court granted anyone convicted by a split jury verdict the right to have their cases reexamined. This means prosecutors can pursue new trials, enter into plea agreements or dismiss charges altogether.

11. The legislature did not pass a bill that would have afforded new trials for this pollution. A second proposal was withdrawn. It would have established a panel of retired judges, a retired district attorney, a retired public defender to review individual cases and determine fitness for relief, which could have been parole.

12. *U.S. v. Brown*, 321 F. Supp. 681, 686 (1971).

13. Recently, Louisiana had the distinction of holding individuals in solitary confinement longer than any other State–at the time 43 years for Albert Woodfox, 41 years for Herman Wallace and 29 years for Robert King (known as the Angola 3).

14. Robert Hillary King, *From the Bottom of the Heap the Autobiography of Black Panther Robert Hillary King* 169 (2012).

15. *Id.*

16. *State v. Burnell*, No. 04-0770, La. App. 1 Cir 08/24/2005 (Guidry, J., dissenting) (recommending that the motion to quash should be reversed and the conviction and sentence vacated).

17. *Brown v. Louisiana*, 143 S.Ct. 886 (2023) (Jackson, Sotomayor and Kagan, J., dissenting).

18. *State v. Williams*, 478 So.2d. 983, 989 (La. App. 4 Cir. 1985).

19. *Id.*

20. *Id.* at 991-2 (Brynes, J., dissenting).

21. The judge ruled that said advice amounted to withholding exculpatory evidence that could have been favorable to Gravois at trial.

22. *State v. Gravois*, No. 7522, Reasons for Ruling on Defense Motions to Quash on the Basis of Prosecutorial Misconduct and for Lack of Notice, p. 9- 10 (April 25, 2017); *See also State v. Gravois*, 234 So.3d 1151, 1162 (La. App. 5 Cir 2017).

23. *See State v. Gravois*, 234 So.3d 1151, 1166 (La. App. 5 Cir 2017). The appellate court did not agree that the charges should have been dismissed so the matter was remanded for sanctions to be reconsidered.

24. According to witnesses, Richard jumped in the water to check on the juveniles, then got back in his boat, returned to his camp and drove home.... As of the publication date, the prosecution was ongoing. Mr. Richard is scheduled to stand trial in September 2023. There have been five continuances in his case to date.

25. In 2016, he pleaded guilty to obstructing a federal investigation of the sex abuse allegations.

26. *Wearry v. Cain*, 577 U.S. 385 (2016) (In this capital case, the SCOTUS ordered a new trial after finding that the prosecutor violated his constitutional rights in failing to disclose evidence in support of his innocence). See further discussion of this in chapter four.

27. *State v. Hampton*, 750 So.2d 867, 882 (1999).

28. *Id.*

29. Wallace was not the only ones accused. Angola 3 member Albert Woodfox was also charged. Wallace was supposed to be tried jointly with Chester Jackson and Gilbert Montague, but Jackson accepted a reduced charge of manslaughter in exchange for testimony that incriminated Wallace. Montague was acquitted. Woodfox presented

an alibi witness. There were records showing Wallace was at work in the tag plant at the time of the murder, statements identifying others as the killer and testimony that exonerated both men.

30. He received far greater concern through magistrate Docia Dalby and Judge Brian Jackson.

31. A medical malpractice claim was settled in Wallace's case.

32. *See Wilkerson v. Stalder*, No. 00-304 (M.D. La.) (Doc No. 374 at 9,10).

33. Report of Professor Laurie L. Levenson, at 2 (Aug. 13, 2019).

34. *Id.* at 8.

35. *Id.* at 8.

36. *Knapper v. Connick*, 681 So.2d 944, 945 (1996).

37. In *Brady v. Maryland*, 373 U.S. 83 (1963), the SCOTUS held "that the suppression by the prosecution of evidence favorable to an accused upon request violates due process where the evidence is material either to guilt or to punishment, irrespective of the good faith or bad faith of the prosecution." Favorable evidence includes both exculpatory evidence and evidence that impeaches the testimony of a witness whose credibility or reliability may determine guilt or innocence. Evidence is material only if there is a reasonable probability that the results of the proceeding would have been different if the evidence had been disclosed to the defense. A "reasonable probability" is that which is sufficient to undermine confidence in the outcome of the trial. In determining materiality, a reviewing court must ascertain not whether the defendant would more likely than not have received a different verdict with the evidence, but whether in its absence he received a fair trial, understood as a trial resulting in a verdict worthy of confidence; Princess P. LaCaze is a white female who was married to a white male. She was having an affair with his Black friend who murdered him. She says her husband committed suicide because he did not want to live with kidney disease. Prosecutors said it was a planned murder. A life sentence was handed down in Princess P. LaCaze's case. At her trial, prosecutors failed to disclose that a witness received assurances that his son would not be prosecuted if he testified. That led to her successful 2011 appeal and new trial. She avoided that trial after entering a plea of guilty to manslaughter in 2017. She is now free. *See LaCaze v. Warden La. Corr. Inst. For Women*, 645 F.3d 728 (La. App. 5th Cir. 06/29/11); In *Wearry v. Cain*, the prosecution hid critical evidence from the defense that almost certainly would have altered the verdict. The Louisiana courts agreed that the prosecutor should have disclosed the evidence but affirmed the conviction, concluding that the withheld evidence would have made no difference to the result. The Supreme Court overturned this ruling, finding that the undisclosed evidence destroyed confidence in the jury's verdict; In *Smith v. Cain*, critical evidence that would have discredited the prosecution's only witness was hidden from the defense. Every Louisiana judge who reviewed the conviction found no violation. At oral argument before the SCOTUS, the Court observed misconduct. This subject is alone a book. What's cited is only for purposes of illustration. It is not a composite picture of the problem.

38. Ivan Moreno, *Louisiana Has A Brady Crisis. Can The Supreme Court Fix It?*, Law 360, Jan. 3, 2023.

39. A.M. "Marty" Stroud III, *Lead Prosecutor Apologizes for Role in Sending Man to Death Row*, Shreveport Times, Nov. 21, 2017.

40. I

41. *Report on Evidence Suppression by Prosecutors in Orleans Parish* (1973-2002), at 3, *available at* During Connick tenure, Orleans Parish District Attorney's Office regularly suppressed crucial evidence in cases, costing taxpa (last visited July 27, 2022).

42. *Id.* at 5.

43. In January 2022, Jay-Z, Meek Mill, Big Sean, Robin Thicke, Killer Mike, Big Sean, Fat Joe, and Vic Mensa are among the artists attempting to change New York law to prevent rap lyrics from being used as evidence in criminal trials; *see also State v. Landry*, 2012 WL 603997 (2012) (where a rap song played by the police during a ride to the police station was used against the defendant at his trial); *State v. Williams*, 833 So.2d 497 (2002) (where handwritten rap lyrics written by an unknown party were located via search warrant used during defendant's trial).

44. His first trial in late 2020 on second-degree murder charges ended in a mistrial when an East Baton Rouge Parish jury could not reach a unanimous verdict.

45. Detective testified that his work with ATF involves assisting with firearms, explosives and violent crimes.

46. This was their second trial. Other attorneys for the defenders were Ron Haley Jr. and Stephen Sterling. At the first trial, the jury could not reach a verdict so a mistrial was declared.

47. There were other witnesses, but not actually observed the crime.

48. *State v. Davis*, 2016 WL 7451365 (2016); The Eastern District of Louisiana dismissed Davis' federal petition for habeas corpus relief with prejudice in 2018.

49. Def.'s App. For Post-Con. Relief ¶ 15; That application raises the following claims: (1) actual innocence; (2) prosecutorial misconduct; and, (3) ineffective assistance of counsel. In 2020, all claims were denied summarily, but the court failed to rule on one claim involving text messages to the star witnesses mother. It remains open. The other matters are all final.

50. Rule 403 of the Louisiana Code of Evidence provides for a simple and well-known balancing test between the probative value and prejudicial effect of evidence as a prerequisite to its admission at trial. La. C.E. 403. Analysis under 403 properly begins with establishing the probative weight of evidence. Probative evidence is evidence "having any tendency to make the existence of any fact...more probable or less probable than it would be without the evidence." La. 28 C.E. 401.

51. *See* Stuart P. Fischoff, *Gangsta' Rap and a Murder in Bakersfield*, 294 J. APPLIED SOC. PSYCHOL. 795, 803 (1999) ("Study results clearly indicate that showing participants the rap lyrics exerted a significant prejudicial impact on the evaluation of a person, and particularly so when the person has been accused of murder.").

52. *See* Rule 3.8: Special Responsibilities of a Prosecutor.

53. *In re Jordan*, 04-2397 (La. 6/29/05), 913 So.2d. 775, 786-7 (Johnson, J. concurring).

54. *See Kyles v. Whitley*, 514 U.S. 419 (1995) (Mr. Kyles' 1984 conviction of capital murder was reversed by the SCOTUS because of the prejudicial prosecutorial misconduct of withholding the evidence that the government's star witness was a paid informant who may have been the actual killer).

55. In a few of these instances some SCOTUS justices have expressed outrage while most Louisiana judges have looked the other way. In *Connick v. Thompson*, 563 U.S. 51, 79 (2011), Justices Ginsburg, Breyer, Sotomayor and Kagan provided this dissent:

From the top down, the evidence showed, members of the district attorney's Office, including the district attorney himself, misperceived *Brady's* compass and therefore inadequately attended to their disclosure obligations. Throughout the pretrial and trial proceedings against Thompson, the team of four engaged in prosecuting him for armed robbery and murder hid from the defense and the court exculpatory information Thompson requested and had a constitutional right to receive. The prosecutors did so despite multiple opportunities, spanning nearly two decades, to set the record straight...a fact trier could reasonably conclude that inattention to *Brady* was standard operating procedure at the district attorney's Office. What happened here...was no momentary oversight, no single incident of a lone officer's misconduct. Instead, the evidence demonstrated that misperception and disregard of *Brady's* disclosure requirements were pervasive in Orleans Parish.

56. *Kyles v. Whitley*, 514 U.S. 419, 455 (1995)(Stevens, J., Gingsburg, J, and Bryer, J. concurring).

57. RULE 3.8 SPECIAL RESPONSIBILITIES OF A PROSECUTOR

The prosecutor in a criminal case shall:

(a) refrain from prosecuting a charge that the prosecutor knows is not supported by probable cause;

(b) make reasonable efforts to assure that the accused has been advised of the right to, and the procedure for obtaining, counsel and has been given reasonable opportunity to obtain counsel;

(c) not seek to obtain from an unrepresented accused a waiver of important pretrial rights, such as the right to a preliminary hearing;

(d) after reasonably diligent inquiry, make timely disclosure to the defense of all evidence or information required to be disclosed by applicable law, rules of procedure, or court opinions including all evidence or information known to the prosecutor that tends to negate the guilt of the accused or mitigates the offense, and, in connection with sentencing, disclose to the defense and to the tribunal all unprivileged mitigating information known to the prosecutor, except when the prosecutor is relieved of this responsibility by a protective order of the tribunal;

(e) not subpoena a lawyer in a grand jury or other criminal proceeding to present evidence about a past or present client, or participate in the application for the issuance of a search warrant to a lawyer for the seizure of information of a past or present client in connection with an investigation of someone other than the lawyer, unless:

(1) the information sought is not protected from disclosure by any applicable privilege;

(2) the evidence sought is essential to the successful completion of an ongoing investigation or prosecution; and

(3) there is no other feasible alternative to obtain the information;

(f) except for statements that are necessary to inform the public of the nature and extent of the prosecutor's action and that serve a legitimate law enforcement purpose, refrain from making extrajudicial comments that have a substantial likelihood of heightening public condemnation of the accused and exercise reasonable care to prevent investigators, law enforcement personnel, employees or other persons assisting or associated with the prosecutor in a criminal case from making an extrajudicial statement that the prosecutor would be prohibited from making under Rule 3.6 or this Rule.

(g) When a prosecutor knows of new, credible evidence or information creating a reasonable likelihood that a convicted defendant did not commit an offense for which the defendant was convicted, the prosecutor shall:

(1) if the conviction was obtained in the prosecutor's jurisdiction, promptly disclose that evidence or information to (i) the defendant or defendant's counsel of record if any, and (ii) the North Carolina Office of Indigent Defense Services or, in the case of a federal conviction, the federal public defender for the jurisdiction; or

(2) if the conviction was obtained in another jurisdiction, promptly disclose that evidence or information to the prosecutor's office in the jurisdiction of the conviction or to (i) the defendant or defendant's counsel of record if any, and (ii) the North Carolina Office of Indigent Defense Services or, in the case of a federal conviction, the federal public defender for the jurisdiction of conviction.

(h) A prosecutor who concludes in good faith that evidence or information is not subject to disclosure under paragraph

(g) does not violate this rule even if the prosecutor's conclusion is subsequently determined to be erroneous.

58. The Louisiana Rules of Professional Conduct impose special ethical obligations upon prosecutors. Louisiana requires a prosecutor to make timely disclosure to the defense of all evidence or information that the prosecutor knows, or reasonably should know, either tends to negate the guilt of the accused or mitigates the offense. This rule embodies and expands the United States Constitution's requirement that prosecutors must disclose material exculpatory evidence to the defense. Louisiana rules also prohibit all lawyers from unlawfully obstructing another party's access to evidence."

59. *In re: Eusi Hekima Phillips*, 19-1779 (La. 02/18/20), 289 So.3d 1023, 1025.

60. *In re Ken Dohre*, 2018-B-0941 (La. 2018); 256 So.3d 978.

61. Jon Campbell, *Fired Louisiana Prosecutor Had 'Whites Only' Sign in Property He Owned*, The Appeal, March 26, 2020, *available at* Fired Louisiana Prosecutor Had 'Whites Only' Sign in Property He Owned - The Appeal (last visited Jan. 11, 2022).

62. Jon Campbell, *Fired Louisiana Prosecutor Had 'Whites Only' Sign in Property He Owned*, The Appeal, March 26, 2020, *available at* Fired Louisiana Prosecutor Had 'Whites Only' Sign in Property He Owned - The Appeal (last visited Jan. 11, 2022).

63. There is evidence of this being done in New Orleans and Jefferson Parishes.

64. *See* La. R.S. 15:625.

65. *See* La. Code Crim. P. art. 419(A).

66. Act 121 took effect in 2021. It allows Louisianans to serve on juries as long as they are not under indictment, incarcerated via home confinement or on probation or parole for a felony in a five-year period before their summons.

67. *State v. Payne*, Hr,g Tr. 8, June 22, 2023.

68. The enslaved could be the source of financial gain in more ways than the obvious. The assessment of fines and fees was another form of financial exploitation. The 1850 Fugitive Slave Act authorized the use of summary procedures to return people to slavery. The commissioner earned a ten-dollar fee for finding that an individual should be returned to slavery and a five-dollar fee if freedom was determined.

69. Most states fund their judicial system through a uniform system. A 2022 report from the Louisiana Commission on Justice System Funding reiterated its mission to

shift funding from defendants to taxpayers, though the panel made no specific proposals to make it happen.

70. Julie O'Donoghue, *Louisiana Public Defenders Expect to Need at Least $4 Million More in Funding*, Louisiana Illuminator, March 23, 2021, *available at* Louisiana public defenders expect to need at least $4 million more in funding - Louisiana Illuminator (lailluminator.com) (last visited March 11, 2022).

71. Radley Balko, *A Louisiana DA Will Let You Out of Your Community Service Obligation — If You Donate to his Nonprofit*, Washington Post, Nov. 1, 2019, *available at*, https://www.washingtonpost.com/opinions/2019/11/01/louisiana-da-will-let-you-out-your-community-service-obligation-if-you-donate-his-nonprofit/?arc404=true (last visited July 9, 2020).

72. *Id.*

73. *See Id.*

74. *See Id.*

75. Andrea Armstrong, *Louisiana Deaths Behind Bars* 2015-2019, p. 5 (June 2021), *available at* LA-Death-Behind-Bars-Report-Final-June-2021.pdf (incarcerationtransparency.org) (last visited Dec. 7, 2021).

76. *Id.*

77. *See* United States Department of Justice Civil Rights Division, *Investigation of the Louisiana Department of Public Safety and Corrections*. Washington, DC: United States Department of Justice Civil Rights Division, Jan. 25, 2023, p.4, *available at* 2023.1.20 LDOC Findings Letter (FINAL FO Approved) (for 508 Review) (justice.gov).

78. In 2017, the Louisiana Legislature passed an ambitious package of Justice Reinvestment laws to reduce the prison population by 10% and save $262 million over the next decade. These laws change sentencing guidelines for many non-violent crimes as well as the Habitual Offender Statute.

79. Sebastian Murdock and Hayley Miller, *Louisiana Sheriff Wants 'Good' Prisoners To Stay Jailed For Their Free Labor*, Huffington Post, Oct. 12, 2017, *available at* https://www.huffpost.com/entry/louisiana-sheriff-steve-prator-prisoners_n_59d faobee4bofdad73b2cded?guccounter=1&guce_referrer=aHR0cHM6Ly93d3cu YmluZy5jb20v&guce_referrer_sig=AQAAAHneHJ9yp2bg6KeKNBLAlN56B9s M8v4GeO9g9REKLxtplpNI1AoysvBZBWY9njPw1eoX1DREgVtk Sw72-LJpx2nrb4X5lyL3xJF7wbV_-nZAjqw7vXsLmkGDMisCoRrdk D0TOFnhaQKAJkH-dgZZLTH2C86GrACgD4YjKqZeoRFP (last visited July 28, 2020).

80. Press Release, 2018 State of the Judiciary Address to the Joint Session of the Louisiana Legislature By Chief Justice Bernette Joshua Johnson (April 23, 2018), *available at* https://www.lasc.org/Press_Release?p=2018-05 (last visited Oct. 10. 2020).

81. Press Release, 2018 State of the Judiciary Address to the Joint Session of the Louisiana Legislature By Chief Justice John L. Weimer, p. 7 (March 15, 2022), *available at* LASC JLW address the Legislature (houmatimes.com) (last visited March 21, 2022).

82. Attorney Mary Howell is one notable exception. It became routine of her to schedule a second autopsy in cases where McGarry had performed the first autopsy.

83. *Williams v. Edwards*, 547 F.2d 1206, 1208 (1977).

84. *Jones v. Gusman,* 296 F.R.D. 416, 431 (2013).

85. *Id.*

86. *Id.*

87. *Id.*

88. After six years of litigation, a settlement agreement calling for daily showers for the three Angola inmates of at least 15 minutes; individual ice containers that are timely replenished by prison staff; individual fans; water faucets in their cells; "IcyBreeze" units or so-called "Cajun coolers"; and the diversion of cool air from the death-row guard pod into their cells was reached. *See Ball v.LeBlanc,* 881 F.3d 346 (2018); When corrections officials met in New Orleans in August 2022, air conditioning was on the agenda. James LeBlanc, the head of DOC, reportedly expressed concerned that eleven of the thirteen states without air conditioning in all their prison living areas are in the South. LeBlanc reportedly indicated that he wants Louisiana off that list due to the extreme temperatures. Most of the various buildings and camps at Louisiana's when air conditioning was new and wasn't contemplated for prisons. The buildings used materials that retain heat.

89. *Lewis v. Cain,* 2021 WL 1219988, p.2 (2021).

90. *Id.* at 5 (granted injunctive relief).

91. Press Release, *PJI on the Mississippi Department of Corrections Hiring of Burl Cain,* May 22, 2020; Cain's tenure at Angola was from 1995-2016.

92. Lea Skene, *Former Black DOC officials: 'Good Old Boy' Network Perpetuates Systemic Racism Inside Department,* The Advocate, June 7, 2021, *available at* Former Black DOC officials: 'Good old boy' network perpetuates systemic racism inside department | News | theadvocate.com (last visited March 22, 2022).

93. Office of the Commissioner, Commissioner Nathan Burl Cain, *available at* Office of the Commissioner (ms.gov) (last visited March 22, 2022).

94. *See* Lea Skene, *Former Black DOC officials: 'Good Old Boy' Network Perpetuates Systemic Racism Inside Department,* The Advocate, June 7, 2021, *available at* Former Black DOC officials: 'Good old boy' network perpetuates systemic racism inside department | News | theadvocate.com (last visited March 22, 2022).

95. *Id.*

96. Letter from William C.C. Claiborne to James Madison, New Orleans, La., January 2, 1804, Dunbar Rowland, ed., Official Letter Books of William C.C. Claiborne 1801-1816, Vol I (Jackson, MI., 1917), 325.

97. *Johnson v. Parish of Jefferson,* 2009 WL 1808718, *4 (2009).

98. *See Washington v. La.,* 2009 WL 2015556 (2009).

99. *Severin v. Parish of Jefferson,* 357 Fed.Appx. 601 (2009), 2009 WL 4885161.

100. *See Washington v. La.,* 2009 WL 2015556, *6 (2009).

101. *See State v. Reine,* 14-0162, (La. App. 1 Cir. 09/19/2014) (unpublished) at 2014 WL 4667595 (where Mr. Reine argued he was penalized with an additional five years for each count although the statute which authorizes the imposition of the five-year enhancement was not included in the bill of information).

102. *See Id.* (Guidry, J., dissenting) (where Mr. Reine argued he was penalized with an additional five years for each count although the statute which authorizes the imposition of the five-year enhancement was not included in the bill of information).

103. Louisiana Department of Public Safety and Corrections and Louisiana Commission on Law Enforcement, *Louisiana's Justice Reinvestment Reforms 2022*

Annual Performance Report. Baton Rouge, La: Louisiana Department of Public Safety and Corrections and Louisiana Commission on Law Enforcement, 2022, p. 5, *available at* 2022_jri_performancereport.pdf (documentcloud.org).

104. Prison Policy Initiative, *New Report Shows Mass Incarceration Doesn't Stop at the Prison Walls*. Northampton, MA: Prison Policy Initiative, May 10, 2023, *available at* New report shows mass incarceration doesn't stop at the prison walls | Prison Policy Initiative.

105. As of 2023, Louisiana is ranked second. Sentencing Project (1st Source): Mass Incarceration Trends – The Sentencing Project World Population View (2nd Source): Incarceration Rates by State 2023 (worldpopulationreview.com).

106. Kanu, Hassan. "Louisiana's Over-Incarceration is Part of a Deeply Rooted Pattern." *Reuters*. Feb. 1, 2023, *available at* Louisiana's over-incarceration is part of a deeply rooted pattern | Reuters

107. Andrea, Armstrong, and Marcus Kondkar. *Louisiana Justice: Pre-trial, Incarceration, & Reentry*. Washington: *Public Welfare Foundation*, 2022, 28, *available at* PWF-Data-Report-Final-Compressed-Nov-2022.pdf (incarcerationtransparency.org).

108. *Id.*

109. There is evidence that Blacks were used as CIA lab experiments at Angola and unknowingly given LSD. There is reason to believe this altered their behavior for the worse, made them subject to enhanced penalties behind bars or violence upon release. *See* Hayden Carlos and Cameron Pontiff, *Trick or Treatment? Confronting the Horrific Intersection of Race, Mental Health, Poverty, and Incarceration in Louisiana*, July 16, 2019, *available at* Trick or Treatment? (americanbar.org) (Last visited July 12, 2021)(discussing Dr. Alfred Tucker Butterworth, clinical director at Angola); *see also Private Institutions Used in C.I.A. Effort to Control Behavior*, The New York Times, Aug. 2, 1977, *available at* PRIVATE INSTITUTIONS USED IN C.I.A. EFFORT TO CONTROL BEHAVIOR - The New York Times (nytimes.com) (last visited July 12, 2021) (discussing the CIA's use of private doctors to conduction unethical and illegal experiences of prisoners and unsuspecting members of the public).

110. Prison Policy Initiative, *Mass Incarceration: The Whole Pie 2023*. Northampton, MA: Prison Policy Initiative, March 14, 2023, *available at* Mass Incarceration: The Whole Pie 2023 | Prison Policy Initiative.

Afterword

1. Maya Angelou, On the Pulse of Morning, cited in James W. Loewen, Lies My Teacher Told Me: Everything Your American History Textbook Got Wrong 137 (1996).

2. This slave revolt occurred Jan. 8-10, 1811, about 35 miles from New Orleans. It is the largest in U.S. history and resulted in the deaths of about 100 slaves. Criminal Case File 195, Territory of Orleans v. .Jaco, the negro slave of the late Mr. Meullion, available at Criminal case file no. 195, Territory of Orleans v. Jaco, the Negro slave of the late Mr. Meuillon, 1811 - page 6 | Louisiana Digital Library (last visited May 7, 2021).

3. Race & Slavery Petitions Project, *available at* Petition Details (uncg.edu) (last visited May 3, 2021)(discussing Thomas Laughlin's petition for injunction).
4. Rickey Hill, *The Bogalusa Movement: Self-Defense and Black Power in the Civil Rights Struggle*, 41 The Black Scholar 3, p. 50 (2011).
5. Countless student leaders reported being in a meeting with then SU President Netterville on the morning of 11/16/72. They all report Dr. Netterville instructing them to wait in his office until he returned from downtown. As they waited, they recall a heavy police presence taking form on campus. Hours later, Denver Smith and Leonard Brown were gunned down after tear gas and shots were directed at the crowd.
6. Norman L. Reimer, The Tradition of Passionate Advocacy, 45 CHAMPION 59, 60 (2021).
7. Angi Porter, *Africana Legal Studies: A New Theoretical Approach to Law & Protocol*, 27 MICH. J. RACE & L. 249, 318 (2022).
8. Id.